THE TEACHER TOOLKIT GUIDE TO MEMORY

PRAISE FOR THE TEACHER TOOLKIT GUIDE TO MEMORY

'We are constrained by our memory skills, especially for students sitting in a class bombarded by facts pressured by an upcoming test, struggling to find relations between ideas and building coat hangers to remember the details, and surrounded by others who seem to find it easy to recall what the teacher said. This book is **M**asterful, **E**vidence-based, **M**emorable, **O**perational, **R**eadable, and the best book for **Y**ou on memory.'

Professor John Hattie, Melbourne Graduate School of Education

'*The Teacher Toolkit Guide to Memory* is a real treasure box for teachers and parents. Packed with accessible information, backed up by research, this book keeps on giving. The practical examples, rooted in classroom practice, will be something teachers can go back to. QR codes with downloadable templates are the icing on the cake!'

Louise Sugden, teacher and MAT lead, @Louiseab72gmai1

'Being research-informed is one thing; having time to do it is another. Solve both issues by reading and acting upon this excellent introductory guide to the theory and practice of memory. Highly recommended.'

Dr Paul S. Ganderton, education consultant, @ecogeog

'Ross McGill has managed to beautifully execute and simply explain the fundamentals of cognitive learning and the importance of understanding the "how" in the context of the brain, complete with wonderful illustrations perfect for the classroom teacher, learner and parent. So, no matter who you are, no matter how successful, no matter how much you already may understand about this topic, Ross has something to offer you.'

Victoria dos Santos, assistant athletic director and pastoral lead

'In my work as a psychologist in schools, staff often tell me about children who have "difficulties with retention". I can now imagine myself recommending this book as a good starting point. Ross has provided an easy-to-access overview of research into memory, as well as an exploration of pedagogy. He has provided practical tips based on concepts from cognitive science and neuropsychology while also incorporating the social and emotional processes which are an integral part of the learning process.'

Dr Jo Taylor, child and educational psychologist, @jgetaylor

'*The Teacher Toolkit Guide to Memory* not only provides concrete, easily implementable teaching strategies, but gives a detailed and clear overview of the intricacies of the human brain. I can't wait to apply this knowledge in the classroom.'

Larissa Gibb, deputy head of science

'This text is long overdue! How can it be that teachers are not taught how their students learn, and how to make that learning stick? This book includes just enough technical information, providing educators with the cognitive and neuroscience research that will be useful and meaningful to them. Thank you for sifting through and translating the research to present practice-based knowledge and strategies necessary to facilitate evidence-based instruction.'

Sarah Oberle, first grade teacher and doctoral student (education leadership and cognitive sciences)

'An impressive collection of findings that draws on the latest research within cognitive science and education. Ross succinctly discusses, clarifies and offers practical, research-informed examples for busy leaders and teachers.'

Mark Leswell, research lead

'The "human teacher first" meets the science. A clear and practical guide to "debunking" teaching practices, with excellent use of analogies and ideas to support teacher development.'

Samantha Torr, Vice Principal: Director of Alpha Teaching School Hub, @alpha_tsh

'A fantastic book that successfully interweaves the breadth of cognitive theory and practical strategies in a clear and accessible way. A great book to begin understanding the science of learning and the complexity of influences on this.'

Sarah Benskin, assistant principal (teaching & learning, curriculum & CPD), @drblearning

'An exceptional effort of presenting the vast and difficult topic of "the learning brain" in a practical and understandable way.'

Yves Moerskofski, educational psychologist

'In this wonderful teacher toolkit, Ross Morrison McGill advocates for more "active learning" opportunities in all our schools. As a cognitive psychologist, I fully endorse the idea that to stimulate thinking, you've got to keep moving.'

Dr Peter Lovatt, author of *The Dance Cure*, @DrPeterLovatt

'This book is informative and accessible for quick reads. The consistent approach to each chapter works really well, especially for utilising the practical applications. The embedded use of diagrams adds to the reader's understanding of some complex concepts.'

Charlotte McLean, SENCO and senior leader

BLOOMSBURY EDUCATION
Bloomsbury Publishing Plc
50 Bedford Square, London, WC1B 3DP, UK
29 Earlsfort Terrace, Dublin 2, Ireland

BLOOMSBURY, BLOOMSBURY EDUCATION and the Diana logo
are trademarks of Bloomsbury Publishing Plc

First published in Great Britain, 2022

This edition published in Great Britain 2022 by Bloomsbury Publishing Plc

A catalogue record for this book is available from the British Library

ISBN: PB: 978-1-4729-8934-5; ePDF: 978-1-4729-8932-1; ePub: 978-1-4729-8933-8

2 4 6 8 10 9 7 5 3 (paperback)

Text design by Marcus Duck Design

Printed and bound in the UK by CPI Group Ltd, CR0 4YY

THE TEACHER TOOLKIT GUIDE TO MEMORY

ROSS MORRISON McGILL

BLOOMSBURY EDUCATION
LONDON OXFORD NEW YORK NEW DELHI SYDNEY

CONTENTS

ACKNOWLEDGEMENTS VIII
FOREWORD BY PATRICE BAIN IX
INTRODUCTION XI
HOW TO USE THIS BOOK XIX
CHAPTER 1: AN OVERVIEW OF THE BRAIN 1
Explainer 3
Practical idea: Direct instruction 10
Worked example 17
Template 18
CHAPTER 2: HOW MEMORY IS SHAPED 19
Explainer 20
Practical idea: Retrieval practice 25
Worked example 29
Template 30
CHAPTER 3: AN INTRODUCTION TO TYPES OF MEMORY 31
Explainer 32
Practical idea: Spaced practice and interleaving 44
Worked example 48
Template 49
CHAPTER 4: LEARNING IS EMOTIONAL 50
Explainer 52
Practical idea: Spaced and active rereading 61
Worked example 65
Template 67
CHAPTER 5: COGNITIVE LOAD THEORY 68
Explainer 69
Practical idea: Managing cognitive load 74
Worked example 77
Template 79

CHAPTER 6: MENTAL MODELS FOR LEARNING . 80

Explainer . . . 81
Practical idea: Using mnemonics . . . 85
Worked example . . . 87
Template . . . 89

CHAPTER 7: BRAIN PLASTICITY . . . 90

Explainer . . . 91
Practical idea: Elaboration . . . 95
Worked example . . . 100
Template . . . 101

CHAPTER 8: COGNITIVE APPRENTICESHIP . . . 102

Explainer . . . 103
Practical idea: Self-explanation . . . 109
Worked example . . . 111
Template . . . 112

CHAPTER 9: WELLBEING AND MEMORY . . . 113

Explainer . . . 115
Practical idea: Prioritising student wellbeing . . . 119
Worked example . . . 121
Template . . . 122

CHAPTER 10: WHAT NEXT FOR TEACHER CPD? . . . 123

Explainer . . . 124
Practical idea: A teacher CPD session on memory . . . 133
Worked example . . . 135
Template . . . 136

BRINGING IT ALL TOGETHER . . . 138

CONCLUSION . . . 143

REFERENCES . . . 147

INDEX . . . 152

ACKNOWLEDGEMENTS

To **Jenni** and **Freddie** who, at home, now think it's hilarious that I forget things. I do wonder if this book title will see me receive a lifetime of jokes for being forgetful! On that note, if I did publish a follow-up to this book, it would be on why and how we forget. There's plenty of research on the brain, memory and remembering, but it's a little harder to find out why we are *all* so forgetful.

My thanks also go to **Hannah**, Helen, Laura and the wider team at Bloomsbury – our sixth book together with another in the pipeline! Thank you so much for all your efforts in the process. Your work is meticulous and it's definitely getting easier and quicker! After several years of reading, research and practice, this book took one year from contract to printing. The fastest turnaround!

A special thanks to **Patrice Bain** and **Dr Pooja Agarwal**. Prior to the pandemic, your retrieval practice research really inspired me and I am so glad we have kept in touch; a huge thank you to Patrice for writing the foreword without hesitation and for being so modest with your expertise.

To **Dr Kripa Sundar** in particular, who kindly offered a critical and scientific eye across the entire text to ensure that the information shared here in relation to cognitive science is factually correct. I look forward to sharing your words of wisdom on my teaching travels as I clarify the terminology and strategies cited in the book. Thank you for your knowledge and feedback.

Finally, thank you to all the teaching colleagues, educators and academics who publish work and share information so that we can learn from one another. These people are mentioned in all the sources I have referenced throughout, including all the academic papers at the back of this book. These people are the real specialists, not me, and there is so much more I could have read and quoted. And to the wonderful teachers who kindly offered to proofread the book before publication – this is for **you**! This is my journey to understanding memory and I hope it contributes to your understanding too.

I guess I should finish by thanking my **Mother** – never miss the opportunity to thank your mum!

Mnemosyne

The one who knows everything, what was, what is, and what will be.

Scan the QR code to listen to a short welcome message I have recorded for you.

FOREWORD

As instructors, we spend years in teacher preparation programmes and professional development focusing on how we teach. Yet how many of us have been encouraged to ask the question, 'How do we learn?' It is not a new question. In fact, it has been asked in many cultures and languages. Although answers vary, a common thread refers to the ability to retrieve knowledge stored in our memory. According to Cicero (circa 106–46 BCE), 'Memory is the treasury and guardian of all things.' If the importance of memory has been acknowledged for over 2,000 years, how is it that understanding how to get information into memory is a field somewhat new to teachers?

I agree with Ross McGill when he advocates, 'All teachers must be research-informed.' The future of our profession lies in methods proven – by science – to achieve the results we want for our students. *The Teacher Toolkit Guide to Memory* boosts us into that future by sharing the how and why of learning and memory. We are better teachers when we understand concepts and questions such as the difference between our students' working and long-term memory. What do neurons and synapses have to do with their learning? How do retrieval, and spaced retrieval, strengthen knowledge retention? Dual coding, chunking, the forgetting curve, cognitive load theory... it's all here in this book, ready to help us boost learning in our classrooms. Understanding the science of learning makes us better teachers. As Daniel Willingham (2017) states in his book, *Why Don't Students Like School?*, 'Education makes better minds, and knowledge of the mind can make better education.'

For too long, teacher preparation programmes and professional development have been burdened with fad theories and pedagogy based on anecdotes rather than measurable, replicable evidence. Although various neuromyths (such as 'learning styles' and differing left-brain/right-brain abilities) were debunked years ago, education writing and advice based on similar unproven ideas are still prevalent.

On the other hand, research that previously had been tucked away in scientific journals is becoming accessible. Teachers around the world are finding, discussing and using evidence-gathered practices. Up until recently, most research studying how students learn was conducted on college campuses with college students. In 2006, in the United States, cognitive scientists began studies on how children learn in primary and secondary school classrooms. When I was asked by cognitive scientists if they could study how children learn in my classroom, I jumped at the opportunity.

A well-respected model of learning includes three steps: encoding, storage and retrieval. The focus of experiments in my classroom was retrieval: how my students improved their retention of material by methods requiring them to recall it. Ross McGill's *Guide to Memory* covers both storage and retrieval. He takes the science and translates it for teachers 'into practice, in a way that works for their classrooms and their students'.

This is key. There is no one-size-fits-all strategy that suits all teachers and all classrooms. I worked with cognitive scientists for 15 years developing the strategies that worked for my students in my classroom. How fortunate for teachers that Ross has made this book available. His layout of chapters includes explanations, practical ideas and examples of techniques that work. He makes his guide even more accessible by including QR codes that lead to downloadable templates. I encourage teachers to understand the science of learning and find what works. For me, doing so allowed me to witness first-hand how the learning trajectory changed for my students. Students who previously had internalised failure now saw errors as feedback that targeted what needed work; a change of strategies helped fine-tune direction for achievement.

When I started teaching, little guidance based in science was available to me, as I wasn't versed in neuroscience jargon and didn't subscribe to the journals where findings were published. I had been taught how to teach, but never received instruction on how the learning happened. Ross McGill, in this book, gives us critical insights into that process. On the first day of school, when all those fresh faces are most alert and attuned, we can say, 'I'm your teacher, and I'm going to teach you how to learn.' Immediately we have made our students powerful partners in what we do at school. And if we can give them insight into the magic of learning, we give them the lifelong gift of how to do it.

Patrice M. Bain, Ed.S.
Teacher

Author: *A Parent's Guide to Powerful Teaching*

Co-Author: *Powerful Teaching: Unleash the Science of Learning* and *Organizing Instruction and Study to Improve Student Learning*

INTRODUCTION
MY JOURNEY WITH MEMORY

If somebody tells you that the ideas in this book are nothing new, they are probably right. You and I are not the first people to have ever wanted to discuss how we learn and how the brain operates. In fact, neuroscience has been developing as a field of study for over 2,500 years. In the fifth century BC, while his contemporaries believed the brain resided in the heart, Hippocrates argued his case for the brain being the centre of both thinking and feeling:

> ‘And [humans] ought to know that from nothing else but (from the brain) come joys, delights, laughter and sports, and sorrows, griefs, despondency, and lamentations. And by this, in an especial manner, we acquire wisdom and knowledge, and see and hear, and know what are foul and what are fair, what are bad and what are good [...] And by the same organ we become mad and delirious, and fears and terrors assail us [...] All these things we endure from the brain.’
>
> **(Hippocrates, quoted in Adams, 1868)**

This book is outside of my comfort zone, but covers a topic I am deeply fascinated with. At some point in our lives, we are all curious about what makes us remember. I wonder about the things people do that make them an expert in their field or societal perceptions of what makes somebody ‘clever’. And we question the times we forget something because we have too many things to do and we become stressed and anxious.

Until recently, memory, and more specifically the brain, was an area I had never become familiar with as a teacher. Despite a very comprehensive teacher training background, covering psychology, child development, subject knowledge and behaviour management, a deeper understanding of the brain and how it works was one aspect of my training that I'd never had. Of course, life gets in the way and teaching is exhausting. If important content is left aside during formal training, there is not much time available for teachers to pursue it as part of their professional learning.

Fast forward almost 30 years, and I have spent the last decade trying to fend for myself (in and around the busy nature of school life) to understand how we learn. Whilst I am neither new to discovering memory nor the first or last person to develop an interest in this area, I wanted to put everything that I have learned on my own journey into a beginner's guide for teachers. From my travels delivering training to schools across the UK and internationally, as well as insights from social media, it is clear that teachers new to the profession are now being trained in neuroscience *and* cognitive science at an early stage in their careers. I am reassured to see teacher training universities in England now offering teachers a good background in cognitive science before they reach the classroom. It has been encouraging to see many school leaders being immersed in cognitive science also. Whilst this is welcome and a wonderful thing, every teacher must initially master their subject knowledge and behaviour management in order to learn how and when to deploy effective teaching strategies in the classroom to help students remember. They need to engage with research and need to be provided with reliable and pragmatic advice to put this information into practice in the classroom.

In my academic life and as a teacher blogger, I have gradually discovered more and more cognitive science and academic research unpicking the world of the classroom. I am slowly beginning to know more about neuroscience and the language used to discuss parts of the brain. One aspect of my own journey has involved reading, taking part in online webinars and connecting with neuroscientists for my website and podcast. Many books have rekindled my affair with memory, most recently *Connect the Dots* by Tricia Taylor (2019), *How Learning Happens* by Paul Kirschner and Carl Hendrick (2020), and *Why the Brain Matters* by Jon Tibke (2019). In addition, I have learned much from the fantastic Learning Scientists (a small team of cognitive psychological scientists working in educational research and translating what appear to be complicated theories into meaningful advice and strategies that teachers can actually use). They have not only influenced me (since 2016) but, in my opinion, many teachers across the profession – and in some respects, English education policy too. Where possible, I will reference these sources throughout and offer some practical techniques based on what I have learned. A final book reference would be *What Works?* by Lee Elliot Major and Steve Higgins (2019), which unpicked the excellent *Teaching and Learning Toolkit* published by the Education Endowment Foundation (2018). The EEF has been publishing education research since 2011 and has been highly influential in transforming 'research-informed practice' for teachers and schools across the UK. I will return to *What Works?* later in this book, but for now I'll leave you with their Bananarama Principle, which resonates heavily with me: it's not *what* you do that counts, it's *how* you do it that matters – that's what gets results. As with this book, it's OK to read the material, but if it doesn't change the way you teach, then we have a problem.

Whilst I am no cognitive scientist, I do claim to be a teacher, a researcher and someone who, having led whole-school teacher learning and professional development in a number of large secondary schools, has a deep fascination with the mechanics of the classroom. This has also become very apparent to me in my life as a teacher trainer. Teaching teachers (crudely) is no different to teaching students per se. We all need information shared in manageable chunks, opportunities to reflect, to receive feedback and, where possible, assessment to gauge what we know and what we have yet to learn. The excellent research published by Barak Rosenshine (2012) does this perfectly. His original six principles of effective instruction evolved into ten and then 17. I have reduced this back to a manageable and memorable sequence for teachers to master: explain, question, practise and feedback. That is the teaching loop to support memory retention.

Understanding how we learn is a journey that everybody should undertake, whether a student, an educator or a parent. Yet, if we are to put ourselves into the position of a teacher or school leader, it becomes critical that we should know more about memory. A fresh-faced university graduate entering the classroom will need to learn how to master the classroom and also develop a wide range of pedagogical strategies – and regularly evaluate them as they teach their students. They will need to learn to adapt those strategies as they teach in different contexts. This is a journey we must all go on as we evolve throughout our career and we each develop an understanding of our day-to-day work and the world around us.

As more experienced teachers and school leaders, we have a duty to inform ourselves of the relevant research and to be able to translate this into bitesize and pragmatic summaries for others around us who are new to the profession and who may be more likely to be bombarded with countless other priorities.

This book is not a thesis on everything and anything to do with the brain, how we learn and how we shape memory, yet I do hope it will become your pocket guide to the key concepts relevant to teaching. I hope it will give you a beginner's grasp of memory, cognition and how we think, which will reassure you on your own journey to discovering more about how we learn. It is also worth noting that, alongside my own personal development in this area, I still hold the belief that learning can happen in a variety of ways and in different contexts. However, the real challenge lies in translating this complicated field of research into practical ideas that teachers can use in the classroom, particularly in schools with large numbers of students, teaching very detailed curriculum plans. What I hope to signpost in this book are some helpful strategies that teachers can use to support their students. As ever, I advocate that all teachers must be research-informed and translate theory into practice in a way that works for their classrooms and their students. Whilst I offer and reference a wide range of practical ideas throughout this book, everyone reading must translate my experiences and my understanding for their own context. Go play with the ideas and theory in your own classrooms and let me know how you are getting on. Use the hashtag **#GuideToMemory**.

What is the number one thing all teachers should know and do?

This subtitle is a phrase I have read, heard and used myself on a number of occasions. Teachers are consumed by all sorts of initiatives, curriculum reform, evidence gathering and research recommendations. The working life of a teacher can feel like a very busy and complicated space. How do teachers filter what's important, and what's important but could be learned at a later stage?

Often, teachers fill their time with trying to streamline their day-to-day: they strive to reduce the marking burden or find more efficient ways to plan lessons. However, when the opportunity arises for teachers to reflect on their own professional learning during the academic year, the vast majority will be engaged with more complex questions about how to make deeper connections with the students and how to make learning more accessible and engaging. They will want to discover and use practical techniques in the classroom to help students to remember and apply key information.

So, how can teachers go about this?

The Great Teaching Toolkit, published by Evidence Based Education (2020), is a comprehensive publication that offers an evidence review route map for all teachers. Peer reviewed by 74 educators (including myself) from 11 countries around the world, this document offers a comprehensive bibliography of some key pieces of education research. 'What are your best bets in terms of making the most difference to your students?' is the key question asked.

The review recommends four key priorities for teachers:

1. UNDERSTAND
the content you are teaching and how it is learned.

2. CREATE
a supportive environment for learning.

3. MANAGE
the classroom to maximise the opportunity to learn.

4. PRESENT
content, activities and interactions that activate students' thinking.

No one can deny that the first priority in this list is essential. Teachers need to have a deep and fluent knowledge of the subject they are teaching, an understanding of curriculum sequencing, tasks, assessments and activities, as well as an appreciation of common misconceptions and sticking points for students. The second and third priorities in the list focus on building effective relationships in the classroom, promoting a positive climate, motivating learners, building classroom routines, and ensuring rules, expectations and consequences are clear and consistently applied. I've always argued that if a teacher can manage classroom behaviour, only then can they develop their teaching repertoire; they must master their subject knowledge and sustain this. These three areas are elements of the teaching profession that all teachers, particularly those new to the profession, need to master before they become proficient. In keeping with the content of this book, we could refine the word 'proficient' and use the phrase 'automated' or 'subconscious' decisions.

In comparison, the fourth priority is something that every teacher has to continually work on and refine on an ongoing basis. This is where I would place teachers developing their understanding of memory and utilising this to best effect in the classroom. This fourth priority focuses on activating hard thinking and *The Great Teaching Toolkit* considers the following to be the key components needed to achieve this:

Structuring

Giving students an appropriate sequence of learning tasks; signalling objectives and progress; matching tasks to learners' needs; scaffolding and supporting.

Explaining

Presenting and communicating new ideas clearly, with concise, appropriate, engaging explanations; connecting new ideas to what has previously been learned; modelling using worked examples.

Questioning

Using questions and dialogue to promote elaboration and to elicit student thinking. (I believe having the ability to ask 30 students a range of effective questions 'on your feet' and keep them actively engaged is a teacher's greatest asset.)

Interacting

Responding appropriately to feedback from students.

Embedding

Giving students tasks that embed and reinforce learning.

Activating

Helping students to plan, regulate and monitor their own learning.

To implement the above recommendations to best effect, teachers must have a secure grasp of memory and how we learn. Only then can they understand how to deliver content, set tasks and ask questions to activate hard thinking, which is where true learning happens. *The Great Teaching Toolkit* concludes that this fourth priority is 'something that some teachers could profitably work on'. I see this priority as the crux of effective classroom practice: the one thing that all teachers should know and do to greatest effect – and it all starts with memory (which is referenced in the 'embedding' stage of this fourth priority). I hope the information and ideas in this book will support you in this endeavour.

What do we mean when we talk about memory?

Where are your shoes for work? Can you find your black dress or your stripy socks? Where did you leave the house keys, and how do you cook a chicken soup? To answer any of these questions, we refer to our working memory: we need to retrieve the relevant information and process it to find the answers we need or to perform an action. The more often we retrieve or organise information, the more likely we are to retain it and remember it quickly when we next need it. If we do not regularly retrieve or organise information, we lose it. However, if we regularly read or deliberately organise concepts, rules or facts, we can be overloaded with information and this information can become redundant (wasted), or worse, lost.

I suspect you may have learned how to ride a bike. Even if you haven't sat on a bicycle for 20 years, after an initial five or ten minutes, it's likely you will soon be able to balance again and begin riding down the pavement with your feet on the pedals. How do we manage to do something again after such a long absence? Why do we retain this information even though we're not using it regularly?

In her book *Connect the Dots*, Tricia Taylor (2019) references the 'wardrobe metaphor', which is the best analogy I can think of when explaining how our minds work. She quotes American psychologist Henry L. Roediger III:

> 'Memories are objects stored in that space; and retrieving a memory is akin to searching for and finding an object in a physical space.'
>
> **(Roediger, 1980)**

The 'wardrobe metaphor' essentially explains the conscious practice of information storage and retrieval. What are the colours of the rainbow? When did Mount Vesuvius erupt and destroy Pompeii, near Naples in Italy? Do you remember when you first tied a shoelace? To answer these questions, we need to look back through the information stored in our memory (the wardrobe) and retrieve the relevant details.

It goes without saying that we can't always rely on our memories to recall the information we need. We can't always find what we're looking for in our wardrobe. To give you an example of a time when the 'wardrobe metaphor' didn't work, let me tell you about one evening when I forgot to lock my garage door. Falling asleep that night, you will not be surprised to learn that I woke up at four o'clock in the morning thinking about it. Knowing that I was not confident that the garage door was locked, my already anxious mind equated this unknown fact to a restless night's sleep! This 'subconscious' risk and fear clearly woke me up to a conscious state in the middle of the night. The key question being asked of my memory was: 'Did I or did I not lock the garage?' You'll be pleased to know that I did go outside that night to lock the garage door. I knew that if I didn't do this I would have struggled to sleep for the rest of the night. There are many reasons why we might not be able to recall information, but this particular case is a good example of the many factors that influence whether we remember or not. This includes sleep, competing demands and even our biology.

The good news is that humans can shape and strengthen their memory to help improve their ability to recall information. Throughout this book I would like you to try out several exercises so I can demonstrate how I can shape and strengthen your memory as you read this book – and how you can strengthen your students' memories in turn. Let's get warmed up with a few examples, starting by using the wardrobe metaphor. Have a go at retrieving the information below.

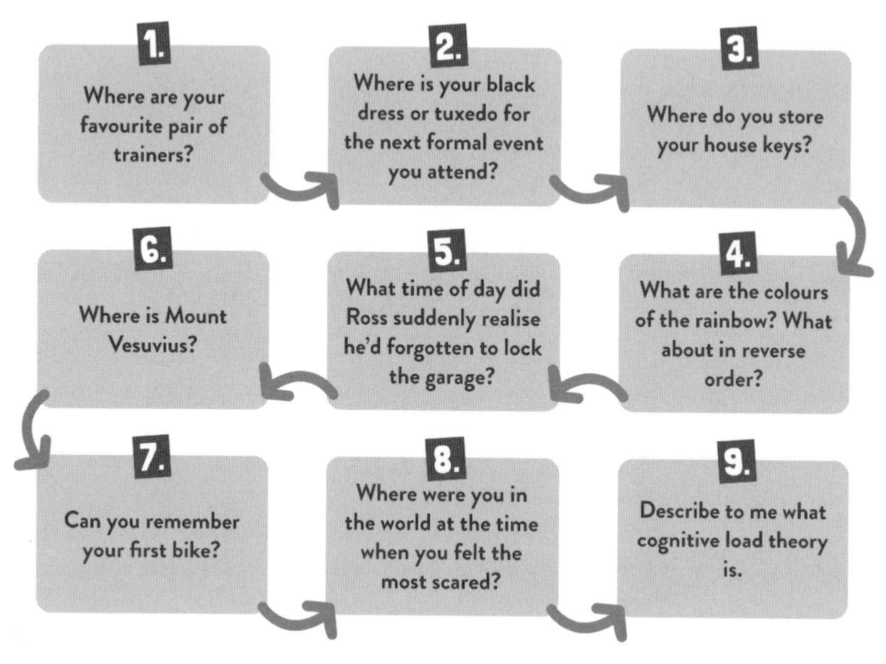

Some of these questions will be easy to answer. Some will require a little bit of a struggle. Others will evoke an emotion or a particular timestamp in your life. Others will require some prior knowledge on your part. Each of these variations in how we respond are some things that I would like to unpick throughout this book. Episodic and semantic memory, intrinsic and extrinsic load, the hippocampus and amygdala are just some of the terms that I would like to share with you from my journey with memory.

Recall doesn't mean you have learned it

From a teacher's perspective, learning is usually identified with the encoding of new knowledge or building upon prior knowledge to help shape schemas: patterns of thought to organise information. We want students to remember things as they develop a degree of self-regulation in their learning and their behaviour.

Schemas are patterns of thought, mental mind maps of how we store and process information and how we decide how this information will be used. I often associate the word 'schema' with a visual mind map or a spider web; this is my schema for recalling what a schema actually is! How memory is shaped and constructed to connect one piece of information to another. Developing schematic knowledge is one challenge we all face; we must connect all the various pieces of information and organise them to make sense of them. In my academic life, for example, I conduct social media network analysis, research and evaluate how conversations spread online, and look at how they are connected. To draw conclusions, I must organise this information to make sense of it. Thinking about schemas supports good curriculum design. Consider the information you are presenting to your students and how you want them to connect this information and organise it to make sense of it. Visual representations of schemas might help us map out a curriculum plan in a visual organiser.

Teachers must build into their curriculum planning schematic maps which offer 'opportunities to retrieve' in and around a crowded curriculum. Most of the research around developing memory – as well as teacher workload – recommends that we 'teach fewer things at greater depth' (see Myatt, 2020). Teachers can support knowledge retention by regularly practising retrieval techniques with their students. Countless pieces of research have shown that retrieval practice produces more learning than engaging in other effective teaching techniques. The crucial question is, if we can recall something, particularly in an immediate scenario, does it mean we have learned it?

We know retrieval is a powerful way to improve learning and memory, and merely studying words once without ever recalling them will produce 'extremely poor performance' (Karpicke and Bauernschmidt, 2011). What teachers must do more is encourage students to practise until taught information can be recalled at a deeper level, and with new information added at specific points. If we learn how to use mass retrieval in our everyday lives, as well as in the classroom, we can each improve our own memory and that of others we work with. The research recommends avoiding the immediate repeating of information. We may be able to recall the answer, but it may not produce any additional gain in learning in the long term. Memory, at least in the classroom when developing subject knowledge, is shaped when we use repeated retrieval – and only then when the repetitions are spaced. As we will see in Chapter 3, the effects of repeated spaced retrieval can be very large.

On the point of remembering, I wish to make it clear that you can use whatever term for memory rehearsal that you wish: rehearsal, practice (the application of an idea or method) and practising (to perform an activity several times to become better), rote learning, retrieval, recap, regurgitate, recollect or remembering. Call it what you want; they are all broadly the same thing. If we want students to remember, they need to repeat from memory their acquisition of concepts, rules or facts to the point of automation. It's worth mentioning that most of these words begin with 're', meaning 'to go back' or to visit 'again'.

As I dig into more details with you throughout this book, I will unpick how we learn and what happens in our brains as we learn. What I would also like to unravel in this book is how some of our personal memories stay with us throughout our lives and what influence emotion has on these episodes. What does this mean for teaching and in particular paying attention to the experiences our students have in the classroom and what we can do to ensure their wellbeing?

I will also draw on a fabulous piece of research, 'Improving students' learning with effective learning techniques' published by John Dunlosky et al. (2013), which offers some robust research into the efficacy of teaching methods to use for developing retention. So important is this article that much of the research and recommendations contained within it inform the practical ideas in this book. Whilst the research paper suggests that there is a low, moderate and high efficacy to the ideas, all of the techniques do have an impact on outcomes. As always, we should define what we mean by outcomes and also consider how these techniques will differ, for example, when used in an Early Years classroom as opposed to a pupil referral unit. Dunlosky et al. highlight that there will be many variables to each technique and that the education sector could profit if 'the benefits of most of the techniques in representative educational settings [could] be more fully explored'.

Why has it taken so long for teachers to get their hands on this knowledge?

In my early years as a teacher, although I set quizzes and competitions, there was little research available to me that recommended carefully planning when quizzing, feedback and questioning would take place across the curriculum. We know this research is in abundance and has been widely available for decades, so why have many of our more experienced teachers not had this academic rigour in their teacher training?

I do think it's largely down to social media that the teaching profession has become more aware of cognitive science in recent years. Good ideas filter to the top and can be spread quickly and far beyond the school gates. This is why we have seen a huge explosion in teachers sharing ideas, connecting with academics directly, as well as having easier access to research, journals, publications and books that can enhance their practice. With apps and technology, all of us can start to locate content that meets our needs at any given time. 15 years ago, this was exactly what I started to do in my classroom. This has now emerged into my writing, my teacher training and my research. I haven't got everything right along the way. I've made many mistakes while navigating this complex world of cognitive science, psychology and academic research. We each go on this journey and what I hope to do is share some of the things that I have been learning with you in this book. Whilst I will ensure information is factually correct and accurate at the time of writing, I make no apologies for exposing my lack of expertise in this complex field. If you're reading this text, you're already taking the necessary steps in your own journey towards research-informed practice.

It is my belief that besides mastering the classroom in terms of subject knowledge and behaviour management, memory is the number one thing all teachers need to know about, and I hope that this book guides you on your journey. I just wish I had written it 30 years ago for myself as a newly qualified teacher entering the profession.

HOW TO USE THIS BOOK

What you'll find in each chapter

In this book, I explore what I've been learning about the brain and executive functions, and why and how I believe this will change the way you teach. As educators, we have important choices to make that will influence how we can hinder or support the learning process. For example, when is it best to use retrieval strategies? Are spaced practice and interleaving preferable to summarisation or using mnemonic devices? When should we pause? And when should we offer a response to an answer?

The key objective for me is to provide you with some initial theory and work hard to turn the content into a practical activity for you to complete as you read through the book, modelling the learning process to you as you move through the material.

Each chapter is therefore divided into four key sections.

1. Explainer

The first part of each chapter covers **what you need to know** about the topic being discussed. We'll delve into the structure of the brain, how memory is shaped, the different types of memory, and key theories such as cognitive load theory and cognitive apprenticeship. The explainers are supported by infographics and diagrams that will promote your understanding of these concepts.

In each explainer section, you'll find a short glossary of **key terms** that you need to know to get to grips with the topic.

2. Practical idea

After the explainer, we'll consider a practical idea that **turns the theory into practice**. There will be step-by-step instructions for implementing the idea in the classroom, as well as recommendations and suggestions for how you might be able to apply the idea to best effect in your context.

At the end of the idea, you'll find a set of **toolkit tips**, which are practical takeaways to support you when putting the idea into practice in your classroom.

3. Worked example

For each practical idea, I'll give you a **clear example** of how it might work in practice. In these sections, I aim to demonstrate how the ideas support the retention of knowledge by devising a series of exercises for you to complete.

4. Template

At the end of each chapter, a **blank template** is provided to help you plan out how you'll implement the practical idea in your classroom. Use the template to make the idea relevant to your students and translate it into your own context. When you're delivering the practical ideas or using the templates with your students, it's a good idea to name the study technique you are using, for example, dual coding or retrieval practice. This will help the students identify each study skill and enable them to use each one in their self-study or revision.

The templates are also available online so you can download and print them. Scan the **QR code** next to each template for access.

Bringing it all together

In the final part of the book, I show you how you can bring all the practical ideas together to support learning across an academic year. I suggest how you might embed the ideas in curriculum overviews, lesson plans and teacher training sessions, so the ideas complement and build on each other to maximise their impact on student outcomes.

CHAPTER 1

AN OVERVIEW OF THE BRAIN

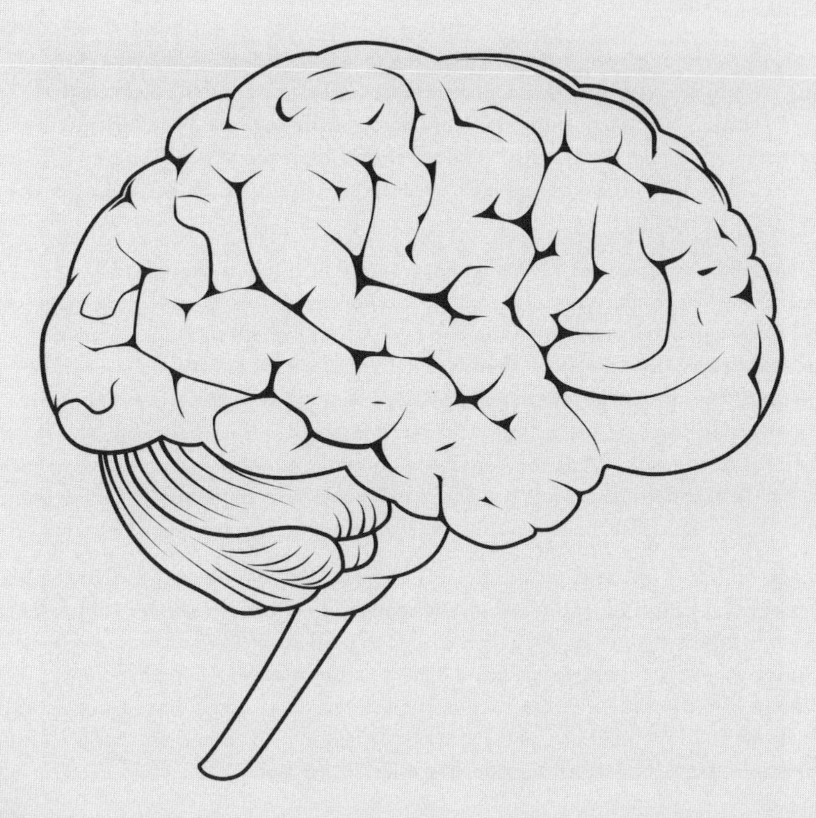

I don't know about you, but every time I attend a conference, I always get very excited when a neuroscientist or cognitive scientist stands up on the stage to talk about the brain and how we learn. In March 2021, the Department for Education (2021a) provided an update on their small-scale research projects. The publication included a comparison of teacher training in 38 countries versus the provision for teachers in England. At the moment, there are certain standards for continuous professional development (CPD) for teachers, but there is no legally specified number of days or hours required per year (see Department for Education, 2016). Unlike England, in 27 of the countries included in the research project, teachers must participate in a legally specified amount of CPD. At the moment, teachers across the UK are generally offered between three and five in-house training days per academic year. This must change if we want our teachers to be engaged with research and cognitive science in order to teach better, and for longer.

On those rare occasions when I was allowed out of school as a teacher, I did my best to craft a timetable for my CPD content to ensure I was exposed to science and research. There's certainly not enough of it available to teachers in their day-to-day work and it's no surprise that teachers are desperate for more support, like me, and lap it up when it is offered. The lust for research and the science of learning is changing, and outside of the accountability, stress and workload pressures all our teachers endure, the interest in cognitive science is exciting and welcome. For every teacher who works in the classroom, there is more work to be done to help them learn how we use our brain and how our memories are shaped, and also how we forget. Much of what we do as teachers, at least in the earlier stages of our career, is very much trial and error. With better training, teachers will get off to a stronger start much sooner.

I believe teachers can become great teachers when they have a deeper understanding of learning, including conscious and unconscious processes, as well as the physiological aspects of our bodies. Although we are still very much at the beginning of a big shift in education here in England, developing a neuroscientific approach to how we teach is essential in all current or future frameworks. This starts with a basic understanding of the brain and how it functions.

In a 2017 research paper, Daniel T. Willingham argues that teachers should work to understand children's thinking, emotion and motivation to aid their practice. He suggests that 'psychology can inspire new methods, and researchers can use scientific methods to evaluate the relative effectiveness' of those methods. If we are to rethink how teacher education trains future teachers on educational psychology, the opportunity to compare different curriculum approaches to instruction and measure the outcomes is an opportunity we should not allow to pass. Whilst the new Early Career Framework in England (Department for Education, 2021b) offers us some hope for a new generation of teachers, it is not yet nuanced enough to consider the wide variety of classrooms and young people we work with.

In this chapter, I would like to unpick some of the things that I have learned about the brain so you can position yourself in a place of good understanding to translate this knowledge back into your work. I believe knowing about some key components of the brain can give teachers a deeper understanding of how we learn and a more secure relationship with memory. Your challenge is to translate this information back to your classroom. I hope the practical elements of this chapter, including a practical idea on direct instruction, plus the toolkit tips, worked example and template, will support you in achieving this.

EXPLAINER

An introduction to neuroscience

For the purposes of this book, it is important to separate two broad and distinct fields of research: cognitive neuroscience and cognitive psychology.

Cognitive neuroscience is focused on the relationship between cognition and the functions of the brain. Cognition can be defined as the mental action of thinking and the way in which we acquire knowledge and understanding. Cognitive neuroscience is concerned with the biological functions and mental processes of the brain. It seeks to understand how the brain achieves the functions it performs.

Cognitive psychology considers how the mind operates and how we develop knowledge and understanding through, for example, thinking, remembering and problem-solving. Cognitive psychology theorises on the underlying mechanisms of learning and creates evidence to test such theories.

As an educator, I have been interested in neuroscience for many years. As my knowledge and interest have developed, I have also become interested in psychology (how the mind operates). It's important for educators to know about the latter, as I suspect if you are a teacher working outside of the specialism of psychology, your journey will perhaps be similar to mine. How far away are we from teacher education developing both of these fields of knowledge for all teachers? In this chapter, I will focus more on the former as it's cognitive neuroscience – how the brain enables us to build knowledge and understanding – that will have the greatest impact in enabling teachers to develop aspects of their teaching and learning repertoire.

The history of neuroscience

As I mentioned in the introduction, neuroscience is not a new field of study. Professor Jeanette Norden (2019), a neuroscientist from Vanderbilt School of Medicine, explains that anyone with an interest in understanding more about the brain can empower themselves to do this. To begin your journey, it may be helpful to take a brief look at the history of neuroscience and how it has developed from Ancient Egypt to today. What I hope to do in this section is summarise some of the things that I have learned from neuroscience experts through the ages. This initial information provides you with an important overview of our human journey with neuroscience, and whilst we have made many incredible discoveries, we have only scratched the surface. This general overview of the history of what we know about the brain will whet the appetite further for those who are deeply interested in understanding how we learn, store and use information.

The key question to ask yourself while you read this is: where are you with your knowledge, your thinking and your understanding? More importantly, how is this influencing the way that you teach?

Ancient Egypt

Reaching back into Ancient Egypt and human perceptions of body and soul, I now know why I should have paid more attention to my son who dressed up as Anubis in his school play during primary school. It might have given me a better understanding of how and why the brains of pharaohs, deemed worthy of embalming, were extracted through the nose and then discarded! The first written record of the word 'brain' dates from Ancient Egypt, in a document written around 1,700 BC but based on texts from 3,000 BC. Nevertheless, the Ancient Egyptians did not consider it an important organ. They focused instead on the heart and other internal organs, which were carefully preserved for the afterlife.

Ancient India

Consciousness was described as the ultimate mystery in Ancient India, with 'gods representing various cognitive centres' (Kak, 1997). This is now consigned to philosophy rather than to science, although there is scope for all of us to develop a more scientific understanding of consciousness (and unconsciousness).

Having read several books by German author Hermann Hesse, including *Siddhartha* (1922), I can begin to understand how my curiosity as a young teacher was well intended. In my newfound freedom at university, in my journey to move away from 'materialism to spiritualism' (Mehmood and Khan, 2018), I read *Siddhartha*, which recounts Buddha's life and highlights how we each encounter struggles with the realities of life. Buddha's life is a 'symbol of modernity of ancient India'. Understanding more about our consciousness (our awareness of the way we think and act) is a journey we all must go on, found in summary texts such as *Siddhartha*, sought physically in the world and enriched by our everyday experiences, or captured together in revered religious texts such as the Bible, Koran or Tripitaka.

Ancient China

As with Ancient Egypt, in Ancient China there are historical examples of methods used to extract the brain from the human skull. Whilst many of us will have some understanding of traditional Chinese medicine, from acupuncture to tai chi or herbal products, few (myself included) will know much about trepanation – the process of making a burr hole in the skull (by drilling, scraping or sawing) to access the brain; an ancient form of craniotomy. Hobert and Binello (2017) unpick some of the ancient 'therapeutic and spiritual purposes' of this with references to inscriptions found on bones or tortoise shells from the time period of the Shang dynasty (1,600–1,100 BC), suggesting that people had knowledge of brain tumours centuries ago.

In 'The records of anatomy in Ancient China', Shao et al. (2020) highlight one of six anatomical maps used to illustrate 'nine places in the head and the spirit in the brain', drawing upon Taoist life. This research highlights not only errors found from earlier civilisation, but also how exploration was evolving at the time and how neuroscience was moving forward in specific directions and cultures.

Ancient Greece

The Ancient Greek philosophers had differing opinions as to the function of the brain. In the fifth century BC, Hippocrates argued that the brain was the centre of intelligence, as we saw in the quote in the introduction to this book. As we move into the fourth century BC, we meet Plato, who began to study the brain and concluded that it was the seat of mental process, but Aristotle contradicted this, bestowing this important function on the heart instead.

ANCIENT EGYPT 1,700 BC: First written record of the word 'brain'.

ANCIENT INDIA Consciousness described as the ultimate mystery.

ANCIENT CHINA 1,600–1,100 BC: Inscriptions found suggesting knowledge of brain tumours.

ROMAN EMPIRE 177 AD: Galen delivered his lecture *On the Brain*, concluding that the brain controlled cognition.

17TH CENTURY Thomas Willis founded neurology.

18TH AND 19TH CENTURIES Franz Joseph Gall's theory of phrenology is popularised.

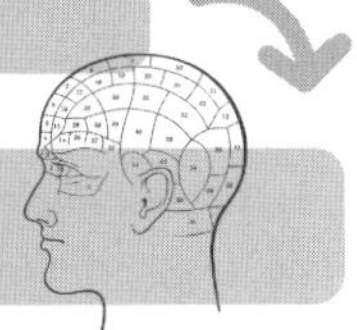

20TH AND 21ST CENTURIES Modern medicine has deepened our understanding of the brain, including its complex functions and faculties.

Roman Empire

Galen (circa 130 to 210 AD) was a Greek physician during the Roman Empire. In 177 AD, he delivered a lecture entitled *On the Brain*. In his lecture, Galen concluded that the brain controlled cognition and was in charge of common sense and memory. Personality and emotion, however, were considered to be generated by the rest of the body, particularly the heart and liver. Records of the pineal gland also date back to Galen. The pineal gland is a small gland in the middle of the head; we now know it produces the hormone melatonin and helps our sleep cycle by producing melatonin in differing amounts throughout the day (see Chapter 9, page 117). At the time, however, its function was unclear and hotly debated. Galen's conclusions 'dominated medical thinking until the seventeenth century' (Lokhorst, 2013).

Seventeenth century

The pineal gland was still under scrutiny in the seventeenth century. René Descartes (1596–1650) believed that the mind exerted control over the brain via the pineal gland. Descartes argued that most parts of the body were paired, but that there might be a single place where the human soul interacted.

In the seventeenth century, English doctor Thomas Willis (1621–1675) founded neurology, the branch of medicine dealing with disorders of the nervous system. Willis researched the nervous system, clarifying patterns of blood flow by injecting coloured dye into arteries. He is best known for his work *The Anatomy of the Brain*, illustrated by Sir Christopher Wren, the architect who rebuilt St Paul's Cathedral after the Great Fire of London in 1666.

Eighteenth and nineteenth centuries

The German doctor Franz Joseph Gall (1758–1828) developed a theory that the shape and size of the brain were connected with intelligence and personality traits. This was known as phrenology. Gall's hypothesis endured into the twentieth century but has since been wholly **debunked**. Phrenology assumed that studying the shape of the skull using examination and measurement would provide information that could determine someone's ability. Gall hypothesised that the brain was divided into 27 faculties, each controlling a different function, from verbal memory to reproductive instincts. It became a popular Victorian method and immersed itself into popular culture at the time, for example, astrology, palmistry and scientific racism to exploit particular groups of people.

Twentieth and twenty-first centuries

Professor Jeanette Norden (2019) explains how the historical understanding of the brain has evolved to such a degree that we are now in a position where we understand the qualities of a person and what may influence them. Through modern medicine, we know that complex functions, for example empathy and compassion, have processes in the brain which are devoted to those faculties. The next time someone fails to accept your point of view or pushes forward with their ideas regardless of the evidence, you could argue that these cognitive processes in their brain are not as developed as yours. A question worth asking is, 'Why do some people have parts of the brain faculties which are not as developed as others? Are there specific things we can do as parents, or as adults, to change the way our brain functions and grows?'

*

There are countless historical references I could have used in this section. The ones I have chosen are snapshots of human evolution and offer a summary of how key discussions have evolved and influenced neuroscience and psychology. One thing I do know is that I'm not the first and won't be the last person to explore this field of research.

Today, we could report back to the Egyptians and inform them that we now know that perception and cognition are separate to the soul and more associated with the mind – the brain has an important job to do, as does modern science.

Parts of the brain

In order to develop an understanding of memory, it's important to have a basic knowledge of certain parts of the brain, for example the amygdala and the hippocampus. This is terminology that most of us may have heard before, but unless we repeatedly learn what these parts of the brain are, what they do and how we can use this information in our day-to-day work, we will struggle to remember. No pun intended.

An introduction to the main sections of the brain

Let me provide you with a beginner's overview of the brain. We'll start with some simple key terms to help us get to grips with the brain as an organ. We will use a simple lateral view of the brain. It's important to note that this diagram **doesn't** precisely represent the true shape of the brain and its parts.

THE HUMAN BRAIN

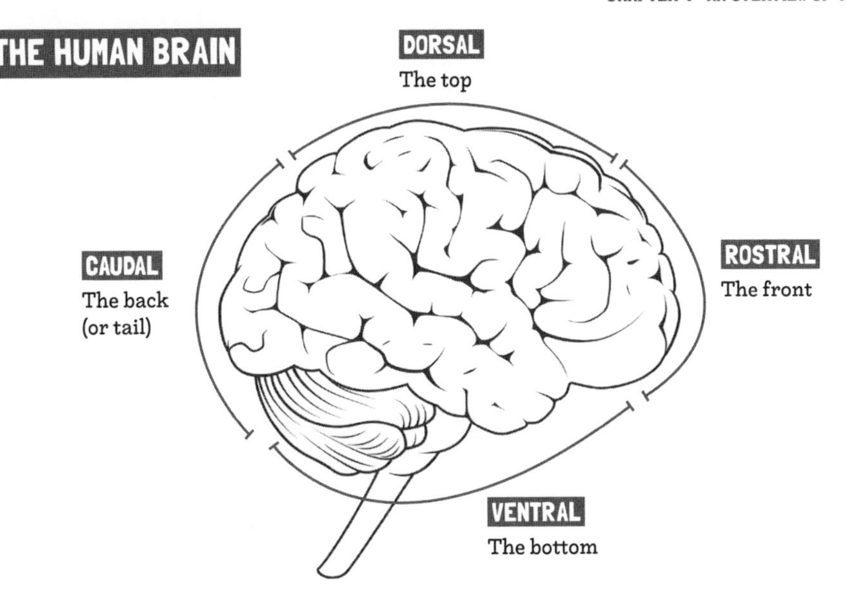

The front of the brain is known as the **rostral** and the back the **caudal** (or tail). The top of the brain is the **dorsal** and the bottom is the **ventral**. One way I try to remember this is using the abbreviation **C.D.R.V.** and tapping my head in a clockwise motion from the back of my head (caudal) moving towards the top (dorsal), the front (rostral) and the bottom (ventral).

The brain can be subdivided (in its simplest form) into five regions.

THE FIVE REGIONS OF THE BRAIN

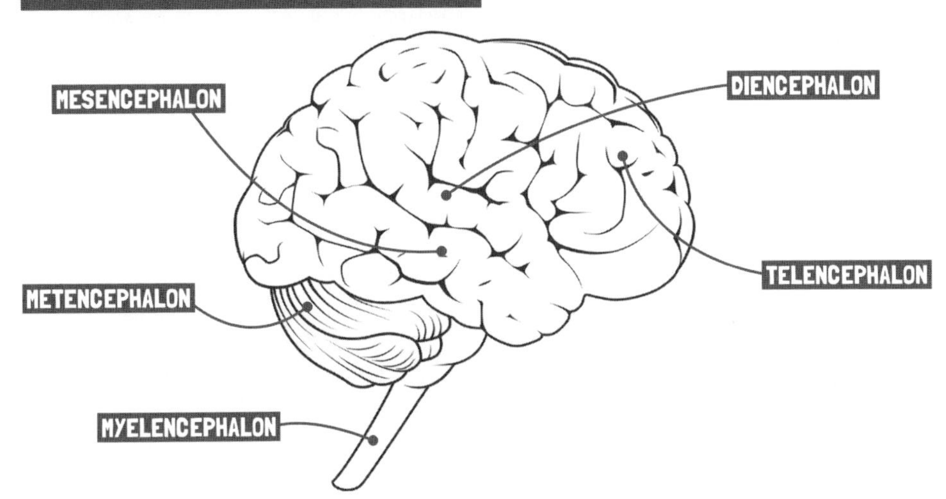

The **telencephalon** is the front area of the brain, which is believed to be the root of our mind. The **diencephalon** is at the centre of the brain and is the 'control room' for the body, for example, controlling body temperature. Another part of the brain is the **mesencephalon**, which involves our motor movement, auditory and visual processing, and reflexes. Underneath this area is the **metencephalon**, which contains the **cerebellum** – Latin for 'little brain'. The cerebellum is the part of the brain that allows us to perform voluntary movements. The metencephalon also contains the pons – the bridge that forms part of our **brainstem** and is attached to the cerebellum. Finally, the **myelencephalon** is the hindbrain and eventually forms the **medulla oblongata**, the lower part of the brainstem that supports our respiration and cardiovascular activities, for example running and swimming.

Brainstem

The brainstem is the stalk at the base of the brain that connects the brain and the spinal cord. It is made up of the **midbrain**, the pons and the medulla oblongata, each with its own function and structure. These parts of the brain help regulate vital systems in the body, such as heartbeat and breathing, enable us to perform reflexive actions, control eye movements, and support visual and auditory processing.

Cerebral cortex

The outer area of the brain is known as the **cerebral cortex**. The cerebral cortex is part of the telencephalon and it is the area that is responsible for higher-order thinking – thinking that goes beyond memorising facts and towards understanding, inferring, connecting, categorising and applying information to solve problems. The cerebral cortex is made up of four different lobes, each with its own individual function. Neuroscience understands the lobes of the cortex are interconnected and when, for example, we move or speak or do both things at once, many areas of the cortex work together to support this functioning.

Frontal lobe: Higher mental functions: concentration, planning, judgement, emotional expression, creativity and inhibition.

Parietal lobe: Sensory processing: sensation from the muscles and skin, for example touch, taste and temperature.

Occipital lobe: Visual processing: sight, image recognition and perception.

Temporal lobe: Association: interpreting sounds and language, object recognition and emotion.

THE CEREBRAL CORTEX, CEREBELLUM AND BRAINSTEM

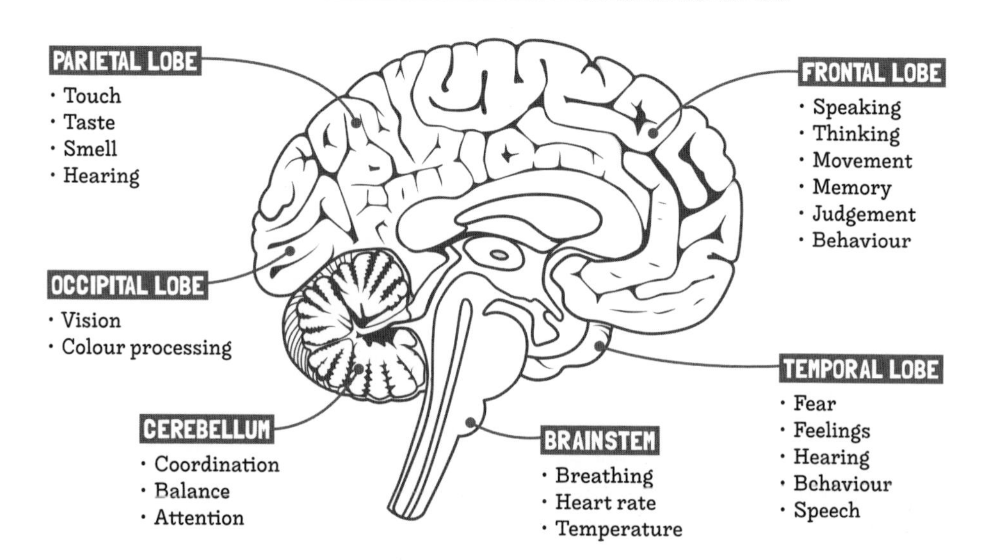

Who knows? By the end of this book when I next pose this question: 'When did Mount Vesuvius erupt and destroy Pompeii?', you may be able to describe what happens to your brain in the **cerebral cortex**, which is situated in the telencephalon part of your brain at the point of answering!

Myth-buster: We know that certain parts of our brain are responsible for specific functions. However, as a result of this, a theory has emerged that some people are 'right-brained' and some people are 'left-brained'. In other words, one part of a person's brain dominates over another and this gives that person specific personality traits and talents. 'Creative' people are said to be right-brained and 'logical' people are said to be left-brained. This theory is a **MYTH**. One of many research papers debunks the theory completely by showing zero evidence that one 'side' of the brain can dominate over the other in this way (Nielsen et al., 2013). The study suggests that there is discrete lateral connectivity between left and right hubs.

The limbic system

The limbic system is a part of the brain that is positioned between the cerebral cortex and the diencephalon. Although the limbic system is linked to many different processes in the body, it is most commonly associated with emotion. The **amygdala** (Latin for 'almond') is considered to be a key component of the limbic system. There are two amygdalae, one situated on each side of the brain at the base. It is where we attach emotional meaning to our memories. The **hippocampus** also forms part of the limbic system and this is where we consolidate declarative memory (concepts, rules and facts). Again, we have two hippocampi, one on each side of the brain. The **fornix**, Latin for 'arch', is the C-shaped nerve fibre that carries information away from the hippocampus. There is only one fornix, supporting the two hippocampi. It's also useful to be aware of the hypothalamus, which is the control centre for our nervous system and which regulates hormone release. We'll look at how the limbic system functions in more detail in Chapter 4.

KEY TERMS

Brainstem: Made up of the midbrain, pons and medulla oblongata, each with their own function and structure.

Cerebellum: Controls our motor responses.

Cerebral cortex: Involved in higher-order thinking and divided into four lobes: frontal, parietal, temporal and occipital.

Diencephalon: The centre of the brain, this is the 'control room' for the body.

Limbic system: Most commonly associated with emotion, the limbic system has multiple components, including the amygdala, hippocampus, fornix and hypothalamus.

Mesencephalon: This region of the brain involves our reflexes.

Metencephalon: Consists of the pons and cerebellum.

Myelencephalon: Part of the hindbrain that contains long pathways where axons travel to the spinal cord.

Telencephalon: The front of the brain; the root of the mind.

PRACTICAL IDEA

Direct instruction

Direct instruction (DI) is a relatively new philosophy I have become aware of over the last decade. Subconsciously using these techniques in the classroom and immersing yourself in the research allows all teachers who are interested in educational theory to refine their teaching techniques. Put simply, DI is a theory which emphasises carefully planned lessons focused on marginal gains, with objectives that are clearly defined with prescribed tasks. Now, I know the cynic in me would question this approach, think that this is 'nothing we don't already know' and perhaps fall into the misconceptions and myths that have blighted many teachers (including myself) for many years. Tackling these myths head-on ensures we support teachers with well-informed strategies.

As we get to grips with knowing more about the brain while we delve deeper into this book, it's important that we tackle some myths and recommendations around DI so that you have some clear strategies to deploy. In an interesting paper published by the National Institute for Direct Instruction, Professor Sara Tarver (1998) tackles ten myths and truths about DI. I've witnessed the impact direct instruction can have. I do know the strategies work effectively, albeit with nuance and in a particular context. On page 11, I've summarised the most common myths Tarver tackles in her paper.

A word of caution: While direct instruction has been proven to be an effective strategy, it's important to acknowledge that there's not just one way to teach. In 2022, Skene et al. published a review of the evidence regarding guided play versus direct instruction in the Early Years. The researchers concluded that guided play had a 'greater positive effect than direct instruction on early maths skills, shape knowledge and task switching'. The key to teaching is to ask yourself 'What works, under what conditions?' in order to devise a nuanced approach to supporting learning and development.

In this chapter, we are going to explore several teaching techniques that support DI:

- **Making abstract ideas concrete:** Presenting ideas clearly and precisely and giving concrete examples.
- **Chunking:** Delivering content in bitesize chunks.
- **Modelling:** Demonstrating ideas and concepts.
- **Dual coding:** Using imagery and text to support learning.

Turn to page 12 to read more about each of these techniques and how to put them into practice in your classroom.

Some people say... MYTH	The evidence from Tarver (1998) suggests... FACT
Direct instruction (DI) is not effective for teaching problem-solving or higher-order thinking skills.	DI can be used to teach basic content, skills and strategies, as well as problem-solving and higher-order content.
DI is not effective for teaching reading comprehension.	DI can be used to teach skills for reading comprehension, including discerning relevant and irrelevant content, drawing conclusions and identifying cause and effect.
DI is equivalent to rote learning.	DI aims to teach generalisations, which permit students to learn multiple items simultaneously, rather than having to learn each item individually by rote.
DI is detrimental to students' self-esteem.	The academic achievement DI can lead to has a positive impact on self-confidence.
DI is not appropriate for students at risk of academic failure or those who are above-average achievers.	DI can be used successfully with students who have a range of abilities. It benefits disadvantaged students, those who are working below expectations, and those who are average or above-average achievers.
DI is less suitable for students with dyslexia.	DI can be used successfully to teach children with a range of SEND, including dyslexia.
DI is better suited to younger students.	DI can work effectively in pre-school, primary school, secondary school and beyond.
DI makes students dependent on their teacher and less capable of independent learning tasks.	DI moves students from acquiring knowledge via structured teaching through to applying this knowledge independently.
DI stifles creativity.	DI provides the prior knowledge and skills required to develop creativity and come up with new ideas.

Making abstract ideas concrete

When you're teaching new concepts, rules and facts, the students in your class will encounter many abstract ideas that they will need to grasp. An abstract idea can be challenging to understand because it is removed from the 'concrete': what you can see in front of you. Some abstract concepts or words may not even have a concrete equivalent, for example 'power'. Expecting students to understand any abstract concepts, rules or facts just by learning a definition is insufficient to support their understanding, particularly if they have no prior knowledge or schemas. Where prior schemas exist, there is some hope, but abstract definitions can still lead to difficulties with learning.

It's essential therefore that teachers take care to be clear and precise in all the verbal instructions, cues and assessment that they use and endeavour to make abstract ideas concrete wherever possible.

For example, if I say the word 'turkey', I have some indication of what you are now thinking. I have made an assessment of what you may already know, based on the fact that you can read this text. The word 'turkey' elicits a schema in your thinking. However, I need to evaluate your understanding and check what your prior schema is retrieving.

What if I say, 'Turkey can be hot'? This is still an abstract statement. Again, without clarity or checking your understanding, as a teacher I'd still have a very low success rate.

In this instance, although we can eat a 'hot turkey', I don't want you to be thinking about the bird. I need you to be thinking about the country. My original abstract introduction was therefore unhelpful. Saying 'Turkey can be hot', without any context, can be misleading.

What I should do instead is offer clarity and a concrete idea. For example:

'Due to the geographical location of Turkey, the country is arid and incredibly hot.'

This example is a little more concrete and provides several keywords which will help connect key concepts, rules and facts. I could remove any two and keep one and still make a difference to my pupils' acquisition of knowledge. For example:

1. Due to the location of Turkey, it is arid and incredibly hot.
2. Due to the geography of Turkey, it can be incredibly hot.
3. Turkey, the country, is arid and hot.

Chunking

Delivering content in bitesize chunks is also essential for successful teaching and it supports understanding and retrieval. Rather than delivering large amounts of information all at once, break it down into smaller, more manageable units. Think carefully about how you organise the information into smaller chunks. Identify similarities and patterns in order to group the information sensibly. This will make it easier to remember.

On page 13 is an example of how this might work.

Example 1 (abstract)

How to build a table

Thanks to the unique construction, this table is easy to assemble, lift and move around.

Unwrap all the products from the outer box. Lay the table top on the floor on a soft carpet or rug to avoid scratching the surface. You should have four self-tapping screws and four legs. Using your hand, turn one self-tapping screw into the hole in the table top. Once the screw is tight, twist the other side of the screw into the hole found in one of the table legs. Repeat steps four and five three times. Turn the table over and wipe it clean.

Example 2 (concrete)

How to build a table

1. Unwrap all items:
   - 1 large table top
   - 4 legs
   - 4 self-tapping screws.

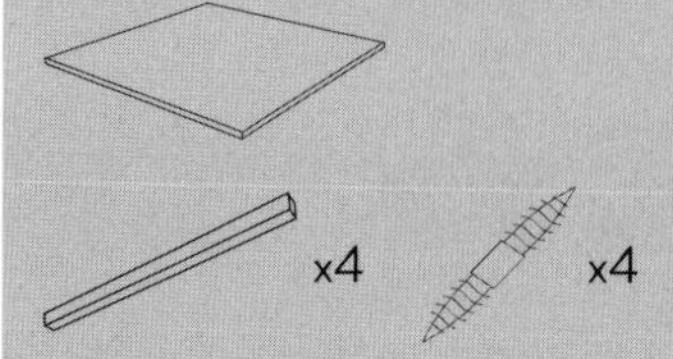

2. Lay the table top on a carpet or rug.

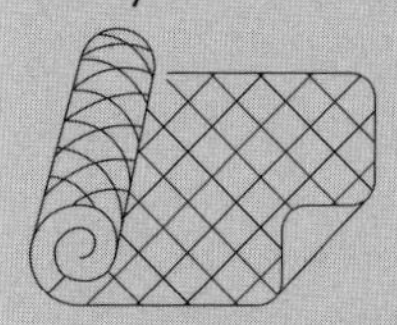

3. Twist all four screws into the holes in the table top until tight.

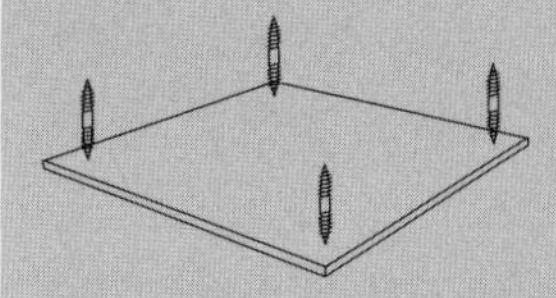

4. Twist one leg into the other side of each screw until tight.

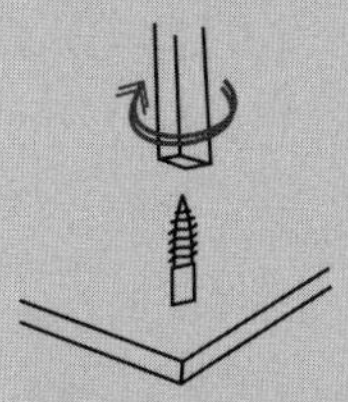

5. Turn the table over and wipe clean.

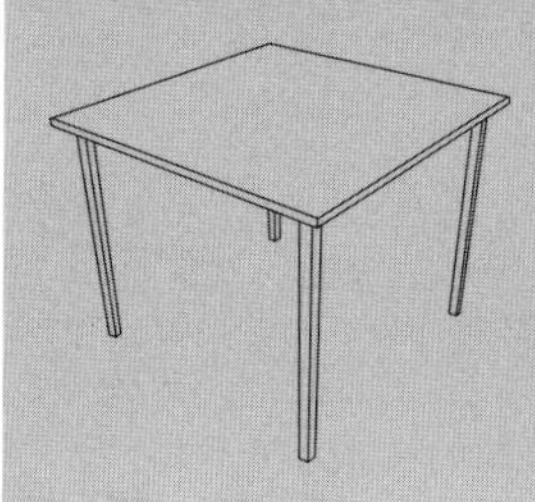

For more on chunking, see Chapter 3, page 42.

Modelling

The most effective teaching also requires good models to make abstract ideas and concepts concrete and accessible. There's much more information on modelling in Chapter 8, page 102.

Dual coding

Dual coding – a theory of cognition and how we think – uses the idea that the formation of mental images aids learning. First hypothesised by Allan Paivio in 1971, dual coding theory states that using imagery alongside text helps to form mental images of text materials while reading or listening. A good example I can give you is the following:

Example 1

Why are volcanoes dangerous?

Magma is the molten rock which sits beneath the Earth's surface. At the top of the volcano is a vent which allows material to escape. It is sometimes surrounded by a crater which is the mouth of the volcano. Lava is molten rock that erupts and then solidifies as it cools. The lava travels up a conduit at great speed. When the volcano erupts, fragments of lava rock smaller than 2 mm are expelled. These are pieces of ash. As there is so much of it, it forms an ash cloud. One example of a volcano is Mount Vesuvius, near Naples in Italy. It is the most densely populated volcanic region in the world. Famously, Mount Vesuvius erupted in 79 AD, destroying the town of Pompeii. During the eruption, the ash cloud rose to 21 miles high.

Example 2

Why are volcanoes dangerous?

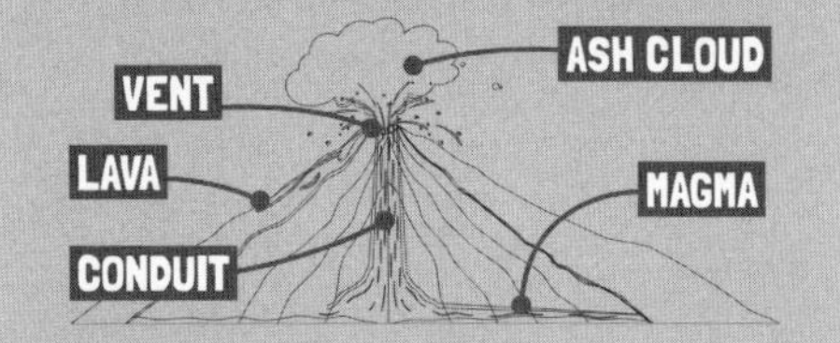

Magma is the **molten rock** which sits beneath the Earth's surface.

At the top of the volcano is a **vent** which allows material to escape.

It is sometimes surrounded by a **crater** which is the **mouth** of the volcano.

Lava is molten rock that erupts and then **solidifies** as it **cools**. The lava travels up a **conduit** at great speed.

When the volcano erupts, **fragments** of lava rock smaller than 2 mm are expelled. These are pieces of **ash**. As there is so much of it, it forms an **ash cloud**.

One **example** of a volcano is **Mount Vesuvius**, near Naples in Italy. It is the most densely populated volcanic region in the world. Famously, Mount Vesuvius erupted in **79 AD**, destroying the town of Pompeii. During the eruption, the ash cloud rose to **21 miles** high.

Which example do you find easier to learn from? As a classroom activity, the terms in bold could be left out, encouraging students to select the right word.

I expect your answer is Example 2. In this example, we are presenting a detailed image of a volcano alongside the text, overlaid with arrows and keywords, to help identify the core parts of the structure.

When imagery is used for enhancing text learning, a teacher is supporting students to develop a mental schema. In a global world, if we think about what a set of instructions looks like when building a piece of furniture, you can often translate the step-by-step instruction manual with images alone (as in my example on page 13). There may be one or two numbers to indicate how many pieces of wood or screws you have in the flat pack. This is a great example of universal language.

Notice that the text is also different in the second example. It is chunked into separate points and some of the words are highlighted; this is another study skill technique referenced in this book to support retention (see Chapter 4). The highlighted terminology allows the student to summarise what could be a difficult paragraph for some.

Direct instruction may be a helpful strategy to use alongside dual coding.

Add a task

When using dual coding, alongside the image and text, you could add an explicit task with an instruction for students to complete it. For example:

Look at the diagram and identify the different parts of the volcano.

Write a paragraph to describe and summarise what a volcano is and each of the key sections labelled.

The parts of the volcano are not labelled on the diagram and the task for the student is to use the keywords listed to accurately identify and place each term in the correct place. This is a very simple and subconscious strengthening exercise that all teachers use and you will see this everywhere in worksheets and textbooks the world over. When a teacher has the opportunity to design these things themselves, it really helps them to think carefully about the curriculum choices, the knowledge that they want to teach their students, and more importantly, how they will develop this knowledge and understanding into long-term retention through a range of pedagogical approaches such as this.

Some considerations for dual coding

It's really important to think about cognitive load theory (see Chapter 5 for a more detailed exploration) when using dual coding. This is the theory that our brains can only process a certain amount of information at any one time and if we overload our brains we inhibit learning. Presenting all the information at once, for example, on a busy slideshow, with lots of images, including irrelevant images, and an ill-thought-out colour scheme will add to a learner's cognitive load. Prior knowledge must also be a consideration, and with this, one can begin to understand how complex classroom life truly is. I can tell you as much as I can about education research, but knowing how to translate these recommendations and apply them on an hourly basis for 30 students in front of me is where the true art of teaching begins to unfold. I also know that you reading this paragraph will be hindered by external distractions or my failure to make the material captivating, by telling stories, keeping information precise or adding in 'dual-coded' images to support what I am saying.

With careful planning and curriculum sequencing, underpinned by very methodological approaches in the classroom, teachers can use dual coding as a technique to help reduce the stress on retention.

Obviously, no teaching technique ever works in isolation. There will be many other factors at play which underpin its effectiveness. If a teacher has poor classroom management, weak subject knowledge and a poor understanding of the curriculum sequence, dual coding or direct instruction for that matter, then pupils will struggle.

For dual coding to be an effective strategy, you need to be selective in the images that you choose because students need to know what they are! You cannot teach a very young student anything substantial about volcanoes if they have never seen one before, have never spoken the word, or know nothing about them.

For direct instruction to be effective, the clear delivery of content through chunking and dual coding, plus routine daily practice that addresses specific skills alongside targeted exercises, is of critical importance. Think about the teaching of phonics in primary schools for a useful example of how these different methods can be brought together in practice.

TOOLKIT TIPS

1. When you're presenting new information, include images alongside the text, chunk the key points and highlight important terminology.

2. Add a simple strengthening task, for example asking students to add keyword labels to an image.

3. Don't go over the top! Make sure all images are relevant and familiar to your students, and dial down the fonts and colours on your slides.

WORKED EXAMPLE

In the worked example below, I have provided you with two potential options to take. In option one, the task for the student is to write a summary of a volcanic eruption when presented with an image of a volcano with some of the key parts labelled.

Alternatively, teachers could try using the dual coding technique (option two) by reversing the information presented. In the example I have provided below, I have offered a summary of a volcanic eruption using some keywords alongside a blank space where the student is asked to draw a volcano and label the key parts. There are potential scaffolding opportunities here where teachers can differentiate the task by providing one or two different versions of the resource. For example, a student who struggles may want a copy of the diagram with arrows already pointing to the right positions. Alternatively, the diagram could have all the words already signposted, but with some letters omitted to help nudge retrieval strength.

Both techniques can be presented in a future lesson as part of retrieval practice (Chapter 2) or a spaced practice method (Chapter 3).

Option 1 Text	**Task: Write a summary of a volcanic eruption**	**Teacher: Provide a volcano with parts labelled**
		VENT ASH CLOUD LAVA MAGMA CONDUIT
Option 2 Visual	**Teacher: Offer a summary of a volcanic eruption**	**Task: Label the parts of the volcano**
	Magma is the **molten rock** which sits beneath the Earth's surface. At the top of the volcano is a **vent** which allows material to escape. It is sometimes surrounded by a **crater** which is the **mouth** of the volcano. **Lava** is molten rock that erupts and then **solidifies** as it **cools**. The lava travels up a **conduit** at great speed. When the volcano erupts, **fragments** of lava rock smaller than 2 mm are expelled. These are pieces of **ash**. As there is so much of it, it forms an **ash cloud**.	

TEMPLATE

Dual coding

Option 1 Text	**Task:**	**Teacher:**
Option 2 Visual	**Teacher:**	**Task:**

Scan the QR code for a downloadable digital copy of this template.

CHAPTER 2 HOW MEMORY IS SHAPED

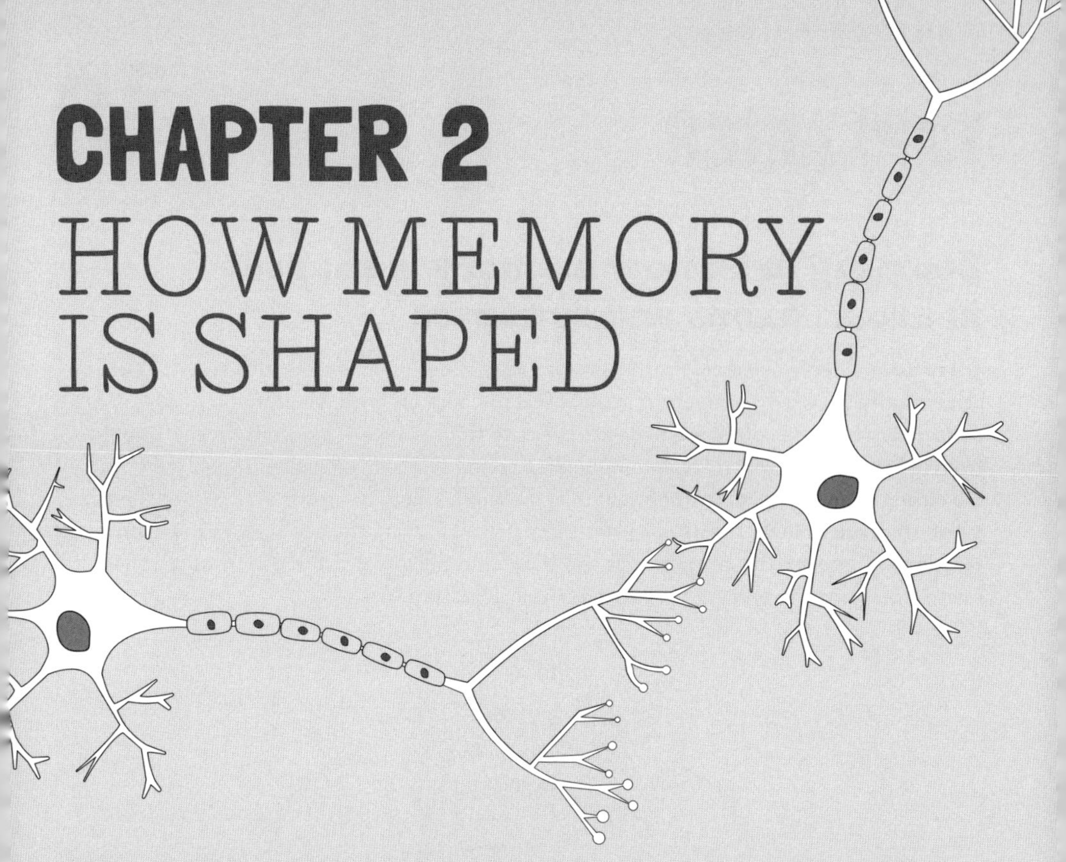

At one point in my school leadership career, I found myself covering for a psychology A level class. I was teaching Year 12 and 13 students (17- and 18-year-olds) without any qualification in the subject whatsoever – just a mere interest and a willingness to take on the teaching of a second subject. I knew it and the students did too! However, this didn't stop me from working tirelessly to revise, attend courses and prepare lessons to the best of my ability. Overall, the students each achieved their predicted grades or better. I look back to that point in my teaching career, over ten years ago, and at that time when social media was emerging and information was becoming easier to access. This is the point in my career at which I started to develop a deeper interest in cognitive psychology and its place in the classroom and in teacher training – almost 20 years too late!

From that moment, I have been seeking out information about how learning happens and that begins with an understanding of how memory is shaped. To develop a basic grasp of this, we must turn our attention to some very important cells in the human body: neurons. Neuroscientists estimate that the adult human brain has between 86 billion and 100 billion neurons (Blakemore, 2019; Norden, 2019). For any of us to imagine this number is staggering. NASA estimates that there are between 100 and 400 billion stars in the Milky Way. Just dwell on that. One adult human brain has 100 billion neurons, which is equivalent to the number of stars in our galaxy!

If you counted out loud in seconds, it would take you 11.5 days to reach just one million, which in human terms is achievable, albeit very hard work! One billion seconds would take you 31.75 years; 100 billion seconds would take you over 3,000 years. I don't think you and I have long enough to live to get close to 100 billion – it's an astonishing number!

EXPLAINER

Zooming in on how memory is shaped: neurons, axons and synapses

A **neuron** is a nerve cell that is a fundamental part of our brain and nervous system. Neurons send information to other neurons in electrical or chemical form. Neurons are made up of **dendrites**, which are soft, branched extensions to the cell body. Dendrites receive impulses from other neurons, which are communicated to the cell body of the neuron. If the impulses are strong enough, a signal is then sent into the **axon**. The axon rises from a part of the cell called the **axon hillock**. The axon carries the signal away from the cell body to the **axon terminals**. These are the axon endings and they send the signal to the dendrites of other neurons, causing the process to restart in these adjacent cells.

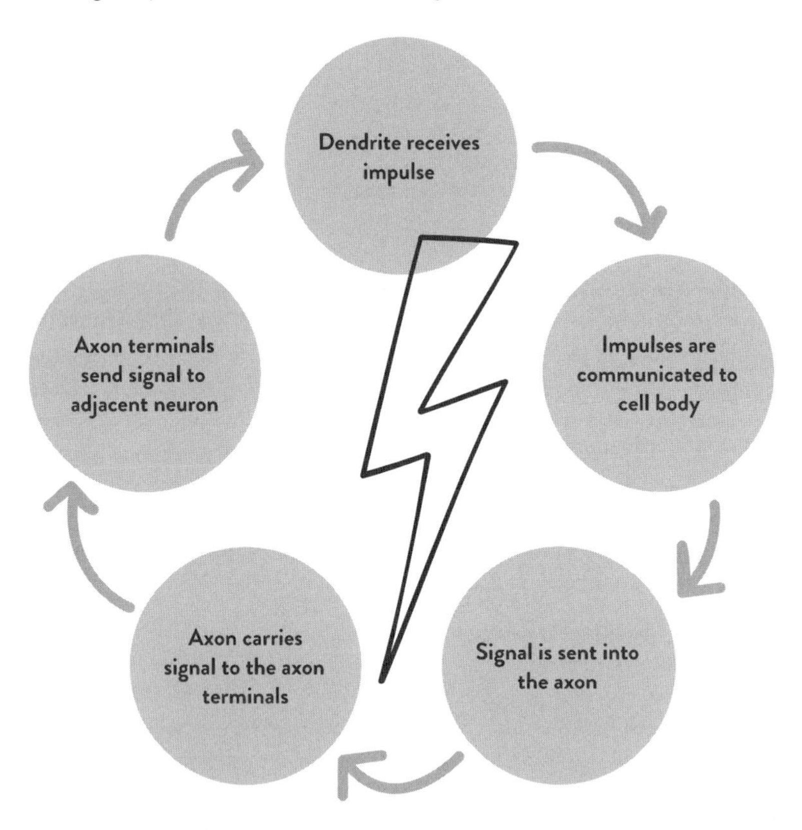

Myelin is a fatty substance that surrounds the axon. It insulates the axon to prevent the signal from degrading. This insulating layer of myelin is known as the **myelin sheath**.

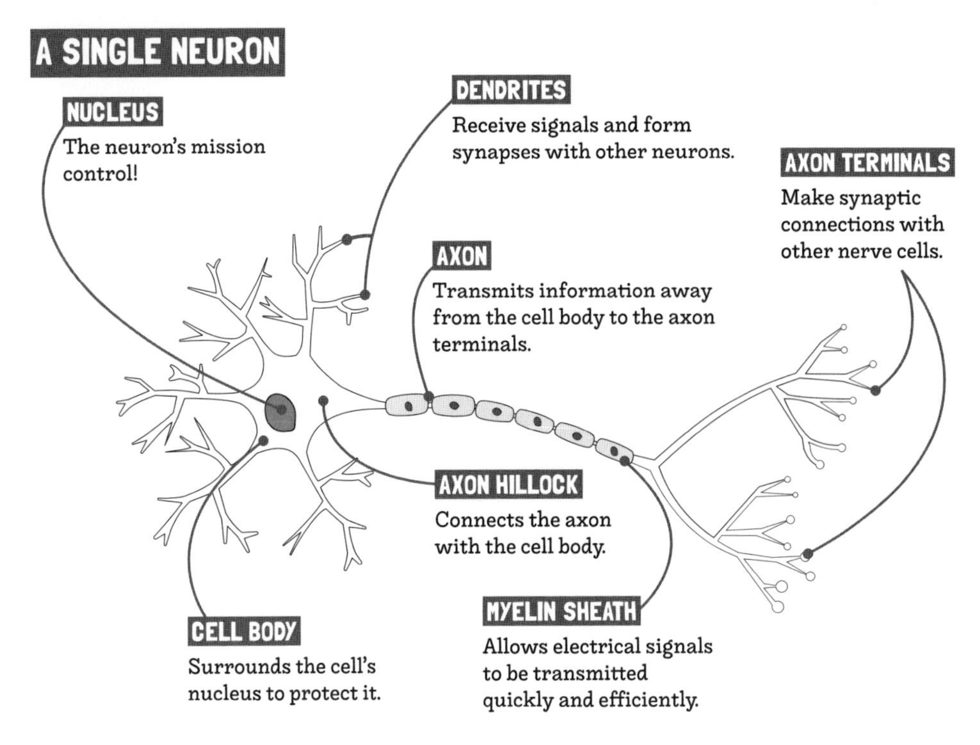

As neurons repeat the process of sending information from one cell to the next, they form stronger **synapses**, or connections. The word 'synapse' derives from the Greek language: to form a connection. Neurons can form up to around **100 trillion connections** – think of the largest spider web you can ever imagine! The greater the connection (the more you practise), the stronger the synapse becomes.

This process is called neuroplasticity – the ability of your brain to create, strengthen, weaken or dismantle this connection between two neurons. This is how we develop the ability to automate our procedural knowledge (everyday actions, such as speaking and movement) and how we can develop these actions without thinking. Neuroplasticity also enables us to accumulate declarative knowledge (concepts, rules and facts). For more on procedural and declarative knowledge, see page 34.

It's also worth noting synapse pruning, something that happens in childhood, adolescence and early adulthood – a natural process that removes connections that are no longer needed.

What happens at a synapse?

A synapse is where two neurons connect in order to transmit information. The two neurons do not actually connect physically – a microscopically small space remains between them, called the **synaptic cleft**. The transmitting neuron (also known as the presynaptic neuron) contains molecules called **neurotransmitters**. When the transmitting neuron is stimulated by an electrical impulse, the neurotransmitters are released into the synaptic cleft. The neurotransmitters then interact with the receptors on the receiving neuron (also known as the postsynaptic neuron). This can cause the receiving neuron to send impulses into its cell body and the process begins again.

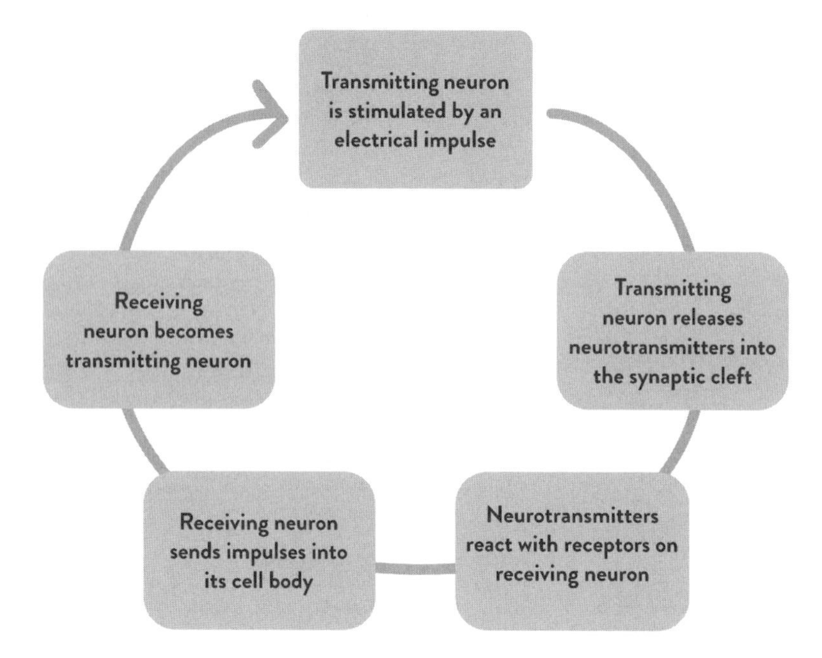

Myelination

Memory is also shaped by a process called myelination, which involves the build-up of myelin, the fatty substance that surrounds the axon. Myelin – think 'insulator' – is referred to as white matter and as it becomes stronger, it forms an insulating myelin sheath around the axon. Most myelination happens before birth and in the early years of a child's life as they develop basic skills, such as motor skills and language skills, but there is growing evidence that new learning experiences can increase levels of myelination at any age (Pan et al., 2020). 'The speed of electrical impulses that travel along axons is greatly improved by the presence of myelin' (Tibke, 2019), and therefore the more we repeat something, the more efficient our brains become at remembering it.

Put simply, myelin protects the superhighways in the brain, allowing increased speed and efficacy of passing signals, and plays an important role in the formation of long-term memories. If the brain can rewire itself, especially in our developmental years, I'd be keen to understand if there are things we can do to form myelination in our older years, or in particular ways for developing learning in the classroom.

Why rote learning is essential

So, we now know that the more we practise the stronger our memories become and the easier it is for us to perform everyday actions and recall concepts, rules and facts. However, it's also the case that we can weaken these connections by not practising often enough. This is why rote learning, recall, testing, exams, retrieval practice or whatever you want to call it is essential for teaching and learning.

Frontiers for Young Minds is an online journal where leading scientists write about their research in a way that is accessible for children. Children are asked to review and edit this cutting-edge research before it is published. What a brilliant concept! Not only do children have the opportunity to learn about science, but they also have the opportunity to be involved in producing a peer-reviewed journal. In May 2020, researchers from Montreal and Tel Aviv (Blanchette Sarrasin et al.) wrote a short paper to help young people learn how to understand their brain. In the paper, a lovely analogy for neuroplasticity is given.

Walking through woodland without a path is challenging. We have to push through the vegetation. But if we continue to use the same path over and over, gradually a track starts to form and the easier it becomes to follow the trail. However, 'if we stop using the trail, the vegetation grows back, and the trail slowly disappears. This is very similar to what happens in your brain – when you stop practising something, the connections between your neurons weaken and can ultimately be dismantled or pruned'.

The challenge for all teachers is how to strengthen these connections on a regular basis. All of us can become bored with repetition, so how can teachers keep motivation high so that the teaching of concepts, rules and facts (in any subject) remains engaging? When we are attentive, we can learn. Teachers then can help link content to whole-school curriculum and the real world so that we can strengthen prior knowledge with developing schemas.

TWO CONNECTED NEURONS

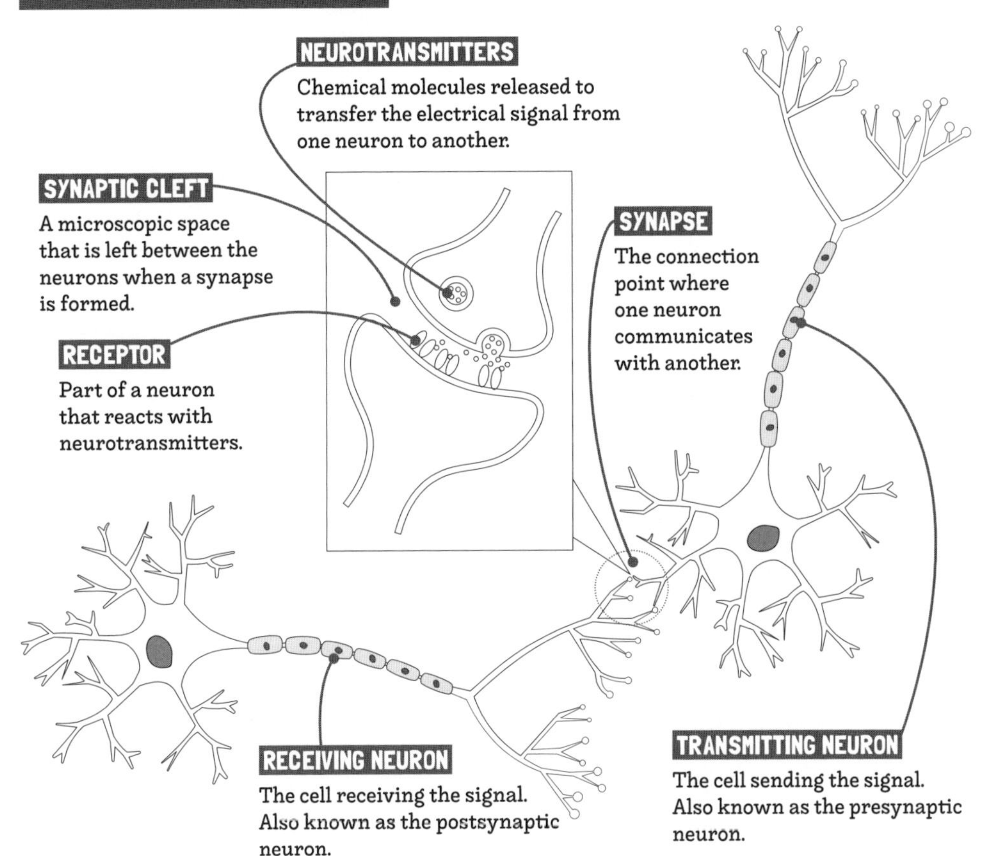

As an addendum, I think it is worth noting that we should all move away from the negative rhetoric about teaching facts and repetition. Every single one of us working inside or outside of the school has to repeat to a point of automation in order to strengthen memory – whether this is mastering a new language, learning how to play the violin or working out how to complete a static social media network analysis for the very first time. On the latter point, now that I have done this several times, I can automate the process. When I did this for the first time, it took me over four hours to complete something I can now do in 20 minutes. It was painful, I thought it wasn't worth it and I became incredibly frustrated. This is where we can all easily give up and why it is important to chunk 'learning something new' into small steps, working backwards from the goal if we are a novice to the point where we can work forwards with a problem if we are an expert (see Chapter 8 on cognitive apprenticeship).

The illusion of knowing

In one of my favourite books I've read on my journey with memory, *Connect the Dots*, the 'illusion of knowing' is described as a situation in which 'the learner thinks they know a lot more than they do, because the material is familiar or because they put a lot of (ineffective) effort into study' (Taylor, 2019). In another brilliant book, *How Learning Happens*, the authors write, 'for immediate retention, cramming sometimes leads to equivalent or even slightly better learning, but for long-term retention, spacing is significantly superior' (Kirschner and Hendrick, 2020).

Here is the challenge for teachers. Two pieces of research with conflicting advice of the benefits of studying through retrieval or cramming. Reading the details and the references and research quoted, different research trials seek to test different scenarios and outcomes. There's an important message for us all here. A technique may work in one context but not in another; it's how you use the findings in your classroom that matters. There are many ways to learn, some more effective than others, but without retesting prior knowledge and building the initial foundations (core knowledge), it's impossible for any of us to recall or develop a more detailed schema.

KEY TERMS

Axon: Part of a neuron that transmits information away from the cell body to the axon terminals.

Axon hillock: Part of the cell body of a neuron that connects it to the axon.

Axon terminals: The axon endings that make synaptic connections with other neurons.

Dendrite: A branched extension to the cell body of a neuron. Dendrites receive signals and form synapses so information can be passed from one neuron to the next.

Myelin sheath: An insulating layer that surrounds the axon, made up of the fatty substance myelin.

Neuron: A nerve cell that sends information to other neurons in electrical or chemical form. It contains a nucleus and multiple fibres called dendrites.

Synapses: Connections that are made to pass information between neurons. They can be strengthened or weakened.

PRACTICAL IDEA

Retrieval practice

Research on retrieval practice goes back nearly a century, but over the last decade, the abundance of research on retrieval practice and the explosion of discussions across the teaching profession on this topic have been nothing short of incredible. Whilst teachers, perhaps subconsciously, have been using these techniques indefinitely, this emerging communication of information is really supporting teachers to identify where they should place their efforts and how they can help students remember better.

Retrieval practice is a low-stakes quizzing method to help strengthen schemas and is a valuable mechanism for teachers to use to determine where students are in the learning process and what to do next. Put simply, retrieval practice pulls information out of students' heads by asking them to write or say it. All teachers must seek concrete answers from their students and insist on a high response rate rather than just hearing from one person. It is important to vary the strategies to suit the learning and student needs.

How you do retrieval practice matters

Remember Lee Elliot Major and Steve Higgins' (2019) Bananarama principle from the introduction? No, probably not! Let me remind you. It's not *what* you do that counts, it's *how* you do it that matters – that's what gets results. Just 'doing' rote learning isn't what's important here. What's important is selecting the correct task, time and format.

Retesting is more effective than restudy

The most important recommendation I can offer from the research I have read is that **retesting is more effective than restudy**. Keep testing students to help strengthen knowledge, rather than reteaching the material.

Whilst we develop 'storage strength' (Bjork and Bjork, 2011) for information to remain, we will find it difficult to recall this information five or ten years later if we don't use it. For example, 'Who was your best friend at primary school?' or 'What was the first movie you ever watched at the cinema?' If the information is hard to recall, it's likely that it has become subconscious, and with some prompts, you will probably get the answer correct (in time). As we sleep, our brain processes what information is relevant and what isn't. We know we cannot have every piece of information accessible and ready to be retrieved. For example, 'What is your employer's phone number?' This information may be inaccessible, you may not need it as it's stored on your mobile phone or you can find it online, but as we are discussing this now, could you recall the number without checking? When you see the number, it's stored (storage strength), but the information weakens because we are not regularly using it (retrieval strength). Put simply, we need to test students' recall to strengthen their knowledge.

How do you choose the most effective way of testing this? Endres et al. (2020), researchers from the University of Freiburg, Germany, concluded that the effects of retrieval practice depend on the type of recall task. They discussed short-answer tasks and free-recall tasks.

SHORT-ANSWER TASKS

- ★ help students to remember targeted information
- ★ support metacognition, as they help learners to identify their knowledge gaps.

Examples:
What is the second planet from the Sun?
Who was the first wife of Henry VIII?
How many pockets are there on a snooker table?

FREE-RECALL TASKS

- ★ help students to remember a broader spectrum of information
- ★ foster motivation, as learners often feel that they have more success in these tasks and can recall information more fluently.

Examples:
What are the colours of the rainbow?
Why do rainbows appear?
Explain how refraction happens.

Our students' motivation levels and the relationships that we have with them influence the success of implementing these strategies. For example, think of the most effective classroom strategy you use: how does this change on a Monday morning compared to a Friday afternoon?

For successful retesting, the research highlights that teachers must:

1. Choose recall tasks that correspond to lesson objectives and goals.
2. Select tasks for retrieval rather than restudying.
3. Factor in retrieval practice tasks with regards to developing self-regulation, behaviour and homework.

SUCCESSFUL RETESTING

It's important not to reframe the learning objective as questions and say it's retrieval practice. Students can only retrieve what they have learned. Given that motivation is a factor too, I'd add that teachers must select when is most effective to introduce their intervention. Cognitive apprenticeship sums this up best; if students are novices they will need more support, with complex end goals broken down into chunks, compared to students who are developing expertise, where feedback and instruction can become more sophisticated. Consider how you will use retrieval practice based on whether you evaluate your student as a novice or an expert.

Desirable difficulties

To strengthen connections between neurons, we must retrieve from memory and activate those connections. This 'struggle' activates learning and some of you will be familiar with the concept of desirable difficulties (Bjork and Bjork, 2011) – learning should be hard. You need to try to find the sweet spot between making learning too easy and too difficult. Evaluate students' storage strength and retrieval strength and devise retrieval tasks that ask them to recall knowledge that is challenging but not impossible for them to remember.

Retrieval strengthens neurons, but keep it low stakes

Sitting tests helps us to remember information rather than just restudying (Zaromb and Roediger, 2010). However, retrieval practice tests must be low-stakes and engaging; this contributes to the strengthening of connections between neurons. When learning is stressful, retention can be hindered and students can become 'overwhelmed with stress which interacts with their metacognitive accuracy' (Silaj et al., 2021), particularly when faced with a high-stakes exam scenario. (It's important to note that exams are summative assessment, not retrieval practice.) In order to reduce this stress, everyday classroom conditions should be motivational and safe and encourage risk-taking. Learning is emotional; so think high challenge, low stress in all classroom scenarios. Mistakes are part of the learning process and teachers should celebrate these moments that contribute towards learning.

If you're using quizzing as formative assessment to determine what knowledge has been acquired, it's important to understand that you should also consider a wide variety of other factors too. Remember the 'illusion of learning': a student might perform well or badly in a test, but that doesn't necessarily indicate how much they have learned. You should also take into consideration the progress a student has made in an academic year, their attendance, what is happening at home, the established relationship you have with the student, and how they interact with the subject, amongst many other factors.

Students should also receive **feedback, feed-up or feed-forward** to know whether they have got an answer correct or incorrect, but remember that how you offer this matters too. It's worth reading about the power of feedback by Professor Rob Coe who highlights 16 feedback influences in his 1998 article 'Can feedback improve teaching?'

Feed-up: Comparison of the actual status with a target status.

Feedback: Comparison of the actual status with a previous status.

Feed-forward: Explanation of the target status based on the actual status. (Hattie and Timperley, 2007)

Feedback on retrieval tests should be actionable. To achieve this, the feedback should be manageable, motivational, meaningful and timely. On this point, Coe (1998) suggests 15 other influences on how feedback is acted upon, including its timing.

Manageable 

The quantity of information you provide should be proportionate to the outcomes that it has for teachers and students.

Motivational 

Feedback should help to engage students to make progress. Offer brief assessment that students can easily understand and that challenges them to improve.

Meaningful 

The assessment needs to have demonstrable outcomes on student learning. In other words, it needs to improve the learner as well as the piece of work.

Timely 

Immediate verbal feedback given in the lesson is much quicker than providing lengthy written feedback weeks after the event.

Words of caution

As with every other idea in this chapter, retrieval practice does not stand alone and work in isolation. If you take a moment to write down everything a teacher does in the classroom, not only would this take quite a long period of time, but you'd also see any theory or strategy is just one aspect of the complex world of the classroom. Retrieval practice is just one of a thousand other things that a teacher can do to be successful and support learning. Although we know the research recommends time and time again that retrieval practice is one of the most secure strategies that all teachers should use in the classroom, it must be underpinned by a wealth of knowledge and pedagogical expertise. This is what makes teaching highly complex and interesting, and no one way works best.

In the classroom, that retrieval practice technique that I use every day may work well on Monday morning but is an awful strategy to use on a Friday afternoon with another class because their levels of motivation, engagement and behaviour are vastly different. This could also be to do with spacing – the amount of time left between retrieval activities – which we will investigate further in Chapter 3. Equally, those 'bingo cards' (or any other strategy) that my students receive for the 18th time may become less effective and a bit long-in-the-tooth unless I mix up the delivery, timing and context. My subject knowledge matters, as do the behaviour management strategies I use, as well as the teaching techniques I select, when I decide to use them and why.

TOOLKIT TIPS

1. Retest key information. Don't just reteach it.
2. Choose retrieval tasks carefully based on your lesson objectives.
3. Find the sweet spot between making retrieval tasks too difficult and too easy.
4. Give timely feedback that is manageable, motivational, meaningful and timely.
5. Don't expect the same retrieval practice techniques to work every time: vary your strategies to suit each individual class.

WORKED EXAMPLE

I hope that you would now know that Mount Vesuvius is near Naples, Italy, and that it destroyed the town of Pompeii. Can you tell me the year when this happened?

So, there is a simple retrieval practice technique. The critical detail rests with how I, as a teacher, present the question and align it with the curriculum design and the resources provided.

In order to develop your schema further, I could introduce some new knowledge building on the foundation blocks of the prior knowledge you have accumulated and present a range of activities to strengthen your synapses. Some examples are:

1. Draw a map of Naples and the surrounding area.
2. Create a graphic organiser to highlight key events around the period of the devastation.
3. Write an account in the first person from someone who witnessed the eruption.

One of the simplest and most powerful retrieval practice resources I regularly refer to is the following layout. Try offering it as a worksheet for students to complete over the course of a lesson, or as an online resource where groups of students contribute into one single document. Alternatively, use the sequence to develop a series of statements, questions or actions.

1 Last month we... **Prior learning...** *We learned that Mount Vesuvius erupted in 79 AD. Vesuvius is near Naples in Italy.*	**2 Last week we...** **Common threads...** *[The students draw and label the key parts of a volcano.]*
4 Today you need... **Clarify misconceptions, quizzing...** *If the plume of ash rose to 21 miles high, estimate what area the cloud covered.*	**3 Last lesson you...** **Key questions...** *We discovered that Eyjafjallajökull has an ice cap of 40 square miles.*

Here's an example script to demonstrate how to use the resource:

Box 1: 'What did we study last month on the topic of Mount Vesuvius? Write it down in the first box on your grid.'

Box 2: [Five minutes later] 'Last week we studied Mount Fuji. Could you write down two facts in the second box that are common threads between Mount Vesuvius and Mount Fuji?'

Box 3: [Halfway through the lesson] 'I'm going to give you a quick quiz on key questions I asked you last lesson about Mount Eyjafjallajökull. Write your answers down in the third box on your grid. Question 1: How many square miles is the ice cap that covers Mount Eyjafjallajökull? a) 30 square miles; b) 40 square miles; c) 50 square miles.' [Note: this should be a quick-fire, multiple-choice quiz with challenging answer options.]

Box 4: [Towards the end of the lesson] 'Write down one misconception you still need to clarify and what you need to go home and study further.'

TEMPLATE

Retrieval practice

Try planning out your next lesson using this retrieval practice template.

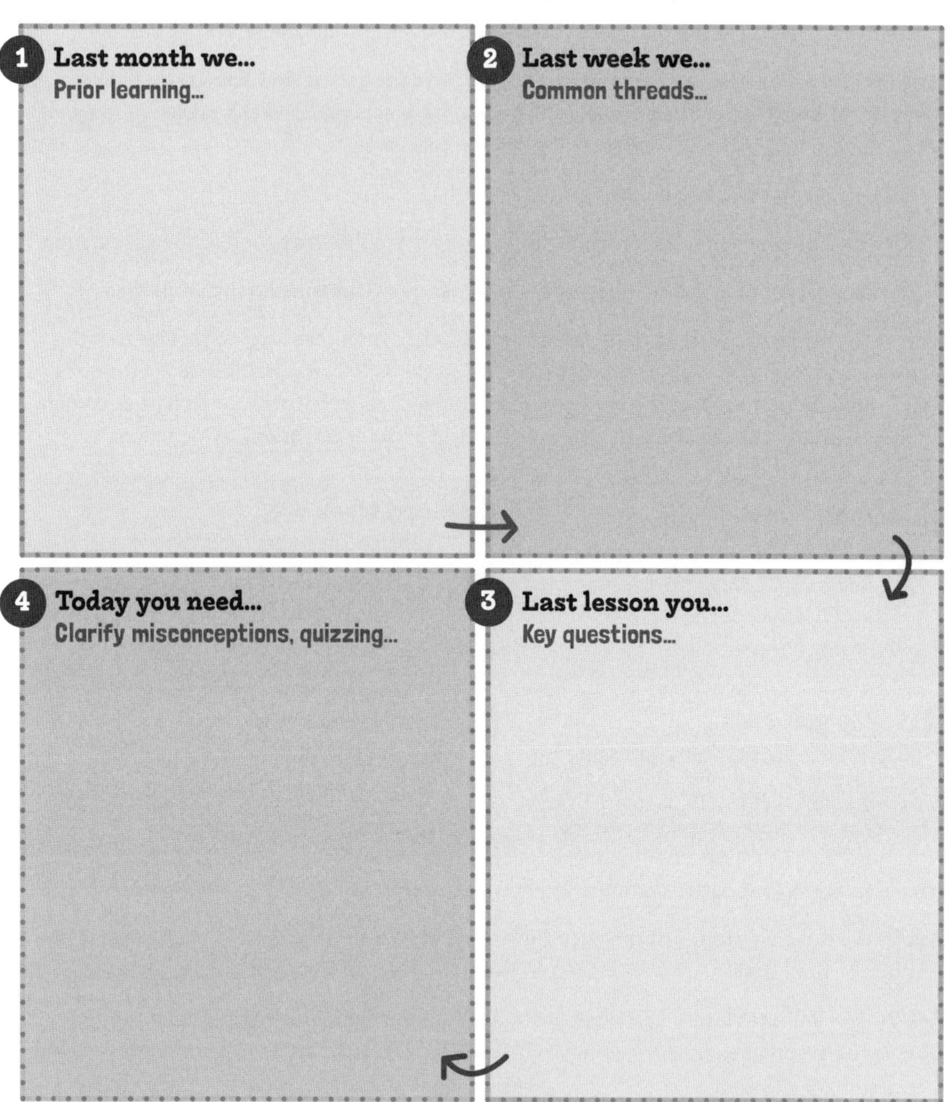

Scan the QR code for a downloadable digital copy of this template.

CHAPTER 3

AN INTRODUCTION TO TYPES OF MEMORY

Scu bap bap bee dee boo do

I mentioned in the introduction to this book (page xv) that one of my favourite analogies for understanding what memory is and how it functions is the wardrobe metaphor (Taylor, 2019). To be able to find information, or indeed our clothes, we need to regularly retrieve this information. Metaphors are always very useful, but they can also lead to oversimplifications. For example, if I am trying to find a white shirt in my wardrobe, are the lights on or off? Am I in a rush or do I have lots of time? How big is the cupboard? Is the shirt at the top or the bottom of the wardrobe and do I need a chair to stand on to reach it? What should I do next if I were to pull out a black shirt?

There are so many permutations and factors influencing our memory and retrieval. After all, we each have approximately 100 billion neurons in our brain. It is important to translate, to define and to consider all the possibilities and not rest with one fixed idea. Information cannot always simply be retrieved. 'There are many things that we can remember that are not like' the retrieval practice teachers have become accustomed to (Claxton, 2021). For example, 'say it' or 'write it down' are different to just 'doing' something. I know how to curve a football but have never explained how to do it. So, there is scope to explore what type of knowledge this is, outside of our usual definitions of being able to regurgitate facts and figures. Why do I remember so well how to 'bend it like Beckham'?

In this chapter, I would like to unpick some different types of memory, consider more deeply how we can support or hinder the development of memorisation and also discuss some of the techniques that teachers can use with their students to help them develop a deeper understanding of how we learn. This will support revision and self-study.

EXPLAINER

Short-term memory

Short-term memory involves memories that are receiving **conscious** attention in that moment. For example, if someone were to list out a set of numbers and ask you to repeat them back straightaway, these numbers would be held in your short-term memory. Conversely, if you were asked to repeat the numbers back again in five minutes' time, the numbers would already have been transferred into your **long-term memory**. In the short-term memory, coding is acoustic or verbal.

Short-term memory is necessary for learning and involves the hippocampus. The hippocampus is integral to the formation and processing of new memories. It also plays a part in consolidating memories. As we learned in Chapter 1, a human has two hippocampi, one on each side of the brain. Generally speaking, the left hippocampus involves verbal memory and the right hippocampus involves spatial memory (Ezzati et al., 2016). The word 'hippocampus' comes from the Greek *hippos*, meaning 'horse', and *kampos*, meaning 'sea monster', a reference to the shape of the structure, which resembles a sea horse.

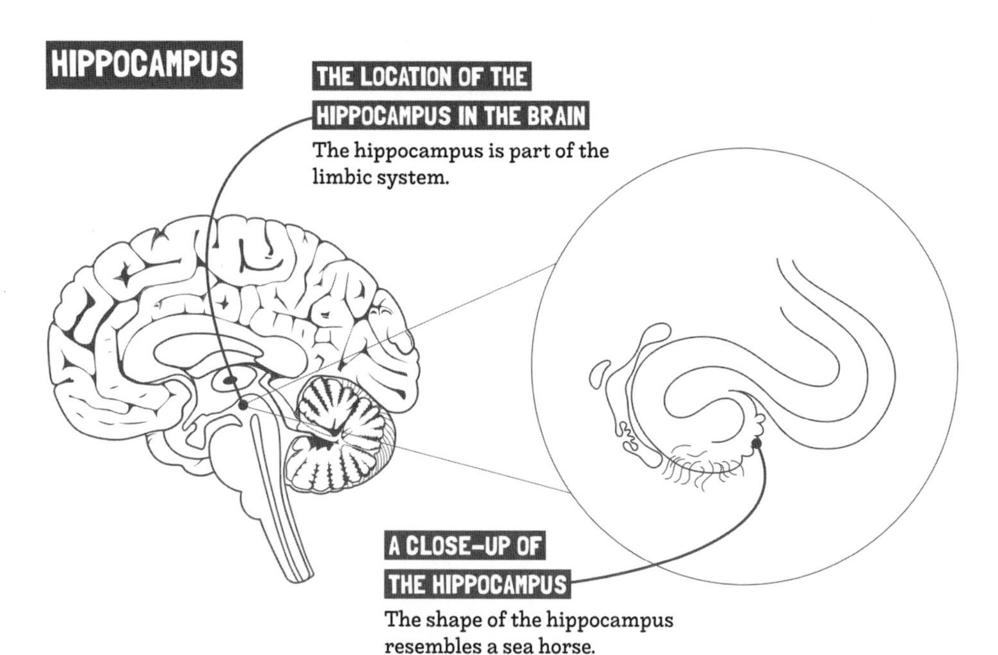

Our short-term memory has a limited capacity. In other words, we can only hold a certain amount of information in our short-term memory at any one time. A critical point to add is that our **prefrontal cortex** – the area that manages our executive functions, such as self-control, planning, decision-making and problem-solving – helps us to consolidate our short-term memories into our long-term memory.

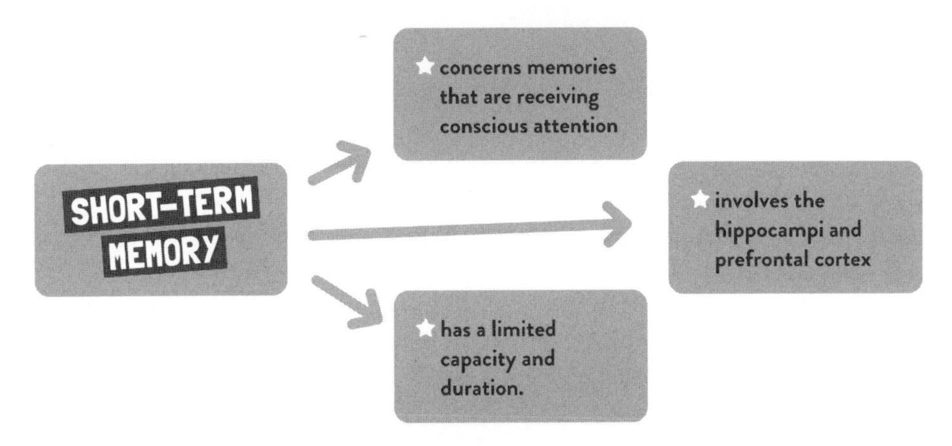

Long-term memory

Long-term memory is where we store large amounts of information waiting to be of service. When describing long-term memory, broadly speaking, these are memories that are not receiving any conscious attention; it is information that has been acquired and consolidated, and it must be retrieved if we want to recall it and use it again. In the long-term memory, coding is semantic (i.e. meanings of words or things).

Many teachers who are already exploring memory will be familiar with Atkinson and Shiffrin's (1968) research on the 'dual store' model of memory. This model argued that information is continually rehearsed in the short-term memory, and without it being rehearsed it would be forgotten. Through rehearsal and association with prior knowledge, information is then transferred to the long-term memory. The more we retrieve this information, the stronger its trace will be in the long-term memory.

The phrase 'rehearsal buffer' is introduced in Atkinson and Shiffrin's paper with an interesting diagram showing information going through stages of 'rehearsal' before being transferred into the long-term memory store or being lost. You can begin to understand why we see cartoon analogies showing a side section of a human silhouette with a 'funnel' inside, depicting how information is squeezed through a small space or is lost.

This model has been heavily criticised in the years since its publication. Even the authors admit that many of its references 'date back many years to an array of investigators' (Atkinson and Shiffrin, 1968). Decades later, where are we now? The world has moved on since 1968, and whilst I do not claim to be a cognitive scientist, I'm confident that the industry has a much deeper understanding of how the brain functions and its components when various neurons are activated. Analogies, metaphors and diagrams help, but they can be misleading.

Guy Claxton (2021) said 'The very idea of "cognitive architecture" is itself a metaphor, of course. Architects design solid structures: things that keep their shape and are meant to last... the metaphor implies that the most important things to know about the mind are likewise structural. But things have moved on in cognitive science a great deal since the 1960s, and the idea of a monolithic mental architecture is no longer universally accepted.' In essence, 'boxology' (Neisser, 1976) tried to divide the brain up into a series of stores and processes, but new discoveries show the idea of separate rooms shunting information between them is a falsehood. Rather, what is happening in the brain is much more fluid and dynamic. Remember, the myth of the right and left brain has been dispelled.

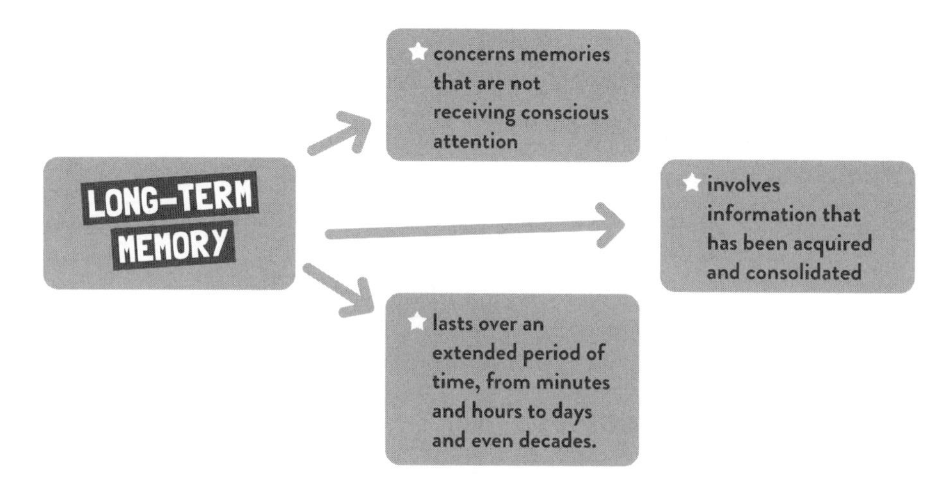

Explicit and implicit memory

Long-term memory can be divided into two categories: explicit and implicit. Explicit and implicit memory form two parts of our long-term memory storage and our long-term memory can be modified by ongoing experiences in our everyday lives. In the classroom, this may be repeated exposure to concepts, rules or facts. Let's break explicit and implicit long-term memory down a little further.

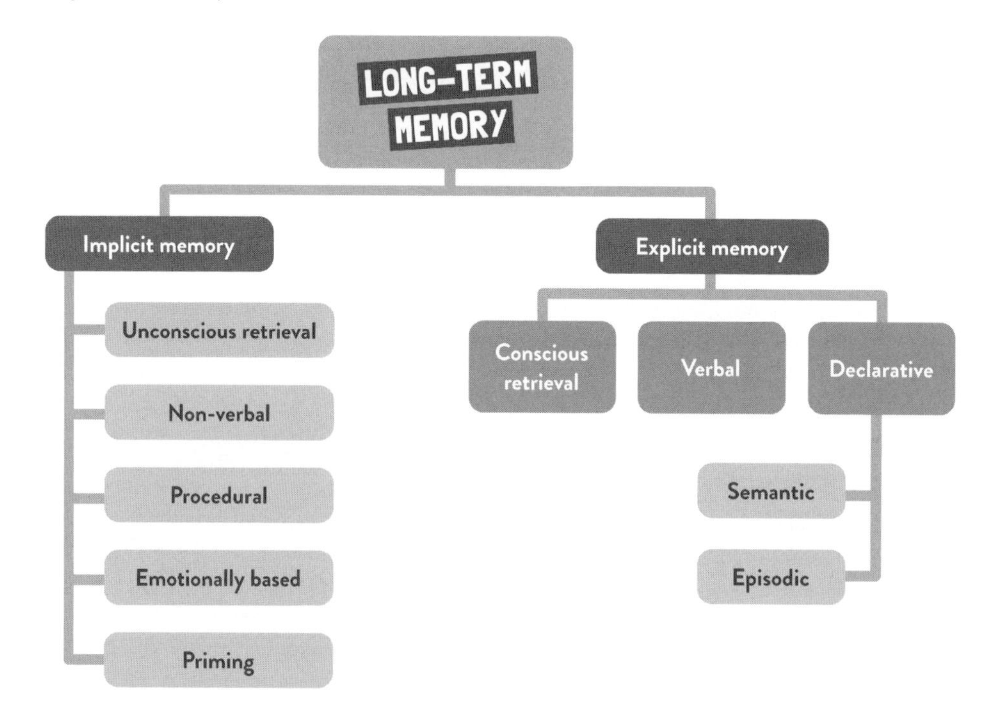

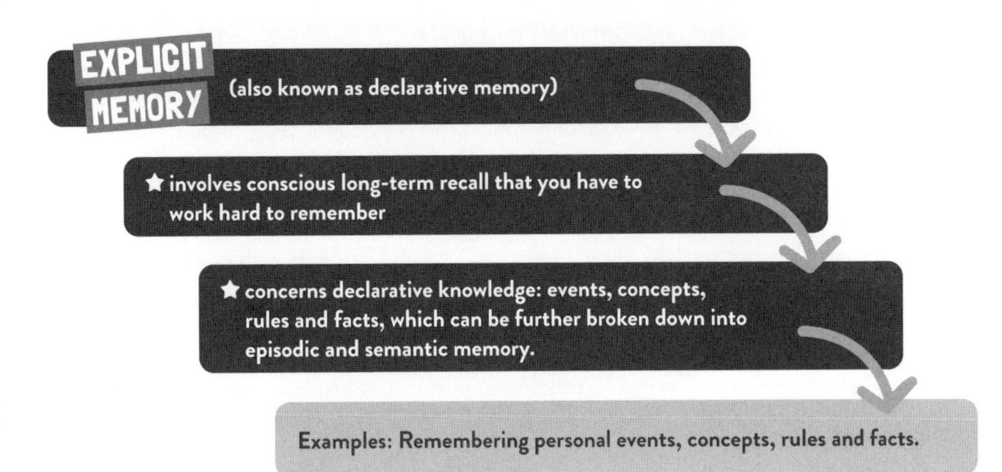

Episodic memory

What did you eat for dinner last night? Episodic memory is your recollection of personal events and experiences from day-to-day living. It's no different to you developing a degree of phronesis in your classroom as you gain experience. Thinking of your life memories as *episodes* is the best definition I can give of episodic memory. It's how you remember certain aspects of your life to date. These are easier to recall because we are 'the movie star in our own blockbuster film'. Retrieval of this information strengthens the neurons. However, in the context of episodic memory, retrieval can sometimes alter the memory with every repeat and therefore the recall becomes unreliable over time. You remember your birth date, but not necessarily the specific things that happened on each of those days that marked it. Episodic memory is a thought-dependent process. The left hippocampus helps form episodic memories, producing our personal autobiographical story. We use this to help shape images, music and ideas in autobiographical form. For example, the pop bands you loved listening to at ten, 18 and 25 years old will likely form part of some personal milestones in your life that you will easily recall the next time you hear the lyrics and the melody played on the radio.

Example: Where were you when the COVID-19 pandemic really took hold in your country?

Semantic memory

Semantic memory is the recall of concepts, rules and facts commonly regarded as general knowledge. Etymologically speaking, the origins of the word 'semantic' derive from the Greek *sēma* (meaning sign), or *sēmainein* (meaning signify), and the word was used from the mid-seventeenth century in French as *sémantique*. The literal meaning of 'semantic' is therefore 'to show sign'.

Example: When did the COVID-19 pandemic begin?

The answer to the question above is a fact. The question asking about your experiences during the pandemic is a personal memory – and a touch unreliable. Of course, episodic memory and semantic memory can interact in our everyday lives. For example, you may have a drink on your table at work. You recognise that it is an aluminium can with a popular liquid drink inside. You can confirm that it is not good for you, unless you drink it in moderation (semantic memory), but it's your favourite drink because it reminds you of lying on a beach during your summer holidays (episodic memory).

Teaching concepts, rules and facts (semantic memory) is the bread-and-butter of the classroom and this is the challenge that lies ahead for all teachers. Helping students to recall, recognise and relearn curriculum material involves teaching students how to shape their semantic memories. One way teachers can do this is by connecting students' personal episodic experiences to their semantic knowledge (Taylor, 2019). Allowing personal experiences to shape more abstract concepts makes for a powerful methodology for teaching, whether students have no prior knowledge or we are aiming to develop further schemas. When you start to think about cultural capital and students with no prior personal experiences that are relevant to the curriculum content, we can start to see how every classroom is not a level playing field. When high-stakes examinations are involved, the challenge becomes a moral dilemma: teachers want to give all their students sufficient knowledge in order to be successful, but this is easier for some students than for others.

Implicit memory

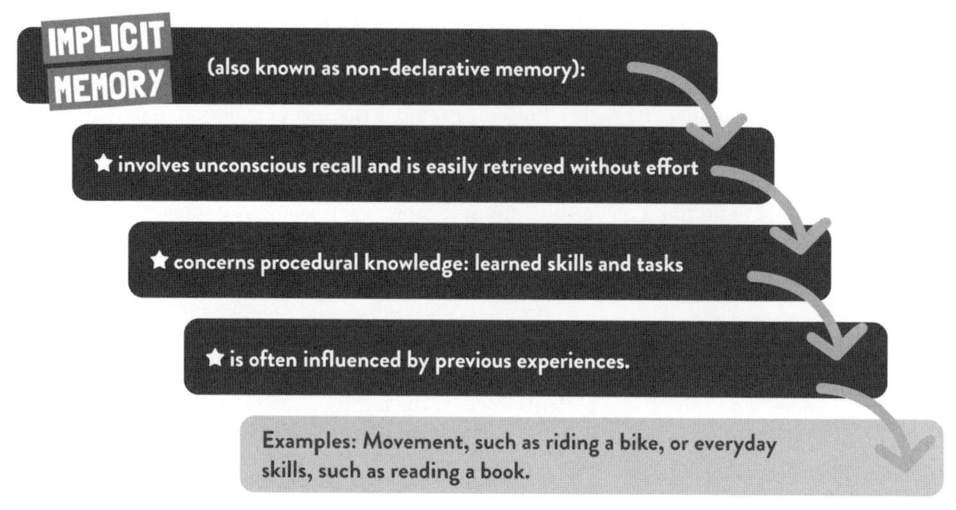

Implicit memory is non-episodic, abstract and subconscious. These memories are often influenced by previous experiences and include everyday skills such as reading this book or walking. These skills involve a degree of automation which is subconsciously produced. Non-declarative memory does not involve the use of the hippocampus. Once these memories are formed, they do not involve any conscious work on our part. For example, how did you manage to tie your shoelaces this morning? You probably don't even remember consciously thinking about it. Previous experiences help us perform these tasks better, without much awareness of what we did before.

There is also an element of our implicit memories that is strongly linked to our emotions and it's important to distinguish this from episodic memory. Episodic memory is about personal events and experiences that we can consciously recall, whereas we also have implicit memories that are emotional and unconscious and can influence our behaviour. For example, we may have developed an unconscious, conditioned response to a certain situation that we perceive as frightening. Shaping emotional memories involves the amygdala. You will be familiar with the phrase 'fight or flight'. This is an example of an unconscious, conditioned response. I will return to this concept in Chapter 4.

Example: How did you find out the country was going into a strict lockdown at the beginning of the COVID-19 crisis? (Episodic memory)

What was your reaction? (Implicit memory)

Priming

If I said the word 'doctor', what do you think of and what words would you use to describe this person? What if I said the words 'turkey' or 'haircut'? Priming is our **implicit memory**: the things we think about when we try to remember events attached to a particular association, for example, a happy or sad time, or an important date or person.

How did you celebrate your 33rd birthday? What were you wearing at the time? My answer to this question takes me back to 1996 when I danced with Sister Sledge to *He's the Greatest Dancer* on stage at G.A.Y. in Soho, London. I had a great night! As for everyone else, I suspect many forgot about it. One thing I do know is that I have a vague idea about the people I was out partying with, but I cannot remember anything about how I was dressed that evening.

Our personal memories are attached to a particular time and place, and they are influenced by our unconscious bias. If we return to the word 'doctor', what words came to mind when I asked you to describe this person? What was that person's gender? What was their skin colour? What were they wearing? How about your birthday: can you remember your 33rd birthday party? Did you have a good evening? What thoughts came to your head when I told you about my five minutes of fame with Sister Sledge? How are your memories of Ross McGill now being formed (or primed)?

The matter in our brains is constantly changing, a fact we'll come back to in Chapter 7. This means that our explicit memory can be shaped, but if our implicit memory is subconscious, it can perhaps become stuck, unless we work hard at retrieval and become more conscious of our thoughts and actions. Priming, put simply, is very hard to unlearn. This is why we battle with stereotypes and inequality for a number of reasons, for example myths and perceptions that are perpetuated through the media, products, conversations or a lack of exposure. To support or hinder learning, teachers must be conscious of what they can do to aid the process of both learning and unlearning.

The interaction of declarative and procedural knowledge

Human beings are not computers. As we learn something, it is stored in our brain like a memory chip, but there are a multitude of factors that will determine what we remember and what we lose.

As we've established, declarative knowledge is the acquisition of facts, figures, numbers and words, while procedural knowledge helps us to perform a task. But have you ever tried to ride a skateboard? Procedural knowledge would allow you or me to be able to explain why and how we stand, push-off and balance on a skateboard without falling off. We could then go into greater detail (if we have any prior knowledge) to explain the decisions we make (declarative knowledge) to turn corners and how to flip the skateboard without falling over. Procedural memory is formed through repetition, strengthening the connections (synapses) between neurons. However, this accumulated knowledge doesn't just get stronger depending on what it is asked to do.

Working memory

I want you to imagine that you are sitting at my desk writing this book. It is the end of a long working day. You are exploring a relatively new concept where you have some prior knowledge; you have two screens to hand, voice dictation, over 15 or so book references, countless academic papers and ten or 20 audiobooks you have been dipping in and out of. In between your reading and writing, the phone rings and an email 'pings' in your inbox.

The phone somehow takes priority, as the opportunity to pick up the phone is limited, although you do know there is an option for a voicemail. Instinctively, you make a decision to pick up the phone because you know that you can read the email later. The person on the other end of the phone speaks very quietly; you have never spoken to them before and they are making an inquiry about your work.

As you put down the phone, you get distracted by the email notification, completely forgetting that you were deeply focused on research and writing. Your mind now wonders about what to have for an evening meal and at what point to stop reading and writing. As the rate of information increases, your performance levels on the original activity start to decrease.

I suspect, like me, your everyday work is similar to the scenario I have just described. This is my example of how our memory can be impacted by a variety of different information. Selective attention can help here. As Ku (2018) states, 'Given the restricted resource of working memory, it is essential to rely on selective attention, the goal-directed focus on certain aspects of the environment, while ignoring other irrelevant aspects.' The above was an actual scenario that happened as I was writing this part of the book.

Working memory is a form of immediate memory but it should not be confused with short-term memory. While short-term memory simply stores static information, working memory processes several different pieces of information simultaneously and forms connections between them.

We know our working memory has limited capacity. However, with practice its capacity can be increased (Claxton, 2021). We all know if we try to do too much, we cannot do any of our tasks adequately and we tend to quit or fail. These limiting factors could be a combination of the individual activities we are trying to complete, our ability and the skills involved. I have read lots of research that suggests we can (on average) manipulate between **three to nine** pieces of information at any one time, **and** we tend to forget this information within **30 seconds** after it has been used. Here's one source to get you started: Singh (2009). As ever, this does differ depending on what you're reading, the topic it covers, what is being tested, who is being tested, and under what conditions.

On the next page are two examples to test these theories. I would ask you to complete them without pausing, getting distracted or stopping to read. Find a quiet time before you start.

Example 1: The working memory can manipulate between three to nine pieces of information

1. What are the colours of the rainbow?
2. How do you spell my middle name?
3. What is your date of birth?
4. What is the second furthest planet from the sun in our solar system?

(That's just four recall questions. Let's push your working memory a little further...)

5. Where is Mount Vesuvius?
6. In which year did Mount Vesuvius erupt and destroy the town of Pompeii?
7. In which part of the brain is the telencephalon: top, bottom, front or back?
8. Think about the opposite side of the brain to where the telencephalon is stored. How do you spell this area of the brain?
   a. Cawdal
   b. Caudal
   c. Caudel
   d. Caudle

Example 2: The working memory forgets information after 30 seconds

Can you tell me what we were talking about on the last page you turned over in this book?

Did you go back a page and check? The concept of working memory demonstrates how easy it is for teachers to support or hinder the learning taking place. If we regularly retrieve information and build on prior knowledge, we can start to achieve a degree of mastery. However, if we overload the working memory with too much information, we run the risk of our students entering cognitive overload and learning can be lost. I will explain more about working memory in Chapter 5 where we explore cognitive load theory.

Redundancy effect

The redundancy effect occurs when the information presented is not necessary. The redundancy effect forms part of cognitive load theory (see Chapter 5). For example, here we are learning more about memory. If I start to tell you about my plans for my 50th birthday, to venture to north-west Scotland with my family, I suspect I have distracted you from the task at hand – memory – and you may now go off into a daydream about your next big day! This risks overloading the working memory. We ad lib these types of conversations in the classroom every day, and whilst there is a place for these types of conversations to nurture great relationships, when we are specifically working on encoding, storage and retrieval activities we need to stick to the task in hand.

Some other types of memory

Here are a few other types of memory that it's worth having a basic awareness of in the classroom. These are worth considering and researching further.

Eidetic memory

This is the phenomenon where some of us have the ability to recall information through images, especially the ability to recall the image after seeing this information once. You'll be familiar with the term 'photographic memory'. There is a lot of scepticism surrounding this, so please do some wider reading.

Sensory memory

Keeping things simple, think of your five senses. We use a very short-term memory store for information that is processed by our organs. It is also worth mentioning 'embodied cognition' here, the idea that the mind is not only connected to your body, but the body influences your mind.

Emotional memory

I will return to emotional memory in Chapter 4 but here's a quick note about it. Learning is emotional and shaping emotional memory involves the **amygdala**. You will be familiar with the amygdala in the context of the phrase 'fight or flight'.

Emotional intelligence (or emotional quotient – the name used for a quantity produced by the division of two numbers) is the ability to understand, use and manage our emotions in a positive way to relieve stress, communicate and empathise with others, and manage conflict.

Context-dependent memory

Students will perform better in examinations and classroom assessments if they study for them with a minimum of background noise. Why? Well, because there is evidence that supports a concept known as context-dependency, which suggests that students are better off studying without background noise, as it will not be present during actual testing.*

Context-dependent memory is not a specific type of memory per se, but instead it refers to the improved memory performance that is present when individuals are tested in the same context in which they learned the tested material.

*Students might insist that music helps them to concentrate better and that they will improve their behaviour if they're allowed to have their headphones in. That may well be the case. However, research shows that students perform better when they study in the same conditions under which they will be tested on this same material. Grant et al. (1998) concluded that students' recall improved in matching conditions (silent study, silent test and noisy study, noisy test) compared with mismatching conditions (silent study, noisy test and noisy study, silent test). It seems that context matters when retrieving newly learned information. It's a question of whether you want to avoid immediate misbehaviour or, for a moment of struggle, help the student achieve in the long term. A similar concept to be aware of is transfer-appropriate processing (TAP), the theory that memory performance improves when 'the cognitive processes engaged during retrieval match the cognitive processes that were engaged when the material was encoded' (APA).

The forgetting curve

Around 2007, I became a school leader and was catapulted in front of hundreds of teachers and thousands of pupils, responsible for whole-school teaching and learning. I remember quite vividly standing in front of hundreds of Year 11 students, advising and motivating them for revision during the exam season. I knew this was far too late in their school career for them to be taught this valuable information.

I introduced those pupils to Hermann Ebbinghaus (1885) and his **forgetting curve** as it is known. His hypothesis concerned the fact that we forget information and the speed at which we forget it: in other words, memory declines over time. His paper, *Über das Gedächtnis* (later translated into English as *Memory: A contribution to experimental psychology*) is technically the first academic reference to retrieval practice. In Ebbinghaus's research, a 'nonsense syllable' was used to design a controlled experiment to measure retention. He invented a 'savings method' to help shape learning and discovered 'that distributing learning trials over time is more effective in memorising'.

It is important to re-emphasise Ebbinghaus's notion of 'nonsense syllables'. How many of us can remember nonsense words? How quickly do you think you would forget this word?

Scu-bap-bee-dee-bap-boo-do

This is a syllabic word I have totally made up. What are the chances of you remembering this word by the end of this book?

If you search online for the 'forgetting curve', I would advise you to be cautious of all the fancy graphics which are presented. Most suggest, for example, that you will forget ten per cent of everything that you have read in this chapter of the book within the hour, and up to 80 per cent within one month – with no regular retrieval. Of course, we know the latter part of this sentence is correct. Retrieval matters. However, the percentage of information that is lost is impossible to predict. Therefore, be conscious of any alluring graphics you find online without unpicking the data.

One interesting point you may not know is that Ebbinghaus conducted the research on himself. His research was also incomplete and it took him five years to conduct it. Perhaps you will remember this interesting fact because it's quite unusual – it is part of the story which shapes our episodic experiences of reading this book.

In principle, short-term memory requires rehearsal of some kind to keep any information in our conscious mind (our explicit memory). We know our short-term memory is limited, so we need to work hard to develop new information into schemas that we can retain in our long-term memory. When we learn any new information, it is easier to learn if it is built upon prior knowledge, which is why it is almost impossible to remember a nonsense word that means nothing to us, like scu-bap-bee-dee-bap-boo-do.

To test these theories, I'd like to conduct a quick experiment. First, read these numbers out loud.

1914191819391945

Can you recall those numbers without checking back? Put your hand over the numbers and try to recall as many as you can.

Do you recognise the numbers? You'll be surprised!

In fact, these numbers *are* in your long-term memory. The way they are presented is not, which means that not only am I hindering the learning process and not allowing you to retrieve, but I am also making the process of teaching a little harder than it needs to be. In a classroom surrounded by your peers, this situation may become more emotional (see Chapter 4), where you start to experience more pressure to perform, and I, as your teacher, either support or hinder your ability to recall in micro-second moments, based on how I deliver and relay information and instruction.

If I don't teach the skills required to acquire knowledge, consolidate and then retrieve, I am more likely to elicit a poorer response rate. Thus, if we do not practise we therefore forget. Key information can also be made redundant if I add irrelevant information (see extraneous load on page 70). For example, what's the weather like where you are today?

In fact, using chunking as a study skill strategy (see Chapter 1), I could work with you to help you recall those numbers. Now, no cheating! Do not flick back to look at what the numbers were. Let's work through this together. Here we go:

19141

Repeat these numbers out loud.

191419181

Repeat them again.

19141918193

And again.

Do you think you could put your hand over the page and repeat them out loud without looking?

Let me remind you again. You do know these numbers. The chances are that you do not remember them in this sequence because when you acquired this knowledge, you learned them in a particular way. You can only retrieve a schema by how you originally learned it. The way in which information is presented and retrieved is crucial to learning, a point we'll explore in more detail when we come across intrinsic and extraneous cognitive load in Chapter 5.

I could have broken the numbers down into smaller chunks to help you remember them, for example 19-14-19-18-19-39. However, if I chunk the numbers in the way you are more likely to have been taught them, it is more likely that you will be able to remember them because you will be able to link them to knowledge that you can retrieve from your long-term memory.

Let's look at the numbers again.

1914191819391945

What about if I presented them to you in this way? 1914 to 1918. 1939 to 1945. You are now probably having a 'aha' moment. You are either happy that you can now recall the numbers, or somewhat surprised or frustrated that the information presented tricked you or made learning harder.

Here is one more example from an excellent research paper published by the Centre for Education Statistics and Evaluation (2017). In my experience, this example works better when spoken rather than read, so you may want to try it on yourself and then on somebody else to see how the results compare.

I would like you to read the following letters.

y-e-m-r-o-m

Now place your hand over the text above and try to recall the letters by saying them out loud.

How did you do?

OK, let's try it again. Here are the letters presented in another way: M-e-m-o-r-y. There is a high probability that you will have the 'aha' moment again. If you try to recall these same letters, you will probably find it much easier. This is because the word 'memory' is embedded in your vocabulary and you can read this sentence and the letters that make the word. This involves a concept known as element interactivity. As your prior knowledge grows, the element size increases, reducing cognitive load. In other words, because you already know the word 'memory', it is easier to remember the word as a whole rather than the six individual letters in the word.

Explicit memory: Conscious long-term recall of declarative knowledge, which can be episodic (personal events and experiences) or semantic (concepts, rules and facts). Also known as declarative memory.

Hippocampus: Part of the limbic system in the brain, which is integral to the formation, processing and consolidation of new memories.

Implicit memory: Unconscious recall of procedural knowledge – learned skills and tasks. Also known as non-declarative memory.

Long-term memory: Information that has been acquired and consolidated. These memories are not receiving any conscious attention and must be retrieved if we want to recall and use them again.

Prefrontal cortex: Part of the brain that manages our executive functions, such as self-control and decision-making. It helps consolidate short-term memories into our long-term memory.

Short-term memory: Memories that are receiving conscious attention in a particular moment.

Working memory: A form of immediate memory that processes several different pieces of information simultaneously and forms connections between them.

PRACTICAL IDEA

Spaced practice and interleaving

Spaced practice

As we've seen, the research on spaced practice (also known as distributed practice) dates all the way back to Ebbinghaus's forgetting curve in 1885. It suggests that retention is significantly improved when students are given a number of practice problems relating to a topic and these are distributed across a period of time. We now know that it's more effective to study fewer things in greater depth, and to retrieve not reteach to help strengthen those connections. The challenge is knowing what content needs to be retested across what might appear to be a crowded curriculum.

In some of the best curriculum plans I have seen throughout my career, intentions are clearly mapped out with a range of strategies and resources, with specific knowledge and applications identified, and formative and summative assessments carefully linked. In an online world, each of these ideas are cleverly hyperlinked to the practical resources that teachers will use and there are coded assessment rubrics to help map individual or group progress.

In an interesting study (Bahrick, 1979), students learned translations of Spanish words, with six repeated sessions to help them retrieve and relearn the translations. The methodology chosen used spaced practice with three variations: zero days between sessions, one day between sessions and 30 days between sessions. Massed practice (or cramming in sessions) initially yielded very strong results. When compared to the students who were retested every 30 days, although forgetting was much greater, there was greater retention (or progress) after the six sessions. This is supported by a more recent paper about spaced practice in the learning of a second language (Kim and Webb, 2022). This study showed that longer spacing has more of an impact on longer-term retention than shorter spacing. In conclusion, retesting after one or several days will reap better retention compared with squeezing everything in at the end.

When considering your teaching approaches as well as your curriculum design, it's clear that spaced study with key retrieval techniques spread out over time (rather than in close succession) will likely reap better results. With spaced practice in mind, it is worth revisiting each of your schemes of work and identifying 'hot spots' where you will deliberately test your students' knowledge on a particular topic, and identify intervals of one, seven or 30 days between when it was first taught and when you'll retest as a methodology for designing your own spaced curriculum.

Interleaving

Evaluation of interleaving practice has started to emerge in education over the last 20 years, but it is notoriously understudied in applied settings. The ripple effect of this research is now starting to reach the classroom floor and offers teachers much promise for curriculum design.

In terms of providing a definition for teachers, interleaving practice is switching between similar content and ideas to help strengthen schemas. Think of a 'fruit salad' of topics, with each ingredient complementing the others, without mixing in 'peas' or 'beans' as disconnected categories. Initially, it may feel harder to teach in this way, but it is beneficial in the long term if we can take the time to think carefully about how we map our curriculum plans and align them to retrieval and spaced practice activities.

What interleaving does is help students to organise and process different content (in an ever-growing schema), which then enables them to select the right skills to solve different problems. My favourite analogy for curriculum growth is the image of a spider web, without broken connections, spiralling out wider and wider as each chord is strengthened.

Developing this foundation of knowledge also frees up our working memory, which means we become more effective at tackling problems, drawing upon prior knowledge (long-term schema). Thus, when teachers interleave topics through the curriculum, and regularly revisit them using spaced practice, students hold information about multiple topics in their working memory, enabling them to make connections between the topics. This improves their understanding and their correct application of the knowledge and skills learned across the topics. In addition, interleaving forces students to retrieve information about the topic or topics learned previously from their long-term memory. This in turn boosts their memory and their retention of this information. Interleaving also supports problem-solving and task completion. The knowledge required for completing a task or solving a problem is already stored in the long-term memory and the relevant information needs to be retrieved. This frees up our working memory (cognitive load) to focus on tackling the problem, rather than being consumed with trying to retain the required knowledge at the same time.

The benefits of prior knowledge

As we established in the numbers and word experiments I presented to you on pages 41 to 43, if we have prior knowledge, we can solve problems more effectively when compared to not having any prior knowledge. For example, imagine I asked you to make me a cup of tea and I stipulated that I like my tea to be very strong, with a dash of milk and no sugar. Assuming that you have made thousands of cups of tea in your life, you should find solving this problem rather straightforward. When you are an expert, and you have prior knowledge, you can work **forward** to solve the problem. When you are a novice – in this case, let's assume you have never made a cup of tea before – not only do you have to battle with how I like my tea to be made, but you also need to work out how to make a cup of tea from start to finish. Because this foundation knowledge is not already stored, it bombards your working memory and makes the task more difficult. This is cognitive apprenticeship (see Chapter 8): moving from novice towards expert, and how Sweller (1988) explains why problem-solving activities cannot be used to learn how to problem-solve if no prior schema exists. When you have no expertise, you have to work **backwards** from the end goal to help solve the problem.

As a solution, if I were teaching you how to make the perfect cup of tea, I would complete each stage in small chunks, providing keywords and some hands-on experience, before letting you go solo. If we use retrieval practice in this scenario, I would regularly quiz you for keywords and information about each step, but not exclusively as we were doing the activity. I'd ask you tomorrow, next week and next month as we developed our tea-making skills!

We need to practise, then re-practise a problem before introducing another problem.

If I were to introduce interleaving practice to help transfer your knowledge of making tea to strengthen your schema, I might now introduce you to the process of making a black coffee. We would establish which connections we could use (prior knowledge) from our experiences of making a cup of tea and establish what information is being transferred. I would model and scaffold the strategies throughout this process and I would fade this support as you developed a degree of expertise using a range of feedback and coaching methodologies.

If you've made thousands of cups of tea before, making a cup of tea or coffee should be straightforward. In this case, I might provide you with another problem-solving activity for the purpose of developing your schema even further, for example, how to make filtered coffee in a busy coffee shop using an espresso machine to make two cups at once!

Now we can begin to understand at what point I would challenge your working memory, and through repeated testing, you would soon become an expert. Taking it further, throughout one day in the coffee shop, we are involved in making 1,000 cups of tea for a dinner party. To add more context, each cup of tea has to be made fresh on order, and all refreshments have to be provided within a 30-minute period during a hot summer's day. You only have one urn which can boil the equivalent of 50 cups of water every ten minutes. We can now work out if this scenario is achievable and how you might solve this problem. Providing you with this example should help you identify how our working memory can be hindered or supported in this sort of situation. I suspect in this case you will become quite stressed very quickly on this hot summer's day! If we started with this last scenario as the first problem, without establishing if you could make a cup of tea, teaching and learning would be hindered.

Increasing the quantity or reducing the time makes anything much harder, including teaching, and this is something you will experience as a teacher when managing your workload, and something you must stay conscious of when providing instruction to students.

Instruction and assessment

The amount of instruction a teacher provides during spaced retrieval practice and interleaving will influence performance. This is what makes teaching fascinating, complex and challenging. Although it 'seems plausible that motivated students can easily use interleaving without help' (Dunlosky et al., 2013), it becomes even more effective for all students when teachers integrate interleaving and spaced practice into their curriculum and lesson plans. The first thing we should all do is return to our curriculum plans and look carefully at how we can warp and weave content over the academic year, with explicit references to retrieval tasks, and where and how new concepts will be introduced and prior knowledge retested (not restudied).

Teachers also have to frequently assess student progress on a regular basis. Without doing so, they risk missing valuable data to evaluate what students know and what they don't yet know in order to move the lesson forward. I think we can safely say that when we are introducing a new topic, or when we are teaching younger students, there will be a greater need for support to help solve more complex tasks. Regular formative assessment will enable teachers to see what is needed and when.

Spacing and interleaving in practice

The following chart demonstrates a scheme of work that considers interleaving and spaced retrieval practice. Students master the basics of Topic 1 before being introduced to some basic concepts from Topic 2. They then return to Topic 1 to deepen their knowledge. When Topic 2 is tackled from Week 5, the students already have some prior knowledge to build on. Two 'hot spots' are identified during Topic 2 to retest information learned during Topic 1. These are at intervals of seven and 30 days.

What might a scheme of work that considers interleaving and spaced practice look like in your classroom?

	Week 1	Week 2	Week 3	Week 4	Week 5	Week 6	Week 7	Week 8	Week 9	Week 10
Topic	Topic 1				Topic 2					
Interleaved materials		Topic 2								
Spaced retrieval						Topic 1			Topic 1	

TOOLKIT TIPS

1. Use spaced practice and interleaving to map out your curriculum.
2. Think carefully about the topics you will teach, when you will teach them and the strategies and resources you will use.
3. Build students' foundational knowledge gradually by teaching in small chunks, modelling and scaffolding. Then provide hands-on experience that enables students to practise and re-practise. Once this knowledge is embedded, introduce another problem.
4. Identify 'hot spots' where you will deliberately test your students' knowledge at intervals of one, seven or 30 days.
5. Embed opportunities for formative and summative assessment in your curriculum plan, and use this data to inform your next steps.

WORKED EXAMPLE

I hope the examples I've been sharing to help you learn about volcanoes have been proving effective so far. In this case, to model this idea and the research about spaced retrieval, I'll provide you with a break in this section of the book – a day off homework, hurrah! – and we'll come back to the topic in the next chapter, where we'll also interleave your knowledge about Mount Vesuvius with a new volcano: Eyjafjallajökull.

This retrieval interval (depending on how long it is between you reading this chapter and the next – spacing) could have a mixed success rate. In keeping with the research on retrieval, and understanding the life cycle of lessons and curriculum design in schools, I would recommend for the purposes of this book that you wait one week before attempting the final retrieval practice exercise on Mount Vesuvius in Chapter 8, page 111.

Where this retesting may have a negative impact is if I design the final test for you in the last section of the book as a high-stakes assessment to determine your future as emotions will come into play (see the next chapter). This is the challenge all teachers have to navigate for their students, and one thing teachers do have up their sleeves is that they see their students regularly and on the whole have a positive relationship with them in every lesson. This can help students develop their metacognition and manage their anxiety in these scenarios.

Scan the QR code for a downloadable digital copy of this template.

TEMPLATE

Spaced practice and interleaving

Here is a template for a scheme of work that takes into consideration spaced practice and interleaving. I have completed an example for design technology and there is a blank template for you to try out.

Year 7	Term									
	Week 1	Week 2	Week 3	Week 4	Week 5	Week 6	Week 7	Week 8	Week 9	Week 10
Topic	Ergonomics				Structures					
Date (w/b)	3rd Sept	10th Sept	17th Sept	24th Sept	1st Oct	8th Oct	15th Oct	29th Oct	5th Nov	12th Nov
Assessment	Knowledge Organiser				Knowledge Organiser		Ergonomics			
Resources	Chairs	Tables	Stools		Bridges	Buildings	Towers	Fencing	Shells	Arches
Knowledge + skills	Add curriculum detail here				Add curriculum detail here					
Interleaved materials		Structures								
Retrieval/Spaced practice						Ergonomics			Ergonomics	

Year	Term									
	Week 1	Week 2	Week 3	Week 4	Week 5	Week 6	Week 7	Week 8	Week 9	Week 10
Topic										
Date (w/b)										
Assessment										
Resources										
Knowledge + skills										
Interleaved materials										
Retrieval/Spaced practice										

CHAPTER 4
LEARNING IS EMOTIONAL

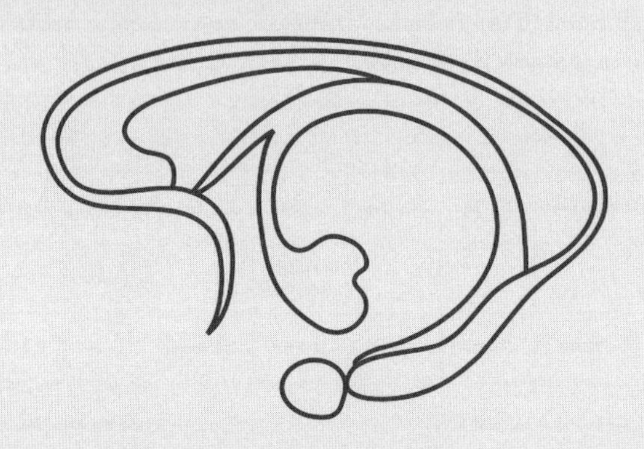

At some point in all of our lives, we each find something difficult to do and we give up. Whether this is learning to play the piano, learning how to code, trying to fathom out how to use Twitter or TikTok, or getting to grips with academic research, paradigms or philosophical and theoretical language. I suspect you have also felt quite anxious – or perhaps excited – when presenting in front of your colleagues during a teacher training session. Due to a multitude of factors, our responses to a number of situations are driven by our emotions and nowhere is this more apparent than in schools. When we think about the classroom, you will know just as much as I that something can go wrong at any moment. Our young people are a hotbed of hormones. They are establishing themselves in the world and in the classroom, amidst the social pressures of growing up and the expectation to succeed.

I am reminded of one of my favourite education books, *The Hidden Lives of Learners* by Graham Nuthall, which was published posthumously in 2007 and which unpicks the author's 40 years of education research. Nuthall spent four decades recording lessons by hanging microphones from the light fittings in research classrooms (with consent, of course!). The first thing that became apparent from Nuthall's very detailed data was how little teachers knew about what was going on in their classrooms. He found that even live observers keeping continuous written records of the behaviours of individual students missed up to 40 per cent of what was recorded on the students' individual microphones. Nuthall's book provides compelling evidence that we as teachers miss so much of what happens in the classroom, as well as the vital peer-to-peer influences that are taking place. Students live in a personal and social world of their own in the classroom. They whisper to each other, pass notes, organise their social life and continue arguments that started in the playground. Strong emotions are at play in all of these interactions and we know that students often care more about what their peers think about them than what their teachers think about them. I see this evolving in my son as I drop him off at the school gates. The older he gets, the farther away I am allowed to say goodbye to him in front of his friends.

More recent research exists to support Nuthall's theories. Professor Sarah-Jayne Blakemore is a leading expert on the teenage brain. In her work, she explores why an adolescent brain differs from those of children and adults, why problem-free children can turn into challenging teens as well as what is physically happening in the adolescent brain as the neural synapses are forming. Blakemore's (2019) research – essential reading for all teachers – confirms what Nuthall may have started to unpick in his research: that adolescents are much more likely to consider the opinions of their peers than the adults closest to them: 'Teenagers just think about what others think of them, nothing else...'. Blakemore describes the 'audience effect' as the phenomenon for why we change our behaviour when being observed by another person. In teenagers, this shift is much more significant than in people like you or me who are a little wiser, set in our ways and more comfortable with who we are. One tip for all teachers is to discipline students in private, away from their peers. The message will be received better, and you won't have to battle with an audience, rudeness or sniggers.

So, what does this all have to do with learning? Put crudely, teachers can influence so much in their lessons, but what a student believes their peers to be thinking may impact the learning process taking place in our classrooms. If this is the case, we must consider students' emotions in the learning experience and seek reliable ways to use our understanding of their emotions to maximise learning potential.

EXPLAINER

Our mood affects everything that we do in our daily lives. Take a moment to think of your favourite music. When are you most likely to listen to it? When you're stressed or relaxed? How does it make you feel? Equally, music can be distracting. For example, I don't have any music blaring in the background whilst writing this chapter. Even though I know it would put me in a good mood and help reduce some of the strain and pressure associated with meeting a deadline, it would likely be distracting and add much cognitive load.

Research on emotions and their relationship to cognition has been on the rise; we are now better equipped to understand how we are affected by stress, relaxation, mood swings and mental health amongst many other factors. We also know that we can influence our mood and that of others. Rather than talking about our emotions in general, in this chapter of the book I will focus specifically on how emotions manifest themselves in the classroom and how understanding emotions can influence our ability to teach and learn better.

The connection between emotions and memory

We can all experience surprise, happiness, laughter and anger to name but a few emotions. Emotions play an essential role in our lives and in our (sensory) memory, and I'd need to write another book to unpick this aspect of our senses. As we grow older, we learn how to respond to the situations around us. Sometimes those emotions bond us together; sometimes they drive us apart...

Can you think about a time when you may have wiped away tears of laughter with your best friend as you both joked about something? Now think about a time when you were being told off by your parents or a teacher. These events create episodic memories and play an important role in our social, mental and emotional development, helping us to form bonds with colleagues and relationships with friends and family members. Emotions are at the heart of these episodic memories.

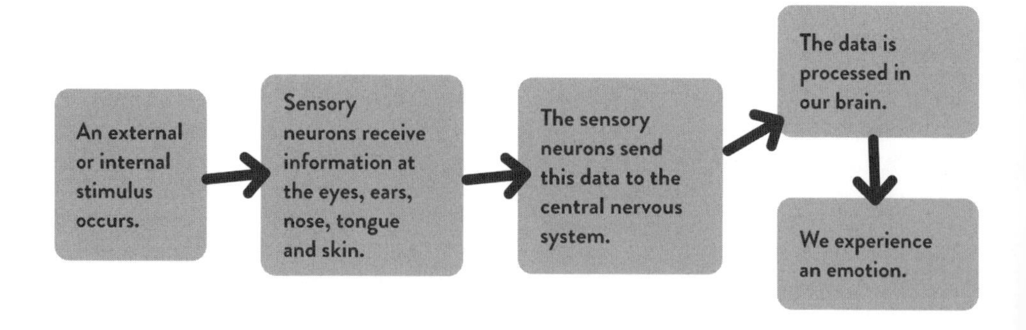

When we experience an emotion, neuroscientists would tell us that our neurons are activated. Sensory neurons receive information at the eyes, ears, nose, tongue and skin. These sensory neurons then send information to the central nervous system and this data is processed in the brain.

The trolley problem

There is a very popular cognitive science test called the 'trolley problem' synonymous with Philippa Foot (1967), which tells us more about the impact of emotions on our memory. I want you to imagine that there is a runaway train carriage hurtling down the railway tracks. On the line ahead, there are five people working, unaware that the carriage is heading straight for them. As a bystander, you are standing between the train and the people ahead; you can intervene. Next to you is a railroad lever that will allow you to change the direction of the train, but you have two options:

1. Do nothing, which will mean that the train ploughs ahead, killing five people on the tracks.
2. Pull the lever, diverting the train onto a side track where it would kill one person.

Which option would you choose?

This moral dilemma relates to the emotional choices we make as humans.

An alternative to this story is that you are watching the train from a footbridge and you see that it is hurtling towards the five people on the tracks. Next to you on the bridge is a large man you could push off the bridge in front of the train to stop it ploughing into all five people. The question here is: would you push this one man off the bridge to save five others?

Foot argues that the decision-making participants faced in this conundrum was a matter of killing five people or one, plus a distinction between 'killing' and 'letting die'. Most participants were willing to pull the lever in the first version. However, they were much less willing to push the man off the bridge onto the tracks in the second version, even though the outcome is the same as pulling the lever – one man dies in order to save five others. The researchers found that 'most people have a strong negative emotional response to the proposed action of pushing the man'.

Researchers also investigated which parts of the brain were activated when participants were faced with these two versions of the problem. In the first version of the problem, greater activity was detected in the areas of the brain associated with working memory and much less activity was detected in the areas of the brain associated with emotion. In the second version of the problem, greater activity was detected in the areas of the brain associated with emotion and much less activity was detected in the areas of the brain associated with working memory (Greene et al., 2001). In this one example, it is clear to see how emotions impact on our daily lives, our decision-making, our problem-solving, our recall and our ability to function.

The trolley problem: A summary

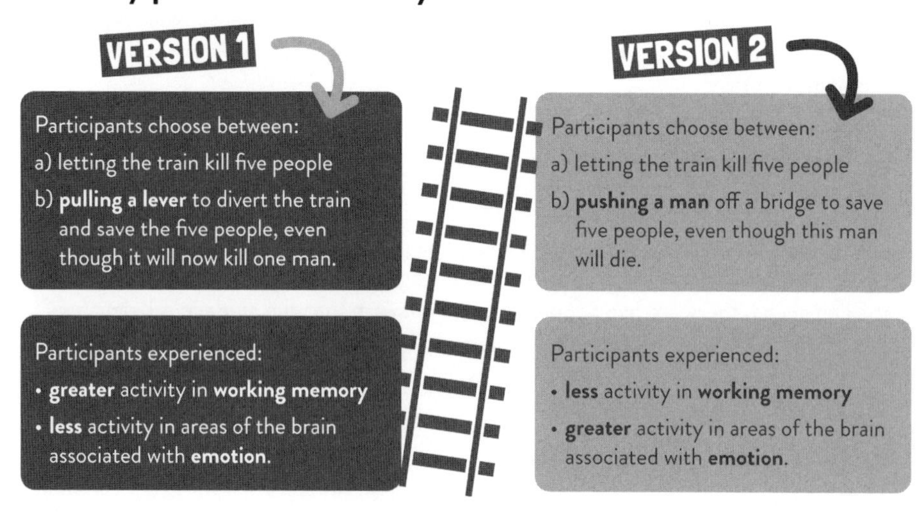

What role do teachers play?

In my journey to understanding memory, I've started to acknowledge that learning is emotional and, as teachers, we have a critical role to play. We can either **hinder** or **support** the learning process through the micro-decisions we make on a minute-by-minute basis in the classroom. There are a million examples of cues I might give out as a teacher, for example, how I pose a question then pause; how I respond to a student's answer; the non-verbal body language signals I communicate to indicate that I want you to expand on your answer; or how my face may signal to you that 'I'm confused' by your response; and how a small gesture back to my body would indicate that I want more information from you.

The classroom is a very beautiful yet complex space in which to work. Psychologist and school teacher Haim Ginott (1972) pioneered communication theory between parent, child and educator and is well-known for his approach to behaviour and the following key quote:

> 'I have come to a frightening conclusion that I am the decisive element in the classroom. It's my personal approach that creates the climate. It's my daily mood that makes the weather. As a teacher, I possess a tremendous power to make a child's life miserable or joyous. I can be a tool of torture or an instrument of inspiration. I can humiliate or heal. In all situations, it is my response that decides whether a crisis will be escalated or de-escalated and a child humanized or dehumanized.'

Despite the complexities of managing motivation, if teachers can consciously manage positive and negative emotions in the classroom, they can support a student's motivation to participate, self-regulate and complete work. Whether by storytelling and bringing the curriculum to life, cracking a joke or raising a stern look, all teachers 'make the weather' and not only do 'positive emotional states accompany an increase in motivation and engagement [but] they also support learning directly by removing a distractor that would otherwise increase cognitive load' (Dudley et al., 2020). If teachers create a positive climate and sense of belonging, students can become motivated to attend class and become more engaged in their learning. Despite the external social circumstances that our young people face, a teacher can reduce these (to a degree) to help support knowledge retention.

The importance of feedback

As an adult, let's consider a time when you received feedback for the work that you did. We know that feedback must be timely and it must be manageable for the teacher; it must also motivate the individual student and be meaningful so that they can translate your feedback into practical action. The same applies to adults in the workplace. Interestingly, when we receive positive feedback for a specific action, we associate any future action with this positive experience. Over the last decade, there has been much shared about Carol Dweck's research on motivation, particularly on feedback, for example, Dweck (2007). If we want improvement, we should praise the effort, not the piece of work. It's important to acknowledge that talent plays a big part in success, but 'effort matters on the margins' and this can yield significant gains (Kirschner and Hendrick, 2020).

When we receive positive (or negative) feedback, it is associated with an event, creating a dopamine (a chemical neurotransmitter) message that influences our mood. This **'reward loop'**, known also as a 'compulsion loop', can be seen everywhere in human behaviour. We seek a 'dopamine hit' constantly: a 'like' from a Facebook friend or five points for squashing the alien on the gaming app on your phone, allowing you to 'level up' and set a new record score. Whatever your compulsion, having 'positive feedback' supports the retrieval process and can – with care – motivate us to put in the hard work to complete tasks, participate with others or simply remain motivated and engaged. It's worth noting that there's a downside too to this dopamine 'reward loop', as it can lead to addictions, to work, drugs or social media to name a few.

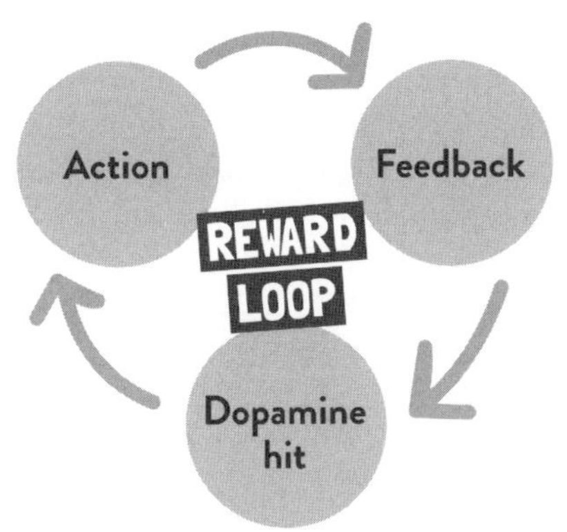

Fight or flight

While experiencing an emotion, the response to this emotion can support the development of memories in certain cases, but it's important to be mindful that negative emotions can also, in fact, hinder the learning process, particularly if they fire up the fight or flight response. This is something we all know, but how conscious are we of our actions in the classroom and the impact they might have?

The **amygdala** (which means 'almond' in Latin) plays a central role in how we process emotions and is a key part of our limbic system. The research on the amygdala is almost 100 years old, so in the grand scheme of things, it is still something we do not know very much about. What we do know is that it is a collection of nuclei in the temporal lobe. Many of us will be very familiar with the role the amygdala plays in the 'fight or flight' response. Neuro-signals are transmitted when we are exposed to a threatening situation; the amygdala helps us to identify a threat and determine if we should choose fight or flight in that environment.

So, whether you are confronted by somebody in the local supermarket or you are dealing with a difficult incident in school, this part of your brain plays a central role in how you respond. It's worth noting that the amygdala a) helps predict *potential* threat to a given situation and b) doesn't evaluate whether the scenario is safe or dangerous. In fact, it's our sensory memory that tells us how to respond. This 'fight or flight' response allows us to evaluate our environment and determine a degree of importance – whether the situation is safe or dangerous. In this 'fight or flight' situation, we learn to make an instinctive decision. Our eyes and ears send data to our amygdala to interpret. If danger is perceived, a distress signal is sent to the **hypothalamus**, which then tells the rest of the body (via our nervous system) to respond with the relevant energy – i.e. to fight or run!

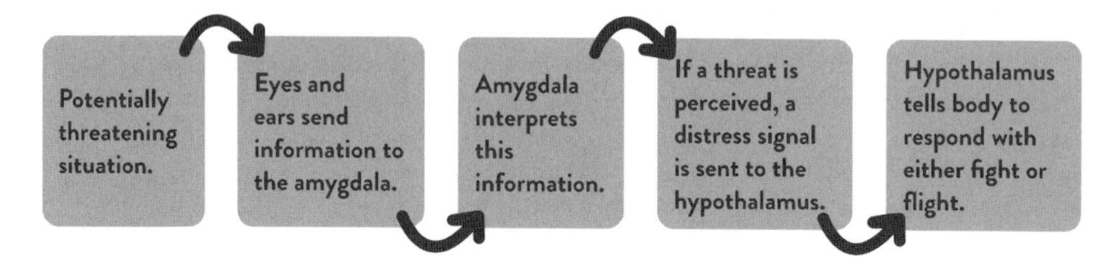

If we return to one of Graham Nuthall's classrooms (see page 50), the teacher is asking the pupils to work in groups to identify the difference between mammals and humans. Following the teacher's instructions, one group decides to divide roles and manage the group's opinions; this is largely determined by one personality. In the aftermath of the activity, one student becomes anxious and is perceived by all the others to be failing to participate. As a result, the dominant personality considers their wishes to have been rejected and takes the opportunity to call them 'useless'. This student responds with a physical 'fisty cuff' moment, and the teacher – also having a micro 'fight or flight' moment – physically intervenes between the two students.

THE LIMBIC SYSTEM

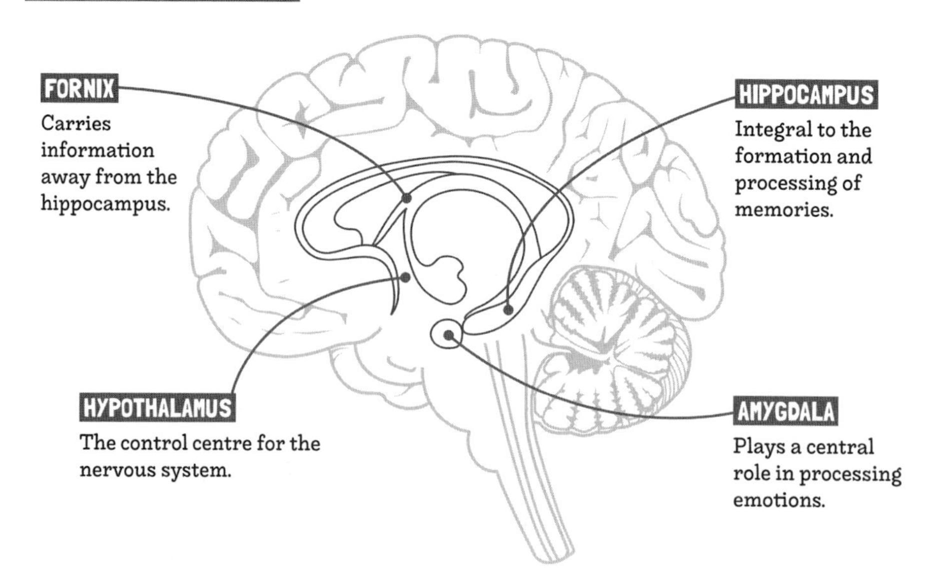

Depression, sadness and disengagement

It's worth making a brief note on the complex factors that may lead to the expression of longer-term conditions and negative emotions in the classroom. On my travels to schools across the country, all teachers report that they lack confidence when dealing with student mental health and managing special educational needs. Increasing mental health concerns, exclusions and off-rolling are just some of the reasons conditions or negative emotions such as depression, sadness and disengagement can be pervasive in the classroom and these issues are by-products of our education system – and a mirror of societal problems. Almost one-fifth of English state school students exhibit 'low or moderately low attitudes' to perceived learning capability, self-regard and feelings about school (GL Assessment, 2018). Mental health problems, such as depression and anxiety, disengagement with the school curriculum, social media and peer networks are a small number of the factors we need to consider.

So, what is the impact on learning? Negative emotions, such as fight or flight caused by anxiety and fear, or withdrawal caused by depression, sadness and disengagement, can all refocus students' attention on the immediate threats they perceive to their safety and wellbeing. This takes up working memory space in order to manage and respond to these threats (Dudley et al., 2020). These threats could arise from situations of extreme stress or duress. Racism is one example, especially when combined with episodic memory. Another example is a fight at home that a student is worried about. As we discovered in Chapter 3, working memory is crucial for learning and therefore these negative emotions only serve to distract from what you are trying to teach your students. Students attending school are not just there to learn stuff. They attend school for social relationships, community participation and countless other 'hidden curriculum' needs. It's also critical that we ensure learning how to learn is a key skill that is explicitly taught across the curriculum in every school.

As teachers, how can we ensure that we create a culture in the classroom that is safe, low stress and supportive in order to maximise the potential for learning performance?

In schools, the role of breaktime and lunchtime has become a more conscious decision, as have the timings of lessons and the start or end of the day. Equally, what food is served in the school canteen has become a prominent agenda across the UK, with obesity in young people increasing year on year. According to the Health Survey for England, around 21 per cent of 10–11-year-olds (Year 6) are obese with 14.1 per cent overweight (UK Government, 2019). Too much stimulus on devices or in food, too few breaks during the day or too much time to get excited around the playground are all carefully managed considerations that influence adrenaline or cortisol levels in young people. Whilst schools can only influence so much, there are conscious initiatives schools are doing to help manage the world our young people are growing up in, for example, mindfulness or active learning, as well as motivational assemblies and a richer breadth of extracurricular experiences.

The role of hormones

Do you learn better when you are angry, happy or frustrated? I suspect like everyone else, you are more receptive to shaping your memory when your brain is operating while composed due to the reasons mentioned above. This isn't to say that we cannot learn during moments of anger, but we might be distracted from the type of learning that is intended to be taking place in the classroom.

I remember vaguely (episodic recall) how my school and personal life was impacted throughout my adolescent years (defined by Blakemore (2019) as approximately between 13 to 25 years old). The views of others were far more important than my parents' opinion in terms of what clothes I chose to wear, how large and painful those spots were on my face, or if attending church ruined my credibility at sixth form.

Another factor we need to consider when it comes to linking memory with emotions is **hormones**. Hormones are chemical substances that act like messengers in the body to control and regulate different bodily functions, from digestion to respiration. They are produced in one part of the body before being sent to another part of the body to evoke a response.

The hormones we are interested in for the purposes of this section are **adrenaline** and **cortisol**. Most teachers will be familiar with these hormones and know they are linked to the 'fight or flight' response. When the hypothalamus tells the body to respond to a perceived threat through fight or flight, it sends a message to the adrenal glands to release a number of hormones into the body, including adrenaline and cortisol. Too much adrenaline and cortisol creates stress, anxiety and increased heart rate, to name but a few side effects. These are not good conditions for learning to take place.

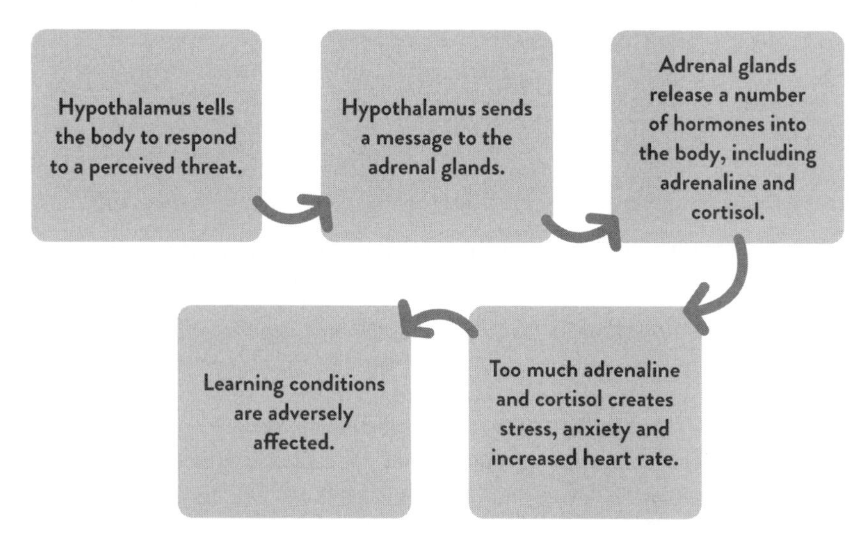

Here's a real-life scenario from my work in London schools. It's the end of the academic year, workload is reducing and it is the annual sports day. A time to relax (somewhat) from the desk job, chat with colleagues and observe students thriving outside of the classroom. As a school leader, one of the many responsibilities I have is to patrol the perimeter of the sports venue to ensure children are safe from the general public. The day is a success. Like most sports day events, I am sunburnt and end up being dragged into the teachers' race and making a complete fool out of myself! However, the only real sticking point on this occasion is having to respond to a group of young people who try to enter the sports ground without permission. These are friends of friends – young people who are not in full-time education – or who are absconding from school in some shape or form. When challenged, one of the students trying to enter the grounds (in a millisecond moment) puts their hand underneath their jumper and mimics a weapon, jerking forwards to insinuate that they are about to run towards me. How do you think I responded to this situation?

Perhaps you may not have experienced the emotions that occur when a young person intends to stab or shoot you with a weapon, and it's something that none of us expects to deal with when we sign up to become a teacher. This 'fight or flight' moment happened in a nanosecond, yet it is something I choose to remember. We could evaluate how much of this memory is semantic or episodic, which parts of the event are concrete or abstract, how this heightened moment generated adrenaline in my senses to determine a reaction, or how any potential cortisol (secreted into my bloodstream) influenced my memory formation, blood pressure or metabolism. I know two of my brothers who are police officers would have chosen 'fight', not 'flight', in this situation, due to the training they receive to handle these scenarios.

All that said, the hormones we produce provide our bodies with balance – and that includes adrenaline and cortisol. Neither too much nor too little is good for the human body in the long term. We need to have a certain level of these hormones in our bodies in order to function, so we cannot and should not eliminate them from our daily lives completely. If we have too little of these hormones in our bodies, we can feel dizzy, moody and can suffer extreme fatigue.

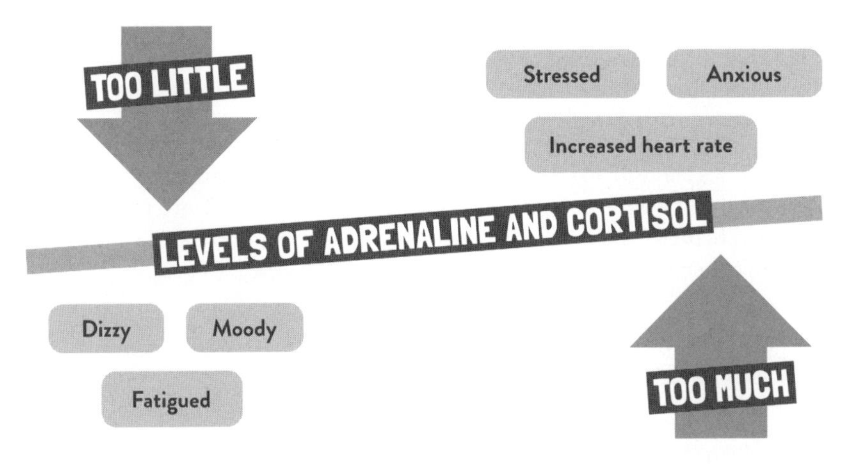

What we inherit genetically will play a significant factor in our ability to regulate our hormones, as well as some of the environmental conditions around us – events that take place in our lives, what we eat and how we live will also impact our cortisol levels. It's therefore important that we learn to understand our bodies, how we can manage them and what influence our emotions have on us.

Hormonal responses, whether they are happy or life-threatening, are essential to our wellbeing and shape our memories. They happen so quickly and subconsciously over time that we are generally not aware of them. Fortunately, we can learn how to manage all of these positive and negative situations, and there are some things we can do in our personal lives, such as exercise and eat a good diet, as well as some of the pastoral aspects of the school environment that teachers can change to support our young people. We'll come back to this when we explore wellbeing in Chapter 9.

Language

Language is one area all teachers help our young people to develop. It's a higher-order cognitive function that plays a fundamental role in all of us. Whether this is verbal, written or non-verbal signals, all human beings are social creatures and we have learned to communicate with one another to give meaning to our everyday experiences. In terms of memory and emotion, language can influence the work teachers do in the classroom. Whether this is teaching students a new language, or chanting or reciting the alphabet in a nursery classroom, the formation of language is critical for how we communicate as humans. Being able to convey information helps form relationships, decode and encode information as well as retain information, and allows us to thrive as an individual.

According to Professor Jeanette Norden (2019), in terms of learning a foreign language 'we appear to lose some plasticity' after puberty. If I unpick my episodic memory of my experiences at school, at some point I studied Welsh, German, Spanish, Italian and French – each for no longer than two years. Moving between schools certainly didn't help my retention or performance, and in the 1980s there was little stipulation across the curriculum that teenagers had to choose a language for final examination. I'm sure I am not the only person with this experience, and in a world where more people are increasingly speaking English, here lies the challenge for us as a British society. How do we encourage more people to speak other languages?

If what Norden reports is true in general terms, would I now struggle to learn a language after puberty? I certainly do have a mental 'brick wall' against wanting to learn a language, but we also know that we can continue to shape neural plasticity well into the latter years of our old age. In Chapter 6, I will discuss some mental models for overcoming any barriers to learning which may hinder us from reshaping our neural plasticity.

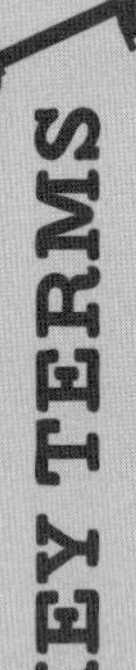

Adrenaline: A hormone that produces more glucose in the blood, giving us a surge of energy to respond in a 'fight or flight' situation.

Amygdala: A key part of the limbic system that plays a central role in how we process emotions.

Cortisol: The body's main 'stress hormone' released by the adrenal glands. It is most commonly associated with fear and anxiety, but it is also essential for many key bodily functions.

Hormones: Chemical substances that act like messengers in the body to control and regulate different bodily functions.

Hypothalamus: The control centre for our nervous system.

PRACTICAL IDEA

Spaced and active rereading

As we've discovered in Chapters 2 and 3, the research on retrieval practice is clear. Low-stakes assessment, carefully spaced at regular intervals, supports the retention of knowledge. The importance of ensuring retrieval tasks are 'desirably difficult' (see page 27) becomes even more evident when we add emotions into the mix. If the tasks are too easy, students might become demotivated, apathetic and disengaged. If they're too hard, we might just risk increasing a student's levels of adrenaline and cortisol to a detrimental degree, causing panic, anxiety and distraction. Teachers who can create the right conditions to learn, where students feel safe and trusted to take risks, will have the biggest impact on shaping students' memories.

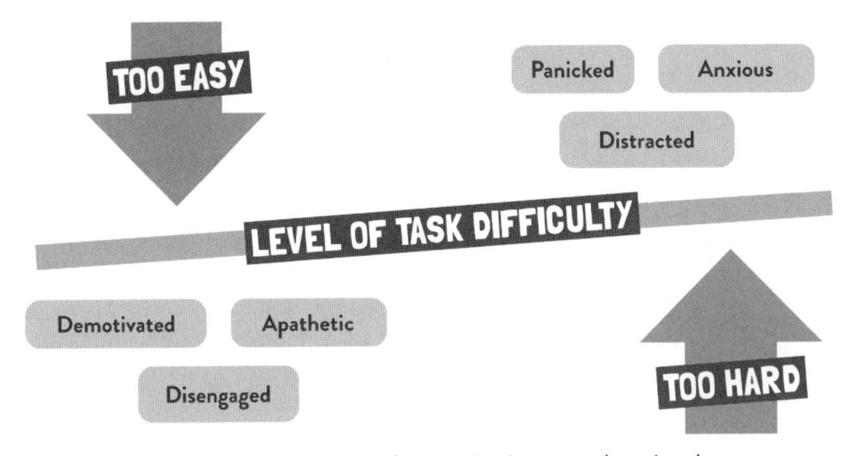

As research-informed teachers, we know that testing improves learning, but to ensure we are creating an environment in which students feel safe and trusted, we need to be cautious about how we use testing in our classrooms. It's understandable that not all students will respond positively to frequent testing, even if it is low stakes, because of the negative connotations they may associate with it in an increasingly high-stakes education system. Students' experiences of testing most commonly involve high-stakes summative assessment designed to evaluate learning. In some cases, our 16-year-old students in England are put through over 30 exams in one academic year. Students must take these exams to get a 'ticket' on results day to grant them access to their next step on the educational ladder. This key moment in one's life 'overshadows the fact that testing also improves learning' (Dunlosky et al., 2013).

Students' views on high-stakes exams are understandable and once or twice a year, you will see and hear an 'outcry' in the media from a range of parents, politicians and even teachers, calling for reform in our examination system. There are many arguments for this and some that I agree with, from the impact high-stakes testing has on children's mental health to the widening achievement gap between disadvantaged students and their peers. Sadly, for some students, when we consider the bell curve and how grades are distributed, the one-off nature of an exam means there are potentially a multitude of factors that could impact their metacognitive performance on the day, including increased levels of anxiety (Silaj et al., 2021).

Of course, low-stakes testing in or out of class to support learning and memory is very different to the conditions used for examinations, and retrieval practice is key to success, but we do need to be mindful about overtesting our students and overwhelming them with constant assessment. There is evidence that retrieval practice can in fact reduce test anxiety in secondary school students (Agarwal et al., 2014). However, if students are put on the spot in front of their peers, this can cause anxiety and distract students from the learning. If you think your students are becoming overwhelmed or you simply find that they need to revisit the content before you try another retrieval task, you could revert to a really simple learning activity that is not just low-stakes but no-stakes and comfortable and familiar to all students: rereading.

Is rereading effective?

Rereading is one of the techniques that we all frequently use when self-regulating our study, particularly when we are revising for an exam. It's an easy, no-stakes technique. We can all do it. Dunlosky et al. (2013) report that 'high-performing students appear to use rereading regularly'. So, if all of us have used this technique, particularly those who achieve some of the highest grades, is it worth the effort and is it effective?

We often think that we are learning simply by rereading, but this is not always the case. This is called the 'illusion of learning', which is when a student thinks they know more than they do because they put a lot of (ineffective) effort into studying – in other words, cramming.

That being said, there is some evidence that rereading can have an impact on learning. The general effects of rereading are 'fairly robust' (Dunlosky et al., 2013), no matter whether students are notified that they will study the material again in the future. This can be explained by the fact that rereading material increases the total amount of information that a student will encode. Another possible explanation is that rereading supports the conceptual organisation and processing of the key ideas in a text. It's important to note, however, that there is almost no research on rereading that has 'involved learners younger than college-age students' (Dunlosky et al., 2013).

So, rereading is an easy technique and it may have an impact on learning. However, as with everything, it is something that must be practised and it's *how* we do it that matters – remember the Bananarama principle from *What Works?* (Major and Higgins, 2019). The teacher acting as an expert must guide the students to learn how to use this technique for effective restudy. How to do this with a four-year-old and a 16-year-old will be very different.

How to make rereading more effective

As with anything, if students are not trained in how to use the technique of rereading, it will have a negligible impact on learning. Here are two ways in which teachers can make rereading more effective so they can help students avoid the 'illusion of learning':

1. spaced rereading
2. active rereading.

So, what do these techniques involve and what might they look like in the classroom?

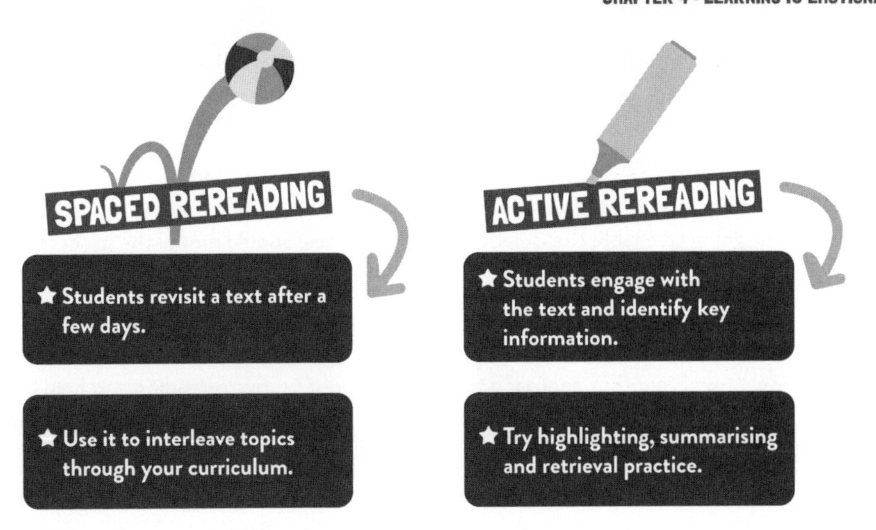

1. Spaced rereading

The evidence suggests that rereading can be effective even if the student revisits the text immediately after the first time they study it. This is known as 'massed rereading'. However, leaving time between initial study and restudy of the text – known as 'spaced rereading' – has been shown to have a greater impact on learning. In a research study from 2008 (Verkoeijen et al.), learners were asked to read a text before being split into three groups: the first group reread the text immediately afterwards; the second reread it four days later; the third reread it three and a half weeks later. All three groups of learners were tested on the material they'd read two days after they'd reread it. So, who performed best? The second group – those who had reread the text after four days.

So, if you're going to use rereading as a learning strategy in your classroom, try spaced rereading. Leave a few days before you ask students to revisit a text. Perhaps you could use spaced rereading to interleave different topics through your curriculum (see Chapter 3, page 44).

2. Active rereading

When students are reading – and rereading – a text, they should be *active* readers. They should be engaging with the text and identifying the key information, concepts and terminology. Rereading should aim to help students to address knowledge gaps identified by retrieval practice.

Highlighting is one study technique that we will all recognise and that can support this. This technique is easy to use and already used by millions of students. It simply involves marking out important text as it is being read. The research I have read on highlighting as a teaching strategy is mixed and this technique has a low impact, but it can have an impact under certain conditions and should not be disregarded. If students actively highlight information as they read, they can become better at identifying and remembering the necessary information. Dunlosky et al. (2013) refer to this cognitive processing as the **isolation effect**: 'semantically or phonologically [a] unique item in a list is much better remembered than its less distinctive counterparts'. In other words, if a piece of information stands out to a student, they are more likely to remember it. If they highlight key information, they isolate it and make it distinctive, and therefore it will stick in their mind. We can also use this method to teach keywords and key terminology.

The challenge is teaching students *how* to identify key information (and key terminology) effectively. We know some students have the tendency to highlight every word on the page! But this is not going to enable the isolation effect. Teachers should model the process of identifying the most important aspects of a text, before fading back their instruction to allow students to develop a degree of expertise (see more about modelling in the section about cognitive apprenticeship on page 102).

Summarising a text is another approach that could support active rereading and help students to process and retain the key information in the text. We'll discuss summarising in more detail in the next chapter.

When students are in the right mindset to return to low-stakes testing, don't forget to support rereading with **retrieval practice** (Chapter 2) and **spaced practice** (Chapter 3) techniques too. Testing students on what they have read is another method of encouraging students to actively engage with what they are reading and will support their long-term retention of the key information.

Dunlosky et al. (2013) conclude, 'We do not yet know the extent to which many of the learning techniques will benefit students of various ages, abilities, and levels of prior knowledge.' Almost ten years on, this appraisal still provides teachers with much to consider. How these techniques are used in Early Years classrooms, in pupil referral units or in large secondary schools is what makes research-informed practice helpful for teachers, but always requires the teacher's wisdom to translate the findings back into their setting.

1. Create the right classroom culture for learning. Students should feel calm and safe but also trusted and challenged to take risks.
2. Ensure all retrieval practice testing is low-stakes to avoid a rush of adrenaline, cortisol and anxiety, which can detract from learning.
3. Don't overwhelm your students with testing. If they're not in the right mindset for a low-stakes test one lesson, try alternative techniques such as rereading. Think high challenge, low stress.
4. Restudy text material with students, but leave a modest gap between when they first read the text and when they revisit it.
5. Teach students how to reread material actively, by using highlighting or other techniques in this book such as summarising and retrieval practice.
6. Consider where best in the curriculum to use summative assessment of the learning so that it informs future teaching and learning.

WORKED EXAMPLE

OK, you should know where this is going now. Throughout this whole book, to model how we remember and how we can teach study skills, I have provided you with some examples about volcanoes. With these examples, we should be able to demonstrate how you as a reader can learn any concept, rule or fact. It's simply a matter of using a variety of techniques to strengthen your synapses.

Here is some new information I would like you to study, this time about the Icelandic volcano Eyjafjallajökull. The learning objective for this paragraph is: 'To learn about the eruption of the Icelandic volcano Eyjafjallajökull in 2010.'

Icelandic volcano Eyjafjallajökull erupted on 14th April 2010 and caused six days of aviation disruption. This ruined Ross's honeymoon in Naples, Italy and it took him eight days to get home by car. Eyjafjallajökull consists of a volcano completely covered by an ice cap. The ice cap covers an area of about 100 square kilometres (40 square miles). It has an elevation of 1,651 metres (or 5,417 feet). Its name means 'glacier of Eyjafjöll' (or more properly 'ice cap of Eyjafjöll') and is made up of the words *eyja* (the genitive plural of *ey*, meaning *eyot* or *island*), *fjöll* (meaning fells or mountains) and *jökull* (meaning glacier). Almost 3,000 small earthquakes were detected near the volcano in March 2010 prior to the eruption. Some damage was caused by a minor eruption in 1821, but there was no major activity between then and the April 2010 eruption. In August 2010 the volcano became dormant. Iceland Post issued three stamps made of volcanic ash to remember the event!

In this study skill example, we are going to use the techniques of rereading and highlighting. So, here is your first set of instructions:

- Read the paragraph on the Icelandic volcano Eyjafjallajökull again.
- Draw a line through any **irrelevant information**.
- Draw a + sign above any aspects of the paragraph that offer **declarative knowledge**.
- Draw a – sign above any text that references any **episodic information**.
- Finally, grab a highlighter and draw over the **key text**.

Now let's complete some further tasks that look at honing in on some key terminology, engaging further with the text and seeing how much you can remember after rereading it. There's also a retrieval question to retest some knowledge we learned in an earlier chapter. To really test the concept of rereading, try completing these tasks a few days after completing the highlighting tasks above. Turn the page to get started!

Now you have reread the text, highlight five keywords about volcanoes and write them below.	**Design two questions to ask another student.**
1. **2.** **3.** **4.** **5.**	**1.** **2.**
Reread the text again. Wait three minutes and then rewrite your own summary of the original text without looking at it.	**Retrieval question: What is the section of the volcano called where lava travels through?**
	(Here are some multiple-choice answers designed to be relatively hard to eliminate, rather than obvious incorrect choices.) **1.** Funnel **2.** Conduit **3.** Pipe **4.** Duct **5.** Passage *(Take a look at the diagram on page 14 to check your answer.)*

If you want to take this one step further, try writing another summary of the original text in two days' time *without* reopening the book to this page and rereading the text. Once you've written your summary, compare it to the first summary you wrote in the box above. How much have you remembered? Did you capture the key information accurately and did you miss anything out?

Why not send me a photograph and tag @TeacherToolkit and #GuideToMemory on social media? I'll send you some feedback.

Now think about how you would use these techniques in the classroom. On the next page, I've provided you with a blank template so you can devise some similar tasks for your students.

TEMPLATE

Rereading

Now you have reread the text, highlight five keywords about ___________ and write them below.	Design two questions to ask another student.
1. 2. 3. 4. 5.	1. 2.
Reread the text again. Wait three minutes and then rewrite your own summary of the original text without looking at it.	**Retrieval question:**

Scan the QR code for a downloadable digital copy of this template.

CHAPTER 5
COGNITIVE LOAD THEORY

In 1988, Australian educational psychologist and academic John Sweller published a research paper titled 'Cognitive load during problem solving: Effects on learning'. It was an initial reference to cognitive load theory. What do we know about cognitive load theory 30 years later and how can it influence the way we teach and learn?

To keep things as simple as possible, cognitive load theory is the theory that we can only process a certain amount of information at any one time. We know from Chapter 3, where we explored different types of memory, that our working memory is where we hold short-term memories and manipulate them in some way. We also know that our working memory is limited by what it can do with any information at any one time. Much of the research that I have read suggests that we can manipulate between three and nine pieces of information simultaneously (see, for example, Singh, 2009), but this depends on the particular study you are reading and the task participants are being asked to do. As we discovered in Chapter 2, cognitive neuroscientists report that the human brain has between 86 and 100 billion neurons (depending on which sources you read), with 100 trillion possibilities of connecting these neurons, so I'd like to believe that there are no known limits to how much information we can store or how it is processed. This information is relatively new for all of us, as MRI scans have only recently been capable of allowing us to study sections of the brain in greater detail and we don't have all the answers yet.

The crux of cognitive load theory is the idea that we can hinder or support our working memory by being intentional about the information we are feeding it at any one time. Is the information relevant or is it redundant? Will it help us to build on prior knowledge to develop new schemas for our long-term memory?

What has evolved from Sweller's research is that various instructional techniques are recommended, which fit in with the characteristics of working memory and therefore unlock better learning potential. The challenge for every teacher across the world is being able to consider carefully what information to give their learners and when – and then regularly assess and determine *how* this is impacting the learning of the students in front of them, before determining how to move on in the lesson. Finally, I also think it is important to mention – despite the popularity of cognitive load theory – that Sweller himself has said it is 'not a theory of everything'. Scan the QR code to hear Sweller talk more about this in an interview from 2012.

In this chapter, I will try to unpick the original research and offer you an overview and my opinions on what you can take away for classroom practice.

EXPLAINER

A summary of Sweller's original research

The aim of John Sweller's 1988 research paper was to discuss whether people can learn through problem-solving, rather than by 'discovery learning'. Sweller's conclusions are clear from the word go. In his opening line he states that 'some forms of problem solving interfere with learning'. The first thing to distinguish is what Sweller defines as 'learning' and what he means by 'some forms of problem-solving'.

How does Sweller define learning?

Are pupils learning how to construct an argument for a history assignment on the Battle of Britain and why Britain's planes outclassed the Germans? Or perhaps we are learning how to construct a tower from building blocks, in pairs inside a Year 3 classroom, as we try to balance a tennis ball at the highest level? Whatever it is, learning needs to be defined. Sweller defines learning as the acquisition of domain-specific knowledge in the form of schemas. He argues that this is the main factor that distinguishes novices from experts. Whilst this definition is very high-brow and academic, for teachers, this is best redefined as our curriculum intentions and how we see the teaching of knowledge throughout the curriculum from day one until a student leaves formal education; developing schemas and strengthening this knowledge across multiple domains.

Sweller discusses one particular study (de Groot, 1966), which derives from investigations of chess matches between players who are masters versus less experienced players. This research indicated that expert players could remember larger sequences of moves.

What does Sweller mean by problem-solving?

The second critical point to emphasise is that Sweller's original paper is focused entirely on problem-solving. He discusses several problem-solving strategies and which strategies are used by 'experts' and which are used by 'novices'.

Strategies selected by expert and novice problem-solvers were different. Novices worked backwards from the goal, often using a process Sweller refers to as 'means-end analysis'. This process involves solving problems one step at a time by attempting to reduce the difference between the problem and the end goal by setting subgoals. Lots of examples are provided in the original paper to elaborate on how problems can be solved (or not) using means-end analysis.

Conversely, experts 'eliminated the backwards-working phase'. Experts 'work forward immediately' because they recognise each problem from previous experience: '... cognitive structures [schemas] allow experts to accurately recall the configuration of a given problem.' (Sweller, 1988) In essence, the person solving the problem can categorise the scenario when they possess an appropriate schema, by using memorised configurations, compared to novices who may not have this prior knowledge. Experts can then apply this same schema to the scenario and solve the problem.

So which forms of problem-solving interfere with learning?

Sweller says it is commonly assumed that practising solving a large number of conventional problems is the most effective way of improving problem-solving abilities, but he argues that this is not the case. Sweller offers experimental evidence of interference between 'means-end analysis' and learning by schema acquisition. Means-end analysis uses heavy cognitive processing. To use means-end analysis to solve a problem, you must consider the current problem, the end goal, and the relationship between the problem and goal, and think about the solutions you're going to use to move from the problem to the goal. This leaves very little cognitive processing capacity for schema acquisition. In other words, when your brain is busy solving a problem, it makes it **much harder** to learn and retain knowledge.

Sweller's research links to our understanding of working memory having limited capacity. We can only manipulate a number of pieces of information at any one time – before additional information becomes redundant. So, there is nothing to contest with here if we accept that cognitive load theory as presented is under the umbrella of problem-solving. However, we know problem-solving in some respects is evident in all subject areas of the curriculum and that developing metacognition in our young people requires a degree of a pre-organised schema.

If you are serious about understanding research, I would recommend reading the original research paper. It's 29 pages in length, but if you have the time and the inclination it's at least worth a skim through the full paper. There is also the original book if you are interested, but it is costly, which is why I think the freely available research paper is probably your better alternative.

Types of cognitive load

Intrinsic load

Intrinsic load relates to the inherent complexity of the material being studied or the learning task being undertaken. *This topic* is a perfect example of high intrinsic load if you are new to this theory.

Intrinsic load concerns information that is directly related to the material or task and that needs to be processed at any one time; in other words, the number of elements that must be simultaneously processed in the working memory and their interaction with each other (or prior schemas). It's affected by both the nature and complexity of the material or task and by levels of learner expertise. You cannot adjust for intrinsic load during instruction. A topic or task is either challenging or it isn't. What you can change is how you present the learning material and decide which tasks you ask your students to complete.

Extraneous load

Extraneous load is a form of working memory load that refers to the load imposed by information elements unrelated to the learning objective or goal of the task, but related to how that task is carried out; in other words, how learning takes place.

For example, I can hinder your understanding of this theory by asking you in what year it was published or what you are having for breakfast tomorrow morning. These irrelevant questions add unnecessary load to the task in hand – in this case, learning more about what cognitive load theory is and how it can be made more challenging with unnecessary information. I trust my irrelevant questions highlight this point perfectly and you may now be distracted and want to find the answers before you read on.

Essentially, these elements can be controlled by the person who designs the learning experience. That's *you*! Think about *how* material is being taught. It can be helpful or harmful...

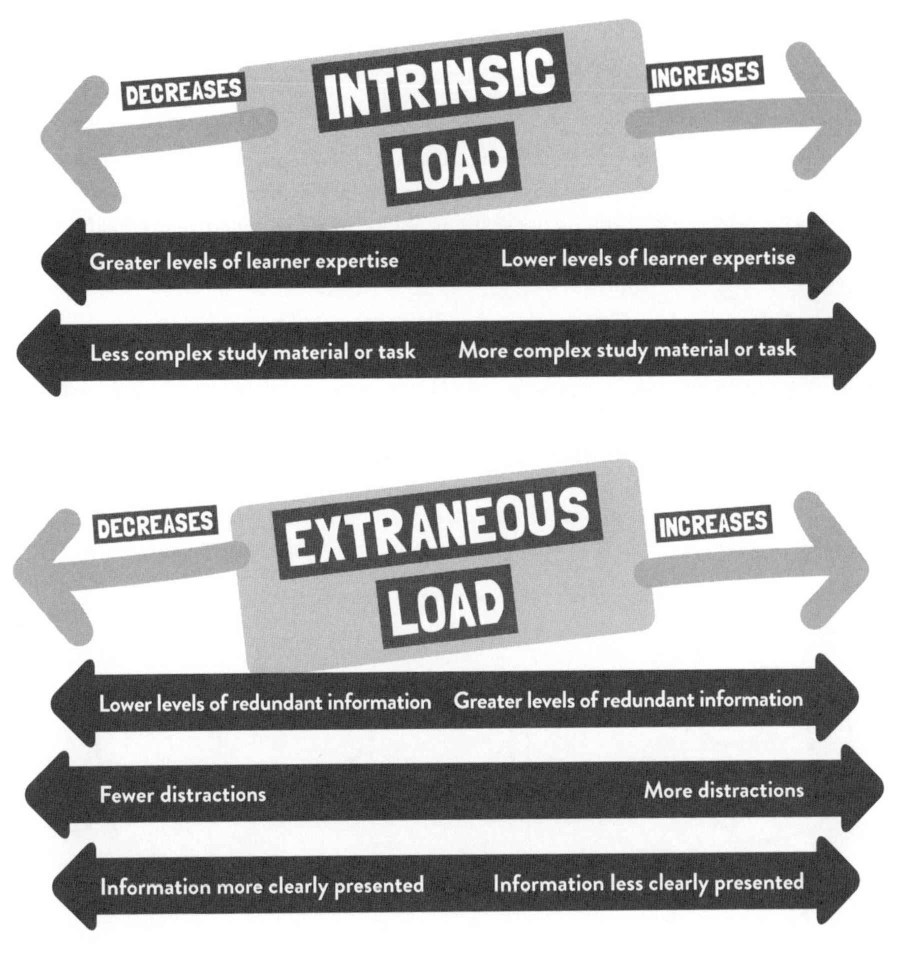

Germane load

Another term to be aware of is **germane load**. This is the mental capacity to link new information with prior knowledge, make connections and learn. You could think of this as the 'aha moment' when you're learning about a new topic and things start to make sense and fall into place. In essence, this is the 'healthy' type of load.

It's important to note that more recent research (Kirschner et al., 2018) suggests that **germane load is a part of intrinsic load**. This research defines germane load as 'working memory resources devoted to dealing with intrinsic load'.

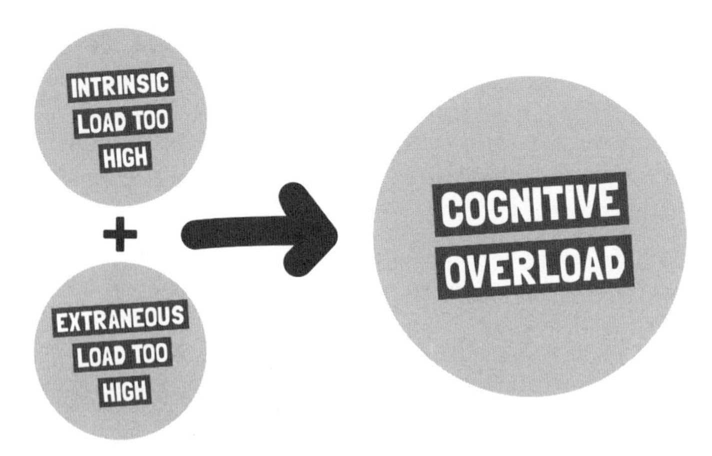

Our capacity for germane load is determined by intrinsic and extraneous load. If the learning task is too complex (intrinsic load) or there are too many distractions (extraneous load), we won't have the capacity for germane load and we risk entering a state known as **cognitive overload**. This is where our working memory becomes overwhelmed and it is much harder to process information.

What this means for designing learning tasks

To help lower cognitive load, teachers should consider well-designed learning activities that have the right level of complexity and balance new information with prior knowledge. It's also important to avoid providing unnecessary information during lesson delivery and to keep distractions to a minimum. To promote germane load, try supporting learning with scaffolding and worked-example resources, particularly for disadvantaged students. In return, specific tasks can help facilitate the development of schemas and automation.

I've produced a simple resource below to summarise the fine balance a teacher must work within.

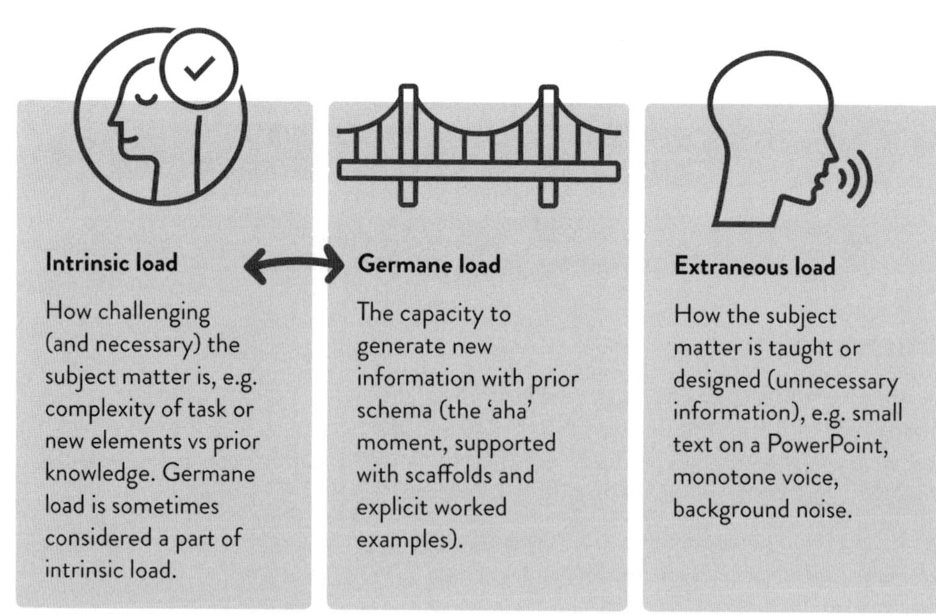

Limitations of the research on cognitive load and working memory

One issue with the research on working memory could be how we interpret the research findings. Sweller's (1988) research tested working memory when problem-solving, while Ebbinghaus's forgetting curve (1885) tested 'nonsensical syllables'. Working memory appears to be a good fit for specific learning conditions. However, where it might be confusing for teachers is when research suggests that 'learning and remembering do not always require working memory,' writes leading cognitive scientist, Guy Claxton (2021).

It is probably worth interrogating any research paper that explores working memory: what precisely is it that the experiments are doing? Is the research conducted in classroom settings or in a laboratory? If we understand this, we can then perhaps reliably evaluate whether any research findings, in this case regarding working memory, are the recommended way to shape schemas. As I dig deeper into this research, I am left with many questions myself.

We should also question whether working memory has a fixed capacity. For example, can it hold up to 'nine pieces of information'? Prior knowledge is a significant consideration here. Remember 'element interactivity'? See page 43.

There are countless pieces of academic research which I could refer to, but one seminal piece of research that has captured my interest is a chapter contribution to the *Handbook of Clinical Neurology* by D'Esposito (2008). There is an interesting breakdown of the cortical areas which contribute to working memory, more specifically our executive and perceptual memory. The paper attempts to rule out what is **not** working memory and how information can be 'retained and coded by the brain in multiple forms from persistent, elevated activity to dynamic trajectories'. The research suggests that 'temporary storage and manipulation of information can be viewed as neither a unitary, nor a dedicated system'.

Whilst cognitive load theory is a difficult subject for all teachers to grapple with, and there is much still for us all to discover in the field of 'working memory', including what factors support or hinder this part of our brain, CLT is a topic teachers should know about and be conscious of when working in the classroom.

Cognitive load theory (CLT): An instructional design theory that argues: a) learners can only process a certain amount of information at any one time and b) teachers should be intentional about how much information they give learners and how it is presented in order to avoid overloading them and hindering the learning process.

Cognitive overload: A state where our working memory becomes overwhelmed by too much information and it becomes much harder to process this information and to learn.

Extraneous load: A form of cognitive load imposed by information that is not directly related to the learning task, e.g. design elements on a slideshow or background noise.

Germane load: The capacity to link new information with prior knowledge.

Intrinsic load: A form of cognitive load relating to the inherent complexity of the material being studied or the learning task being undertaken.

PRACTICAL IDEA

Managing cognitive load

When designing classroom tasks, teachers need to consider how to manage the levels of cognitive load involved in order to promote learning. This is three-fold: choosing tasks that have the right level of intrinsic load (challenge); minimising extraneous load; and promoting germane load. Here are some practical ideas to help.

Finding the right level of intrinsic load

The best advice I can offer here is to think of a classroom task, particularly the end goal. If you want students to be able to see how they can reach the completed task, it is essential that the teacher breaks down the task into chunks.

For example, to make a pepperoni pizza for the first time in a food technology lesson, I would show the students the completed product, then work backwards. Here are the pieces of equipment you will need, the ingredients and the step-by-step instructions to reach each stage. This is why a recipe card can help all of us to cook and is an excellent worked example. I may also consider examples of pizzas that 'didn't work' or variations of the recipe once students have mastered the task. The key point to remember is: how difficult is the task? Remember, any task, no matter how easy it is, can be made more challenging by reducing resources or the time available.

Minimising extraneous load

In the above example, I would need to consider if students were novices or experts (see the chapter on cognitive apprenticeship, page 102) and determine how I will scaffold my instructions (what I say) and interventions (resources). Too much detail? My students will become confused and stressed (high burnout) about what they have to do. Too little? They become bored and demotivated by the task, making key information redundant. The key part to remember is how I help my students access the subject matter by the way that I teach it.

Promoting germane load

To help develop knowledge, again using the pizza example, I can use retrieval practice. Assuming all my students have seen a pizza and have tasted one, I can draw upon this knowledge with retrieval quizzing activities. Checking to see how many students have made a pizza, a teacher should then use curriculum connections to help make implicit knowledge more explicit. For example, 'What is dough?' Elaboration tasks can also be helpful: 'Apart from a pizza base, in what other food products would you find dough?'

An example task: writing a summary

Summarising is a simple learning task that can promote germane load – when designed well, of course.

We have probably all been there at some point in our life, writing new summaries of lengthy pieces of work. For example, we might have had an assignment where we copied extensive notes or been in an exam where we needed to re-shape information into bullet points. But you might be surprised that summarising can be used as a study technique to help you remember.

Summarisation enables students to access higher-order concepts and thinking, helping individuals to identify, organise and process key information, and then extract meaning. We translate everything we've learned into a short summary to help us remember the key points. This schema works as a trigger to shape key concepts, rules and facts, unlocking further knowledge that can be recalled and used, and also making connections with prior knowledge to deepen understanding. For example, what are the colours of the rainbow? How does refraction work?

Writing summaries is a complex task because you first need to understand what you are reading, identify what is important and then consider how different concepts, rules and facts connect to one another. However, it is possible to control the intrinsic load of the task by choosing a text based on the domain knowledge students have already learned. It can also be beneficial to train students on how to summarise effectively. Being able to identify the main points of the text, summarise highlights and discard unimportant or irrelevant information takes practice. So, use scaffolding and worked examples to demonstrate these skills to students. It is important to build in time for your students to learn the strategy.

Summarising is a useful alternative strategy to verbatim copying. Although it is difficult to evaluate the success of this strategy because how it is implemented across different studies makes its efficacy 'difficult to evaluate' (Dunlosky et al., 2013), it is important to emphasise that the instructions provided by the teacher, or what is written on the exam paper, will help students to succeed.

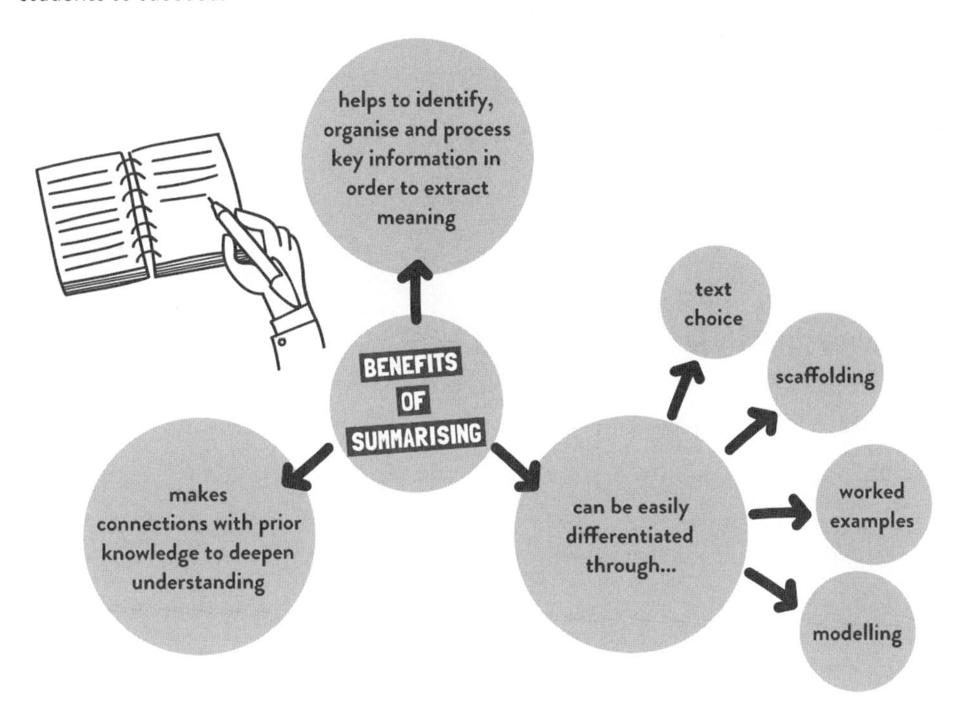

Sketchnoting

Sketchnoting is becoming very popular among online educators, and as a design technology specialist, it is a technique I have used in my own teaching and have encouraged in students as they develop their design thinking.

Sketchnotes are essentially drawing-summaries and are critical for communicating visual representations of concepts. It warms my heart to see academic research advocating sketchnoting as a learning tool to support long-term retention. Gansemer-Topf et al. (2021), for example, describe sketchnoting as an 'active learning tool [that] has shown potential for influencing student learning'. We also know from Paivio's (1990) theory of dual coding (see Chapter 1) that 'deeper learning occurs when individuals process words and pictures rather than words alone'.

So instead of written summaries, why not try asking students to create visual summaries to capture key concepts? As with written summaries, it's important to model and scaffold the technique of sketchnoting so students can learn to identify key information and translate this into visual form.

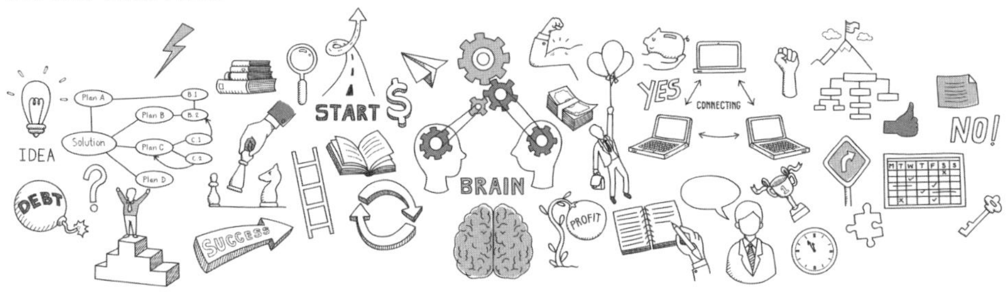

If you want to introduce sketchnoting into your classroom as a study skill, or want to use it for your own professional development, then I would suggest grabbing a copy of *How to Sketchnote: A step-by-step manual for teachers and students* by Sylvia Duckworth (2018), one of the most popular visual notetakers in education in the USA. In her book, she reminds us of sketching as an effective tool for memory retention. It calms us down as well as helping us to develop a schema, making connections between concepts.

TOOLKIT TIPS

1. Ensure tasks have the right level of intrinsic load. Hit the sweet spot between not too easy and not too difficult.
2. Minimise extraneous load by avoiding distractions when delivering content, such as background noise and unnecessary graphics or instruction.
3. Use scaffolding and worked examples to support germane load.
4. Consider using summarising as a learning task, in place of verbatim copying.
5. Model summarisation to students before setting it as a task: demonstrate how to identify and record what's important and how to discard irrelevant information.
6. Remember that summaries don't always have to be written. How about trying sketchnoting as a visual alternative?

WORKED EXAMPLE

Summarising can include single-word instructions, sentences and paragraphs in varying length, or it can involve speaking aloud. Obvious though it may sound, how would you summarise *this* chapter of the book? Where would you start? How would you determine which information is critical and sits at the heart of the concept of cognitive load theory? Which parts of the text are not so important?

To demonstrate summarisation, let's revisit the paragraph about Eyjafjallajökull, the Icelandic volcano. I would like you to read this paragraph, reread it, and then follow the next instruction. The learning objective for this paragraph is: 'To learn about the eruption of the Icelandic volcano Eyjafjallajökull in 2010.'

Icelandic volcano Eyjafjallajökull erupted on 14th April 2010 and caused six days of aviation disruption. This ruined Ross's honeymoon in Naples, Italy and it took him eight days to get home by car. Eyjafjallajökull consists of a volcano completely covered by an ice cap. The ice cap covers an area of about 100 square kilometres (40 square miles). It has an elevation of 1,651 metres (or 5,417 feet). Its name means 'glacier of Eyjafjöll' (or more properly 'ice cap of Eyjafjöll') and is made up of the words *eyja* (the genitive plural of *ey*, meaning *eyot* or *island*), *fjöll* (meaning fells or mountains) and *jökull* (meaning glacier). Almost 3,000 small earthquakes were detected near the volcano in March 2010 prior to the eruption. Some damage was caused by a minor eruption in 1821, but there was no major activity between then and the April 2010 eruption. In August 2010 the volcano became dormant. Iceland Post issued three stamps made of volcanic ash to remember the event!

Once you've read the paragraph twice, try completing the four tasks in the table on the next page. As you're writing your summaries, think about which parts of the paragraph are declarative knowledge and which are redundant information.

If I can offer a suggestion, I would summarise the paragraph into the following five points. **DO NOT** read the below answer suggestion until you've turned over and given the tasks a go yourself!

1. Eyjafjallajökull erupted on 14th April 2010.
2. There were six days of aviation disruption.
3. Around 3,000 earthquakes were detected in March 2010.
4. Prior to this, there had been no major activity since 1821.
5. The volcano is now dormant (since August 2010).

To build on the idea of sketchnoting, you could explore concept maps: graphic organisers or visual representations of knowledge. Scan the QR code to find out more about concept maps from Dr Kripa Sundar.

Write a detailed summary of the paragraph about Eyjafjallajökull.	**Now summarise the content in five bullet points.**
	1. 2. 3. 4. 5.
Highlight the keywords in your summary above and then write them below.	**Now try sketchnoting the key points in the paragraph.**

TEMPLATE

Summarising

Here is a simple template that you can use to redesign this summarisation process for your students. You can amend this template to incorporate other techniques in this book, using each strategy to build up study skills and memorisation over time.

Write a detailed summary of the text.	**Now summarise the content in five bullet points.**
	1. **2.** **3.** **4.** **5.**
Highlight the keywords in your summary above and then write them below.	**Now try sketchnoting the key points in the text.**

Scan the QR code for a downloadable digital copy of this template.

CHAPTER 6
MENTAL MODELS FOR LEARNING

Sometimes we learn from being taught, and other times we need some rigid support. There are also times we discover things for ourselves and we can each have our own 'Eureka moments' at any point. These latter moments tend to happen because we already have prior knowledge subconsciously stored. When learning is hard, it's often because it is new, but depending on how the information is shared and what the task is, techniques can guide us or provide scaffolding for stages along the way.

When learning happens, it may be in the classroom, it may be in our garden or it may be on the journey to and from work. Wherever it happens, learning is part of our DNA (deoxyribonucleic acid), our evolution and our survival as a human race. We experience the world around us, we listen to one another, we observe and we practise. We use our past experiences, make models, or do three or four takes to make that perfect social media video. These are just some of the ways that we are always learning. But sometimes, we need to find ways to learn very specific things and in this chapter I want to focus on some methods that lend themselves to this, including mental models and mnemonics. It's important to note that these methods must be evaluated prior to adoption. If they are wrong, they can lead to implicit biases and negative consequences. If they are right, they can support learning.

EXPLAINER

What is a mental model?

A **mental model** is a representation of how something works and how we understand the world. We all see things from different perspectives. Let's take the example of a student whose behaviour has improved. A teacher may perceive this student is now behaving as a result of a classroom task. A form tutor may observe this improved approach to learning as a result of an intervention put in place the day before in conversation with the student's family. A school leader could view this remarkable change in attitude in relation to how well the school behaviour policy is now working and the pep talk they had with the student in between lesson changeover. Whilst we know all these factors are intertwined and contribute to the overall picture, each person will look at the situation from a particular perspective and through their own mental model of how they view the world.

In this example, a mental model helps each person simplify the complex cogs that are turning as they try to make sense of the situation, breaking it into manageable chunks and establishing a mental model for working more effectively. In other words, mental models are a framework for thinking which creates a mental map (schema) for working through the topic. In many cases, mental models are formed unconsciously: they are shaped by our experiences and perspectives. However, we can also use mental models *consciously* to help us to learn.

Mental models are fantastic for all of us in a number of scenarios; they offer a representation for unpicking our thought processes. They give us a better way of working and help us to improve our decisions. Feedback loops, scripts and knowing when to introduce pivot points are some of the many examples for using mental models in our everyday work.

FEEDBACK LOOPS

Feedback loops are designed to help students complete a task, receive feedback and adjust their actions using selected strategies to achieve a goal.

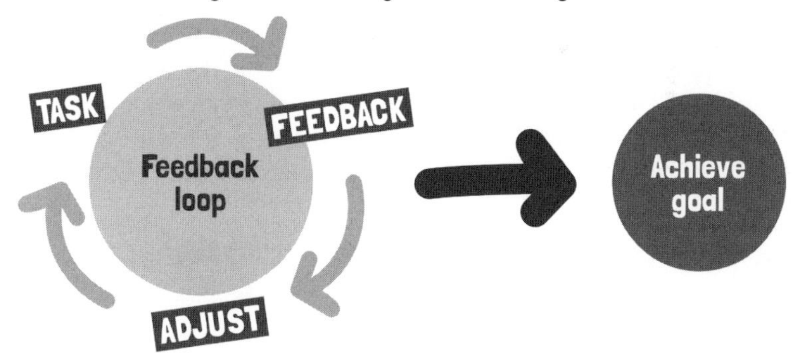

It's also worth considering types of feedback:

Feedback: comparison of the actual status of work with a previous status
Feed-up: comparison of the actual status with the target status
Feedforward: explanation of the target status based on the actual status

SCRIPTS

Having a script to follow helps to keep conversations concise, structured and focused.

Use them with, for example, classroom feedback, behaviour management in the corridor, or lesson observation feedback with a colleague.

PIVOT POINTS

Use these as key assessment moments in the teaching and learning process, with questions that differentiate accurately and instantly. For example, use self-explanation ('Tell me why...') and elaboration methods ('Show me how you reached this point...').

As well as the example above, think about your life as a teacher. Given the busy nature of school life, with one teacher interacting with 30 students at any one time, we know the working lives of teachers are incredibly busy and that they must target their efforts on a minute-by-minute basis. Not only is this exhausting, but teachers regularly suffer from cognitive overload in their day-to-day job. This is why it's helpful to create our own mental models to help us go about working life.

Mental models can be supported by rote memory practice. I myself have to work hard to use techniques to make day-to-day living a little easier. I'll use the example of locking the door again because I continue to suffer from this problem... I tend to, but don't always, lock the door when I leave the house and jump into a taxi or into my car on the way to work. One or two minutes later, there I am panicking, thinking, 'Have I locked the door?' To avoid this scenario and any anxiety caused, when leaving the house, whether I am in a rush or just ambling, I now simply say out loud that 'I am now locking the door' two or three times so this information becomes embedded. When I need to do this, it is clearly a sign to me that I am trying to manage too many things at once and not protecting enough time between events. Using this mental model helps me take things more slowly and establish a concrete action being completed. More importantly, using this over and over creates a lattice of thoughts and techniques to help automate that process in the future. I use words and actions to make this specific moment memorable.

What are mnemonics?

Mnemonics are also a very useful, but different, mental strategy. A mnemonic is a memory device used as a learning technique to help retention or retrieval. The Greeks and Romans used signs or pictures to aid memory and mnemonics create more of an 'artificial' memory that has been trained and developed through the learning and practice of a variety of mnemonic techniques. Mnemonics can come in a variety of forms such as a song, rhyme or acronym.

Why are mental models important?

Mental models help shape our behaviour and understanding. They can be used to help solve problems, understand concepts, and in general, use thinking tools more effectively. They also help to reduce our cognitive load (see Chapter 5; Yilmaz, 2020). An example of a mental model that can be used consciously to shape our thinking is the popular concept the **Pareto Principle** (or the 80/20 principle), named after the Italian economist, Vilfredo Pareto: that 80 per cent of consequences come from 20 per cent of causes. Switching from an economic perspective towards education, this theory could be translated in the following examples: that 80 per cent of our marking could be done in 20 per cent of our contact time, or that 80 per cent of all behavioural issues found in any school come from 20 per cent of the pupil population. Using this mental model, we could achieve more by focusing to a greater extent on the 20 per cent in our work.

In terms of revision, students may spend their time revising topics that 'pop up' time and again, requiring students to spend more time on these questions during the exam. Rather than spreading themselves thin and covering lots of topics, students should find the core 20 per cent of material and understand this in (80 per cent) greater depth. For teachers adopting this principle as a workload strategy, when the most important tasks are identified and completed, there is less pressure to complete everything else because the most essential tasks are done. Where possible, do the most important tasks first!

Why are mnemonics important?

Developing mnemonics as a study skill strategy is incredibly powerful for learning.

What are the colours of the rainbow? Does the letter 'i' usually come before 'e' or the other way around? How many days are in each month of the year?

How do you remember these conventions? It is likely that when you learned these things at home or school, the memorisation technique you used was mnemonics. Using this as a technique is a great shortcut for building memory. In Ancient Greek, 'mnemonic', meaning 'of memory', was known as the 'art of remembrance' and related to the goddess of memory in Greek mythology, **Mnemosyne** (the original title for this book!). Legend has it that Mnemosyne presided over the River Lethe in Hades and that anyone who drank from the river experienced complete forgetfulness. Today, we are likely to assume that these stories are fables and myths, somewhat romanticising bygone times. However, we can see how words have evolved in our language, and in this case, how the word mnemonics has evolved.

In essence, mnemonics are used as shortcuts (perhaps auditory phrases or presentations in visual form) to help retention. The most obvious one you can try right now is to clench both your hands into a fist and bring them together so they touch. If we now recall the 12 months of a calendar year, January, February and so forth, we can start to use the knuckle shapes to retrieve how many days are in each calendar month. One obvious challenge for some will be that if you have never done this before, it will be more difficult to retrieve the information.

When I was a young boy attending our local church, I learned to play the trumpet. Part of my music lessons involved learning how to read music. When I learned how to read the C major scale, the musical notes were F, A, C, E and the notes on the lines were E, G, B, D and F. What was drilled into me from an early stage was that I could translate these letters into memorable words or phrases. For example, FACE, or Every Good Boy Deserves Football.

It's important to remember the mnemonic *and* what the information is telling you, not just the story or a strange word or rhyme. Stories work well as does 'movement', both of which activate our neurons. Mnemonics offer a familiar framework for unfamiliar information.

One final point worth making on the historical evolution of mnemonics is that there are different types. Musical, auditory, models and imagery to name a few. If we think back to the theory of dual coding (see page 14), teaching keywords alongside an image or propositional code may support storage. **Propositional theory**, developed by Dr Zenon Pylyshyn in 1973, suggests that mental relationships between objects are represented by symbols or meaning-based descriptions and not by mental images of the scene. Imagery helps us to solve problems and influence our decisions. For example, if I gave you £50,000 to buy a new car, what are you now imagining? Can you visualise the interior, the smell, how the engine sounds and the smooth ride? In order to visualise the car we'd buy, our brain pulls together symbols or descriptions of all these different elements.

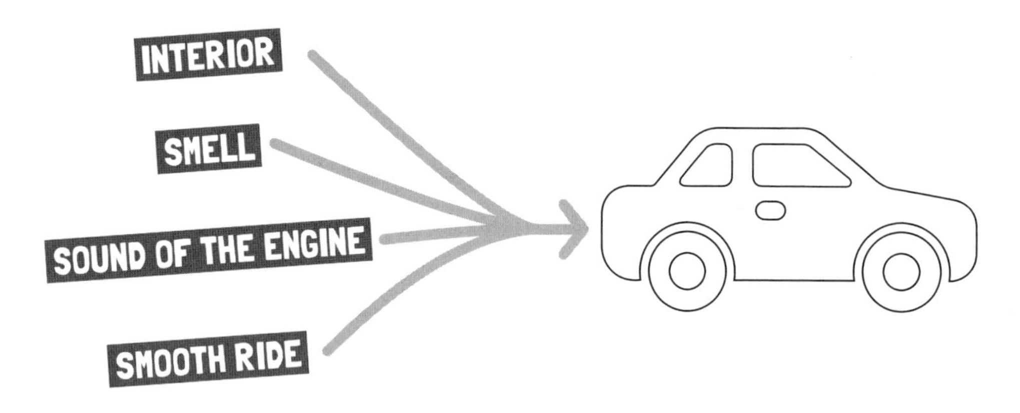

We might use this as a technique for retrieving information. This is when we have to create a mental image, for example, a rainbow. We can draw upon a mnemonic as a strategy to help recall the colours and hopefully we will then be able to explain how refraction works.

It is worth noting that as a learning approach this particular strategy is much harder to use if there is no prior knowledge in place, so when working with students, I'd suggest that using dual coding in the classroom is a more beneficial strategy for students who are learning new concepts, rules and facts.

Mental model: A representation of how something works and how we understand the world.

Mnemonic: A memory device used as a learning technique to help retention or retrieval.

Mnemosyne: The goddess of memory in Greek mythology.

Propositional theory: A theory developed by Dr Zenon Pylyshyn that suggests mental relationships between objects are represented by symbols or meaning-based descriptions and not by mental images of the scene.

PRACTICAL IDEA

Using mnemonics

If we return to the colours of the rainbow, let's try to recall each colour: red, orange, yellow and so forth.

Most people should be able to do this, give or take one or two colours incorrectly listed in the wrong place. However, if you have taken the time to practise a mnemonic device for this particular fact, you could potentially turn the first letter of a list of items into a memorable word or sentence. So, you may be able to recall R, O, Y, G, B, I, and V. As a mnemonic, this could suggest a name, ROY G. BIV, or be a rhyme or story: Richard Of York Gave Battle In Vain. This example is only useful if you're familiar with British history and have this prior schema, but I will assume you understand and are familiar with the idea. I have observed some schools redesign this mnemonic to encourage diversity: Respect Others You Grow By Including Variety. It may not be very well known to you, but you can understand how mnemonics can be used, adapted and encouraged in other contexts.

Let me give you two examples of **mnemonics** that I have used every day in my teaching career as a design and technology (DT) teacher.

K.I.S.S. = Keep It Simple, Stupid

K.I.S.S. is a design principle used by the US Navy in the 1960s. The premise is that things work better when they are simple, whether we are considering a simple teaching and learning policy or a beautiful piece of design, such as the iPhone or the Taj Mahal building in Agra, India. K.I.S.S. is a design strategy I regularly used with thousands of students when developing design ideas for DT projects.

I use this KISS methodology on my teacher resource websites, keeping blogs short and concise, making resources straight to the point, with templates teachers can use in their classrooms the very next day! I mean, who can remember the last time a 30-page teaching and learning policy had any impact across a school? Over 16 million teachers have read content on my website, with the average reading time being 70 seconds. What does that tell you? With students, the same philosophy applies. Now we know more about cognitive load (Chapter 5), we understand how important it is to keep direct instruction (Chapter 1) clear and precise. Supporting students' retention becomes more meaningful over time.

M.I.N.T. = Materials, In or out of seats, Noise level, Time

M.I.N.T. is an instruction methodology I first learned as a trainee teacher in the 1990s. This effective mnemonic has served me well for my entire teaching career. It helps teachers follow a scripted methodology for explaining activities or tasks to a room full of students. I didn't know it back in the 1990s, but this now appears to be a brilliant strategy for managing working memory and cognitive load. From developing my own understanding of working memory, I actively use this script in classroom and teacher training scenarios. Although I was aware of this methodology, reflecting back on my teaching career, I know that I allowed this to slip into my subconscious, rather than making it an explicit teaching strategy that I used every lesson.

A methodology for introducing and using mnemonics

So, how can we use mnemonics to make our curriculum come to life and help content stick? Try this five-step process to introduce a mnemonic and use it to embed learning:

1. Surprise: Offer an interesting thought or question.
2. Structure: Explain the cause and effect.
3. Simplicity: Translate a complex idea into engaging content.
4. Specificity: Be concise and precise.
5. Subtext: Underpin this with medium-term and long-term thinking – the big picture.

(Great news! To help you remember this process, it forms a simple mnemonic in itself: SSSSS or the 5 Ss.)

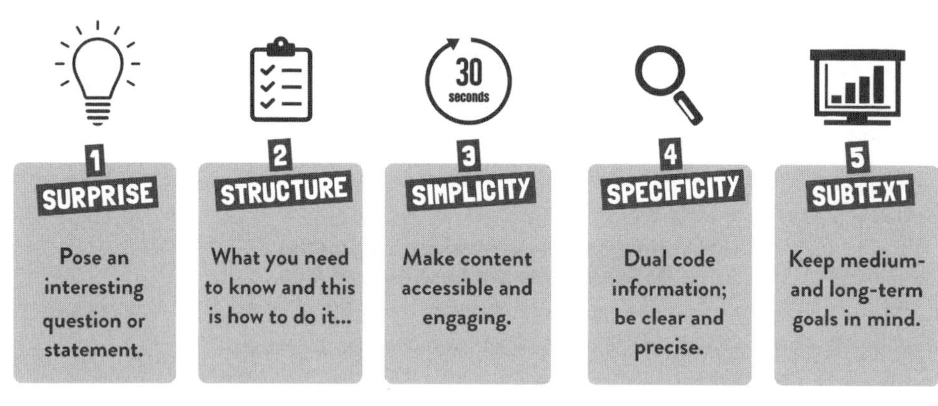

On page 89, I have provided a template to help you plan how you will use this methodology in your own context.

TOOLKIT TIPS

1. Come up with mnemonics to help embed key information you want your students to learn and retain.
2. Ensure the mnemonics you devise are familiar to the students in your context. Make them relevant and ensure all students have the required prior knowledge to access and remember them.
3. You could ask the students to come up with their own mnemonic as a group. This will help ensure the mnemonic is relevant to your target audience and only uses knowledge that is already embedded.
4. Try using the KISS and MINT strategies to keep your teaching clear and to the point. This will help you to manage students' working memory and cognitive load.

WORKED EXAMPLE

Let's try recapping what we know about the Icelandic volcano Eyjafjallajökull. I realise that I should have unpicked with you how to pronounce this word already. By not doing so, writing about it in the previous chapters could be considered poorly placed. Depending on your location and age, you may have some memory of an Icelandic volcano disrupting our aviation routes, but not much more than this, unless you have actually visited Iceland and learned from that episodic experience some semantic knowledge of the country and its topography.

So, the pronunciation should have been explained. You won't be surprised to learn that I've done this on purpose to demonstrate that teachers should never assume students have the required prior knowledge without checking; and even if it has been taught, it must be tested in order to determine what to teach next.

In this case, especially when we read something for the first time and when we have no prior knowledge, we need to be careful to focus on delivering key information in bitesize chunks. If you provide too much information at once, you risk all the information, including the key information you want students to learn, becoming redundant. For example, if I started explaining to you how to pronounce Eyjafjallajökull while also telling you what I had for dinner last night, not only is the information about my diet redundant, but I risk making the key information about Eyjafjallajökull redundant too. What we do to support this new knowledge to become embedded is key.

To design any mnemonic device for pronouncing Eyjafjallajökull without having visited Iceland personally or being able to speak Icelandic or having any degree of expertise in volcanoes and glaciers poses a challenge. However, as teachers we are experts in pedagogy and, having a good grip of memorisation techniques, we can translate this new information into classroom strategies which can shape our neurons. I can begin to offer some examples.

Without any prior knowledge of how to pronounce this word, I've used what schema I have to find out where I could hear someone say the word out loud. I repeated this audio over and over again, then used phonic decoding (identifying individual letters) to help blend phonemes (sounds) to identify the word. You can hear the audio yourself by scanning the QR code. I've since learned how a native Icelandic speaker would help someone to pronounce Eyjafjallajökull phonetically in English. So let's fix it now.

Eyjafjallajökull

1. Read the name of the volcano above. Place your hand over the text and ask yourself, 'How do you pronounce this word?' without peeking below! Try pronouncing the word out loud now.

2. Phonetically by sound, you can begin to pronounce this name as: **Eh-ya-flat-lie-yuk**
3. Let's try again with a mnemonic.
4. Hey-ya Flat Lie Yook
5. To make it easier, sometimes the volcano is referred to as E15.
6. Its name means 'glacier of Eyjafjöll' or 'ice cap'.
7. It may just be easier for you to recall E15 unless you've now mastered reading Eyjafjallajökull and when reading these letters, you are now able to say out loud, **Eh-ya-flat-lie-yuk.** Impressive, eh?
8. On that note, let me burst your bubble! Returning to what the name means, this is potentially redundant information if we have not worked hard at retrieving this information too.
9. Let me give you a bit of help. **Hey-ya-flat** or Eyjafjöll means 'ice cap'.

The 5 Ss

Remember the 5 Ss from the practical idea?

1. Surprise
2. Structure
3. Simplicity
4. Specificity
5. Subtext

Let's look at an example of how we can use the 5 Ss to teach the pronunciation of Eyjafjallajökull.

1. **Surprise:** Offer an interesting fact about Icelandic as a language, for example: 'You may think that Icelandic is a very challenging language to learn, but in fact the US Foreign Office rates it as easier to learn than Arabic and Japanese for native English speakers.'
2. **Structure:** Explain that knowing how to pronounce Eyjafjallajökull will make it easier to remember the name of the volcano and then to remember some key information about it. Ask the learners to try pronouncing Eyjafjallajökull – you can have some fun with this! Then say that we can learn to pronounce it quite simply through a mnemonic that allows us to relate the phonemes to recognisable words in English.
3. **Simplicity:** Introduce the mnemonic and try it together:
   Hey-ya Flat Lie Yook
4. **Specificity:** Explain that the name of the volcano means 'glacier of Eyjafjöll' or 'ice cap of Eyjafjöll'. Show a photo of the volcano and invite the learners to take a look. Point out that the volcano is completely covered by an ice cap.
5. **Subtext:** Now they have mastered the pronunciation, ask the learners to recap what they know about the volcano. Invite them to share with a partner the information they can remember, this time confidently talking about the volcano using its proper name.

TEMPLATE

Mnemonics

1 SURPRISE

Pose an interesting question or statement.

2 STRUCTURE

What you need to know and this is how to do it...

3 SIMPLICITY

Make content accessible and engaging.

4 SPECIFICITY

Dual code information; be clear and precise.

5 SUBTEXT

Keep medium- and long-term goals in mind.

Scan the QR code for a downloadable digital copy of this template.

CHAPTER 7 BRAIN PLASTICITY

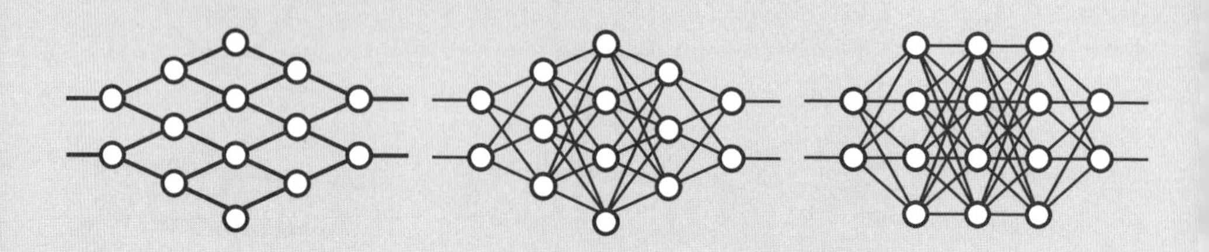

Like me, I'm sure you too have said on many occasions, 'I can't do this.' Never having learned to play the piano or the guitar, and not being able to speak another language, are beginning to become some of my life regrets. Not taking the time out to learn how to do something; to dedicate hours to learning a new skill. However, even though I am 48 and a half years old at the time of writing, I feel sure that you can still 'teach an old dog new tricks'.

Now that you have this book, I wonder how much time you are willing to invest in developing your knowledge of memory. If we just pause for a moment and I ask you to name the five regions of the brain, can you remember them without having to turn back to Chapter 1?

Learning happens when there is a shift in our long-term memory. In Chapter 2, I explained some of the key parts of the brain and how learning requires our neurons to form a synaptic connection. We need to keep repeating small chunks of content to the point of automation in order to strengthen these connections.

In this chapter of the book, I would like to discuss brain plasticity. Neuroscientists would explain how a change in protein synthesis occurs when our neurons begin to change and the synaptic plasticity of the brain enables it to reshape itself continually to make new connections and reorganise its existing structure. This is particularly interesting when we consider what can happen when someone develops an illness, suffers a serious accident or trauma and enters into a coma, and how the brain responds to help heal the body. In the classroom, we know students are going through a phase of rapid growth, as well as synaptic pruning. When we consider all the complex social, emotional and mental health needs our young people require support with, not to mention any special educational needs and disabilities that we are aware of, we really start to understand that the classroom is a very complex space. We sometimes (foolishly) try to evaluate it with little or no understanding of brain development. So, as teachers, how can we use brain plasticity to our advantage in such a dynamic environment?

EXPLAINER

What is brain plasticity?

Let's start with some definitions.

According to the Oxford Dictionary, 'plasticity' is 'the quality of being easily made into different shapes'. However, this is an engineering or physics definition. In neuroscience, a better term to use is 'neural plasticity', which is the ability for neurons or neural networks in our brain to change through being reorganised or through growth.

The term 'plasticity' was first applied in the context of neuroscience in 1890 by William James, a professor of psychology at Harvard University. In *The Principles of Psychology* (1890), James first proposed 'that the brain and its functions were not fixed throughout adulthood'. It was almost 100 years before his proposal was reconsidered in the 1970s. This is quite astonishing given all the research and discovery in the earlier part of the twentieth century. It also suggests how much we have still to discover.

In neuroscience today, 'plasticity' is generally understood as the ability of the brain to change its neural pathways. Give or take the 100 billion neurons that we have in our brain, they are constantly being produced and introduced into our **central nervous system**, which consists of the brain and its connection to the spinal cord.

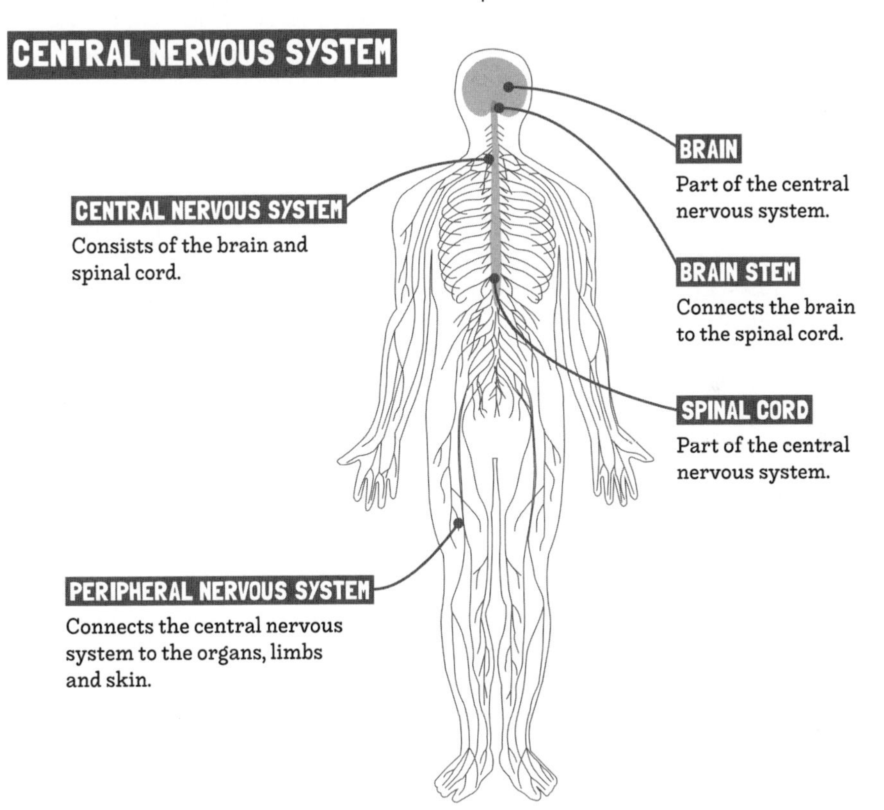

Learning causes physical changes in our brain

When we learn something, the physical change in our brain happens at a synaptic level. Neuroscientists call this **synaptic plasticity**. One neuron connects to another neuron through information acquisition, consolidation or retrieval, changing the structure of our brain. This suggests that our brain is dynamic and reshapes itself as we learn. Now, I know this may appear obvious to qualified psychologists and neuroscientists, but for me, as a teacher increasingly fascinated by memory and the structure of the brain, this is something I believe I should have had signposted during my teacher training – these obvious statements aren't so obvious after all! Perhaps this is something to consider for training providers.

In addition to learning, synapses are also shaped by experience and this may explain why our memories evolve over time. I have mentioned in Chapter 3 that our episodic (personal) memories fade over time and become increasingly unreliable. Our parents' portraits of us as young children, shared through storytelling around a dining room table, may not be as accurate as described. Of course, photographs help, which is why so many of us like to look back on episodes in our lives.

Long-term memory is likely to involve changes in our neuron structure, and this can happen structurally or physiologically. There are different types of neurons which are created to do different things. Something that I've only mentioned briefly in this book so far is **neurotransmitters**. As we discovered in Chapter 2, these are the chemical molecules released to transfer electrical signals from one neuron to another. The neurotransmitters are released by the **presynaptic terminal** on the transmitting neuron. Digging into the details, the more neurotransmitters that are released at a synapse, the greater the potential for a strong synaptic connection to be formed. When these synaptic connections are used repeatedly through retrieval practice, they are strengthened. If they are not used, the synaptic connections are pruned. This is plasticity.

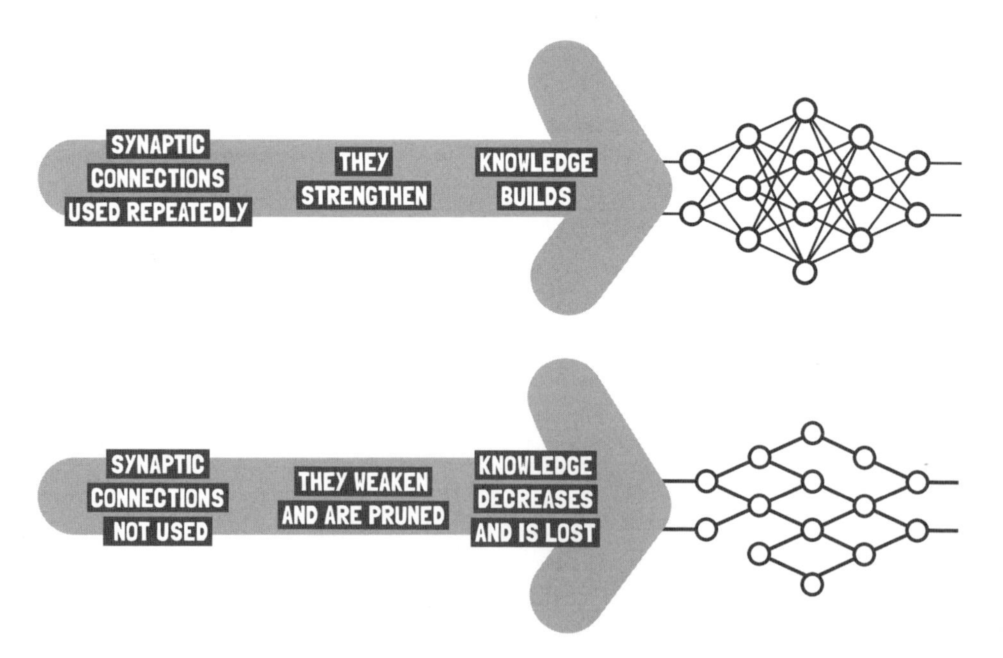

From novice to expert

Brain plasticity can enable us to move from novice to expert in a particular task. Through the acquisition of domain-specific knowledge and repeated practice and recall, we develop a series of strong synaptic connections. Over time, these connections give us the ability to perform the task with such skill that it becomes automated. As an example, let's consider how children learn to walk.

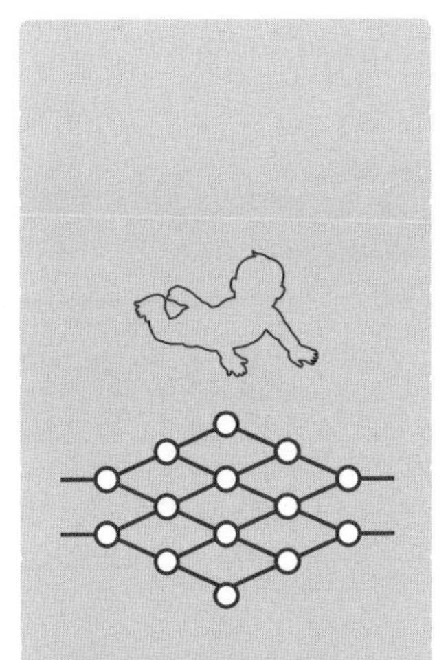

Novice

When a child first learns to walk, they spend many weeks and months on their tummy, gradually learning to crawl, then stand, before tentatively taking their first step. Eventually, they are able to make one or two steps forward unaided.

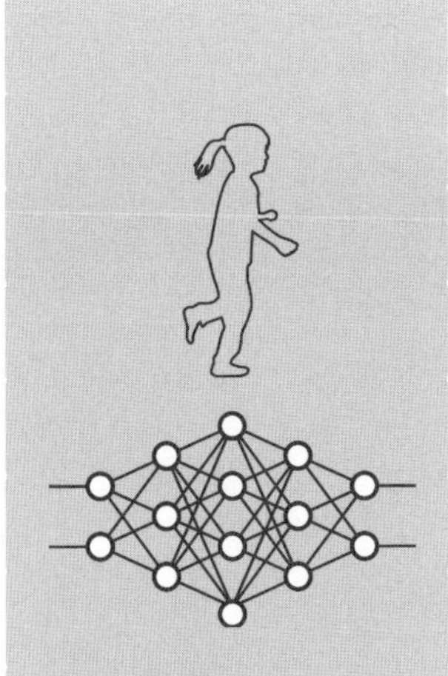

Intermediate

During early childhood, we learn to run, hop and skip. As we grow, we come to understand the differences between running and walking – and even sliding across ice.

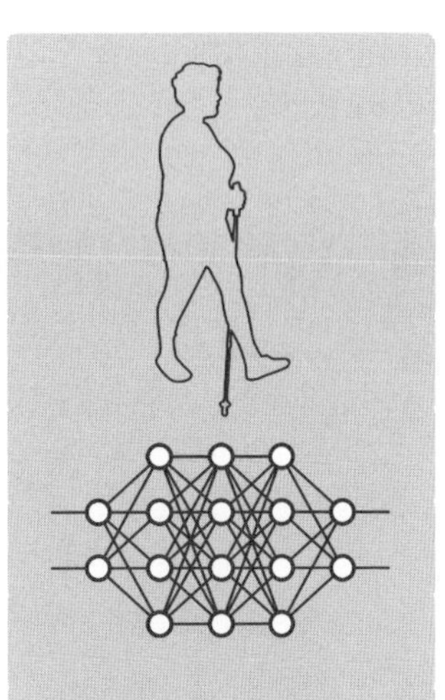

Expert

Experienced walkers can walk for miles in one day, even climbing very high mountains with specialised equipment, being aware of uneven surfaces and conditions that impact traction, speed and effort.

For an example based more on cognition, consider these three equations:
Novice: 3 + 3 = ?
Intermediate: 9 x 12 = ?
Expert: 9 – 1 ÷ 1/3 + 1 = ?

Shaping synaptic plasticity

If we want to shape our synaptic plasticity, we have to experience acquisition, consolidation or retrieval, but we need to be targeted and deliberate about this if we want to develop expert knowledge in a specific topic or become proficient at a specific skill. For teachers, this is what we work to do in our classrooms every day and therefore you would assume it was quite easy for us, right?

Well, no. We know teaching is incredibly complex. There are countless nuances to consider, even when we are signposted to read various books, attend training courses or use specific techniques. Add into the mix 30 children at any given point in the academic year and then you have countless scenarios, each of which requires a different approach. All I can offer are the techniques that I use and recommend from my work in secondary schools and as a teacher trainer. As ever, you must translate this theory into your own classroom and then practise to see what works for your students.

More information

In some of the *Understanding the Brain* lectures, Professor Jeanette Norden (2019), who has a background in nervous system development, regeneration and plasticity, provides a comprehensive overview for teachers who wish to take a beginner's interest in memory to a more intermediate level. It's definitely worth digging into Norden's lectures if you want to read more about the science behind neural plasticity. You can find the lectures on Audible by scanning the QR code.

KEY TERMS

Central nervous system: The brain and the spinal cord.

Neural plasticity: The ability for the brain to reorganise itself and continually make new connections through neurons.

Neurotransmitters: A chemical substance that sends signals between neurons or nerve cells.

Presynaptic terminal: A part of the axon that contains neurotransmitters.

Protein synthesis: The creation of proteins in a cell.

Synaptic plasticity: The ability of synapses to strengthen and weaken over time.

PRACTICAL IDEA

Elaboration

Elaboration is the process of developing or presenting concepts, rules or facts in further detail. It's a technique that can be embedded in curriculum plans, in questioning and in learning tasks. Elaboration helps learners to make connections between prior knowledge and new, more complex information, increasing the number of synapses in their brain and moving them from novice to expert in a particular topic area or skill. Posing 'Tell me more...' or 'Why?' questions back to students helps them to elaborate on their thinking to analyse and synthesise concepts.

Embedding elaboration in curriculum plans

Teachers will be familiar with developing prior knowledge, shaping schemas or having a knowledge-rich approach to curriculum. In essence, all of these involve elaboration. Subconscious strategies that teachers already use will involve simple references to what has been taught before and retrieval tasks, before moving on to new or more complex related material. When teachers do take time out to think more carefully about how they can shape schemas, a focus on classroom resources that draw out and build on prior knowledge is a critical part of developing a knowledge-based approach to teaching – and elaboration is a great tool for doing this.

Try this methodology for planning curriculum coverage. The questions in the first column will help you consider more consciously what you're covering each week and why. Think about how each week builds on what was taught the previous week. How does this enable learners to make connections, deepen their understanding and move them from novice to expert?

	Week 1	Week 2	Week 3	and so on...
What?				
Why?				
How?				
When?				
Where?				
What if?				
What now?				

Questioning for elaboration

Questioning techniques used in the classroom for elaboration can be as simple as prompting students as they share their thinking. For example, you could use:

'Say it again, but better'

This encourages a learner to go into more detail in their answer, increase their accuracy and use more complex terminology (Lemov, 2016).

Pose, pause, pounce, bounce

Don't accept 'I don't know' as an answer and instead coach students towards a correct answer. A 'high challenge, low stress' way to do this is to bounce the first answer around the class for elaboration before returning to the original source.

'Why?', 'How?' or 'What next?'

Simple elaborative questions take students' responses to the next level. 'Compare and contrast' is another potent teaching strategy that works and is often being used in the classroom already.

The important part of the process is that we should be aiming for students to explore explicit knowledge and make connections between prior knowledge and new, more complex information.

Moving from the abstract to the concrete

Another useful way teachers can encourage students to elaborate is to ask them to provide concrete examples, rather than simply describe abstract concepts. With context in mind, we should be seeking for a student to be able to articulate their first response in a more concrete way. For example, to be good at making a work table, you will need to consider materials, scale and weight in order for the design to meet its unique purpose. You will need to consider costs, how the material is fabricated and the selection of tools that will be used in order to ensure the specification is met and that a high-quality finish is achieved. The selection of materials and the development of paper models considering scale, accuracy and availability of tools will all feature in the design process.

Here's an example of what this process might look like using elaborative questioning in the classroom. Of course, this is an elaborate example (no pun intended), but I want to give you an example of some of the things that a teacher should be seeking when asking a student to elaborate.

Example: A one-to-one conversation

On the following page is a one-to-one conversation between a teacher and a student. The teacher is seeking a shift away from abstract language and examples to more concrete terminology, definitions and knowledge. The teacher first asks the student what they are making and the student replies that they are making a table. The teacher then delves deeper...

Teacher: What type of table are you making?

Student: It's a four-legged work table.

Teacher: How does this differ to a dining table?

Student: This table is slightly smaller; it includes specific areas for a computer, paper and for writing. It is small and portable, and the material used is lightweight.

Teacher: How did you select the material?

Student: I started with gathering secondary research on types of tables and the most common materials used. I then looked at costs and started to narrow down what I could do in the time to best fulfil the brief.

Teacher: Did you survey any potential clients to meet the brief? If so, what did you ask them?

Student: In my primary research survey, I presented clients with a range of resistant materials and asked them to select a solution based on their needs and a number of design factors. For example, height, cost, material, weight, colour, size of surface...

Teacher: And how did you narrow down the range of resistant materials available to use?

Student: Well, most people are happy to spend between £100 to £1,000 for a large dining room table that could sit between four and eight people. I narrowed this down based on material costs, including softwood, hardwood, non-ferrous metals and thermosetting plastics.

Teacher: Great! Which material did you settle on, and what is more expensive for a table that sits eight people? Does the material become more expensive with size?

And so on. It's important to prime students to connect the dots around the key schema. Other strategies in the book, such as summarising and sketchnoting, can help.

Elaboration in group and whole-class learning tasks

When using elaboration techniques as part of any learning task, teachers need to model the process of elaboration so that students learn how to articulate their thinking.

To begin with, I would probably recommend that teachers ask students to work in small groups or pairs in order to practise this technique to develop a degree of confidence. To support this, you could display sentence starters for younger students. Self-explanation can also be a good starting point for the more reserved students. Of course, context is key depending on your subject, your students and their prior knowledge, but all teachers will need to regularly check the learning to ensure that students are developing a degree of expertise before asking them to share examples with the whole class. If students already have good oracy and practice, then a teacher may just want to get straight on with business!

During the learning tasks, teachers will need to regularly check the learning in order to reassess where to move the lesson next, or what to teach in the next lesson; this requires a degree of accuracy and systematic 'on-your-feet' assessment. Other considerations teachers need to factor into lesson plans include:

- self- and peer-assessment techniques
- allowing students time to think and generate their own responses
- the type of response required, e.g. written responses, for example in an English class, or physical responses, for example in a drama class (for physical responses, you could ask the question: 'Show me how...').

Here are two examples of learning tasks using elaboration: a group discussion and a whole-class discussion.

Example: Group discussion

When students are working on a group activity, the teacher will of course navigate the room and monitor independent practice. When working with different groups of students, the teacher will be using their conversational data to support and challenge student thinking. Here's an example of how this might work.

Teacher: OK, using this resource [points to resource on table], I would like you to quiz one another [points to one pair] on what each of you know about volcanoes in general and Mount Vesuvius. Read these instructions [points to the exact section in the resource] carefully, then check one another's answers without looking at the resource. Please make sure you reply to your classmate with: 'How does...?' to ensure that you can draw out detailed information. Understood [signals with a thumbs-up]?

Student: Sir, what should we ask if our classmate only replies with a one-word answer?

Teacher: My suggestion would be to insist on a detailed explanation as practice for your speaking assessment. For example, pose the question, 'Why did...?' or 'What makes you think...?' in response to your classmate. [If the students are ready for more detailed intervention, I would add:] It's important to ensure you can each link to extra detail in your answers to determine cause and effect, prediction, explanation, rationale or opinion. These are just a small number of examples to help draw out this information so that you each have time to prepare for your speaking examination.

Example: Whole-class discussion

Teacher: Right! Year 9. Pens and mini-whiteboards ready? [Pause] Before writing anything down, [big emphasis] I want you to remember that whatever you write on your board, you should be prepared to explain in greater depth to someone else – including me [raises eyebrows with a smile]. Ready? [Long pause] 3-2-1... Without writing anything, think about two facts about the volcano Mount Vesuvius [waits for ten silent seconds]. OK, write it down in silence [waits ten silent seconds]. Now, hold up your board and show me in 3-2-1, [quick pause] go!

Students are then given an opportunity after this instruction to respond to teacher questions or to take a moment to explain what they have written down to somebody else or the whole class.

Think it, write it, say it out loud!

Taking this further

Following the above example, a teacher will have many routes to take next depending on 'checking for understanding', the time remaining, the purpose of the lesson and where the teacher needs to get the students to. After a 'show me on your whiteboard' or a 'think, pair, share' moment, it's worth moving on and then returning to this retrieval exercise later in the lesson or soon after.

TOOLKIT TIPS

1. Embed elaboration in your curriculum by using sequencing that enables students to build on prior knowledge.
2. Use questioning techniques that prompt students to elaborate as they share their thinking to help them deepen their knowledge and make connections.
3. Encourage students to provide concrete examples to support elaboration.
4. Incorporate elaboration techniques in group and whole-class learning tasks, but model the process beforehand and regularly check the learning through 'on-your-feet' assessment.

WORKED EXAMPLE

The table below is to be used as a checklist by the students to help draw out their thoughts. You will need to adapt this according to the age of your students and the content you are teaching. We know that we learn new information based upon some prior knowledge, so this table is designed to ask the students questions and offer prompts to help them retrieve information and elaborate on it in order to strengthen their understanding. This resource is most appropriate for secondary school learners. Dr Kripa Sundar offers an excellent example for younger learners on her blog. Scan the QR code to access it.

	Methodology	Classroom concept, rule or fact to be assessed: ______________
1	Make a list of the key ideas.	*The student writes a list of the key ideas they have learned in relation to the topic.*
2	Why do these ideas work?	*The student elaborates to explain why the ideas work.*
3	How do they work?	*The student elaborates to explain how the ideas work.*
4	Check against which classroom material.	*The student (or teacher) identifies which sources will be used for checking their answers.*
5	Check what you know without materials.	*The student tests their knowledge. This can be self-assessment or peer assessment between classmates.*
6	Check what you don't know with materials.	*The student identifies any knowledge they are unable to recall.*
7	Verify that all your answers are correct.	*At this stage, the student checks their sources for the correct answers.*
8	What connections can be made to prior learning?	*The student explains how the information connects with learning in previous lessons.*
9	What connections can be made to future learning?	*The student identifies information they have not yet learned but that would be valuable to explore further in relation to the topic.*

TEMPLATE

Elaboration

	Methodology	Classroom concept, rule or fact to be assessed: ______________
1	Make a list of the key ideas.	
2	Why do these ideas work?	
3	How do they work?	
4	Check against which classroom material.	
5	Check what you know without materials.	
6	Check what you don't know with materials.	
7	Verify that all your answers are correct.	
8	What connections can be made to prior learning?	
9	What connections can be made to future learning?	

Scan the QR code for a downloadable digital copy of this template.

CHAPTER 8
COGNITIVE APPRENTICESHIP

Printed in 1991 in the journal *American Educator*, the article 'Cognitive apprenticeship: Making thinking visible' (Collins et al., 1991) is important reading for teachers serious about education research. Cognitive apprenticeship requires the student to become the expert. This research was offered as a framework to help point the way towards the redesign of schooling so that students could develop robust problem-solving skills. Almost 30 years later, where are we now?

In the opening paragraph of this 18-page paper, the authors write:

> 'In ancient times, teaching and learning were accomplished through apprenticeship: We taught our children how to speak, grow crops, craft cabinets, or tailor clothes by showing them how and by helping them do it. Apprenticeship was the vehicle for transmitting the knowledge required for expert practice in fields from painting and sculpting to medicine and law. It was the natural way to learn.'

This on-the-job education has largely been replaced by schooling (or teaching and learning) as we know it today and as policy and research evolve, so do the subtle methods we use. In this paper, an alternative model of instruction is proposed that refers back to the traditional methods of apprenticeship but is also applicable for the modern classroom. The researchers call this model cognitive apprenticeship. As a teacher, you can imagine my heart started to sing at this snapshot summary of the approach: 'Put simply, students see the processes of work.'

In his book *The Future of Teaching*, cognitive scientist Guy Claxton (2021) offers a useful definition of cognitive apprenticeship: 'The coaches' job is to model, design activities and provide feedback and to introduce only as much theory as directly supports the learners' here-and-now skill development.'

In this chapter, I want to go into more detail about what cognitive apprenticeship is and how it can be used to best effect in the classroom.

EXPLAINER

Apprenticeship: a vehicle for transmitting knowledge

Do you remember a period in your childhood when your family or friends taught you *how* to do something for the first time? Perhaps tying your shoelaces or riding a bike. Or maybe you remember when you attempted to construct an acute or obtuse triangle in a maths lesson for the first time. Whatever it is that you remember learning how to do, in each of these scenarios you will have had to move from a position of novice to expert: to the point where the task was automated by following a series of steps.

As children, we watch our family members do something at home. We may watch our parents employ a tradesperson to build something and we pick up small tips and tricks so that we may be able to use this knowledge in the future. Even if we consider ourselves to be qualified, we can choose to watch someone with more experience perhaps create a website or construct a garment to learn to do something at a deeper level. These are all forms of apprenticeship.

Traditional apprenticeship

Most outsiders to teaching feel that schools are working with a curriculum largely divorced from what most people do with their lives in the real world. Rewind a generation or so in the classroom and we can assume that teaching would typically show the student how to do a task, watch as the teacher practises on stage, and then provide the student with more responsibility until they are proficient enough to do the task themselves. This is traditional apprenticeship. The basic concept is that the teacher would show the student and help them achieve it. Whether this model is outdated or irrelevant to the real world or for developing a degree of proficiency in an academic subject is up for debate. There are many ways to teach another person something and it is important to note that this model of teaching will vary significantly depending on age, time of year, prior knowledge and subject.

There are four important aspects of traditional apprenticeship: modelling, scaffolding, fading and coaching.

1. Through **modelling**, the teacher makes the target processes visible.
2. The teacher then **scaffolds** the activity to provide the support required for the student.
3. As the student acquires expertise, the teacher slowly **fades** the support.
4. The teacher **coaches** the student through a range of activities.

Observation also plays a key role in traditional apprenticeship; it aids learners in developing a conceptual model of the target task prior to attempting to execute it (Lave, 1988).

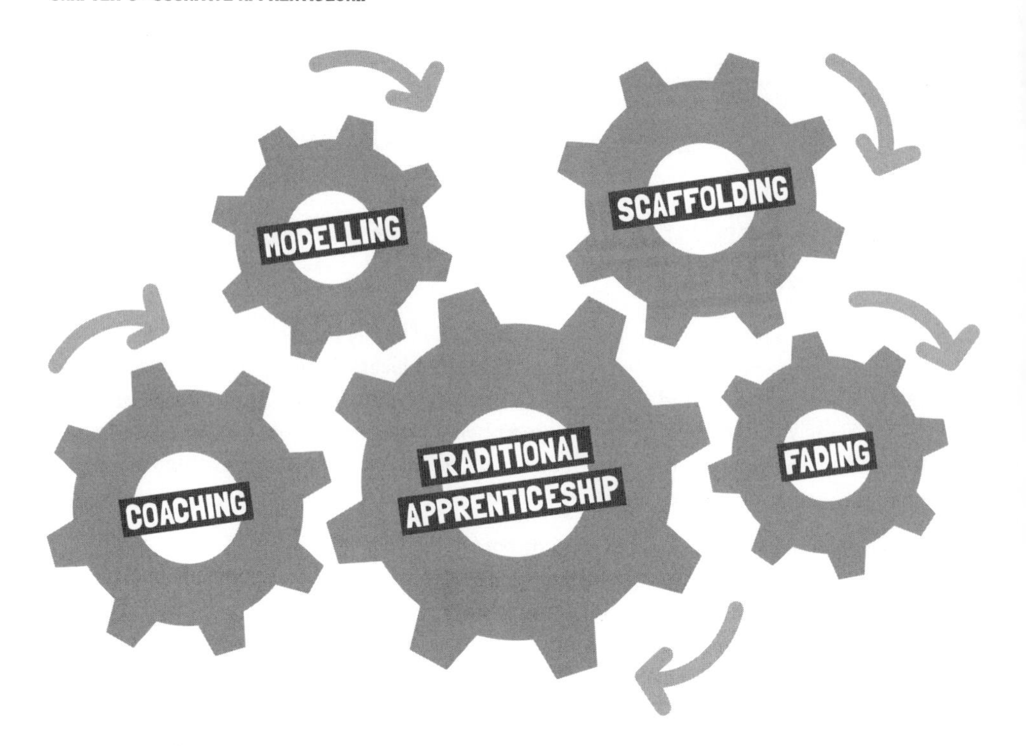

Towards cognitive apprenticeship: making thinking visible

While traditional apprenticeship is about learning a physical and tangible activity, cognitive apprenticeship is about the teaching and learning of cognitive skills. It's a model of instruction that works to make thinking **visible**. The research on cognitive apprenticeship looks at how to adapt the techniques of traditional apprenticeship so they are suitable for teaching cognitive strategies that are central to integrating knowledge and skills in order to accomplish meaningful tasks.

The research (Collins, 1991) cites important differences between traditional and cognitive apprenticeship models:

1. In traditional apprenticeship, the process of carrying out a task is easily observable. In cognitive apprenticeship, the teacher must bring the thinking to the surface and make it visible.
2. Tasks that can be taught through traditional apprenticeship come up as they arise in the world, with students naturally understanding the reasons for the finished product. Cognitive apprenticeship is to situate the abstract tasks of the school curriculum in a context that makes sense to a student.
3. In traditional apprenticeship, the skills to be learned are the task itself. It is possible that students encounter situations in which they fail to transfer the skills required to other situations. Much of our curriculum reform today demands that students be able to transfer what they learn and apply it. Cognitive apprenticeship teaches students how to transfer and apply their learning to other contexts.

Traditional apprenticeship	Cognitive apprenticeship
Involves the teaching of a concrete task.	Involves the teaching of metacognitive skills.
The task is visible and easily observable.	Thinking is invisible and the teacher must make it visible.
The task is concrete and has a tangible end goal.	Thinking is abstract and the teacher must contextualise it for students.
The skills learned are relevant to the task at hand only.	Learning needs to be transferred and applied to other diverse contexts.

Three teaching approaches for cognitive apprenticeship

The research article 'Cognitive apprenticeship: Making thinking visible' (Collins et al., 1991) recommends that, to translate the model of traditional apprenticeship to cognitive apprenticeship, teachers need to approach teaching in three explicit ways:

1. **Identify** the processes of the task and make them visible to students.
2. **Situate** abstract tasks in authentic contexts so that students understand the relevance of the work.
3. Vary the **diversity** of situations and articulate the common aspects so that students can transfer what they learn.

Identify	Situate	Diversify
Identify the task and make the processes visible to students. *Example: Saw the wood.*	Place the abstract task into an authentic context. Make it relevant. *Example: Check the plans.*	Vary the situations and state common aspects. Help students transfer what they learn. *Example: Make a table.*

A framework for cognitive apprenticeship

Cognitive apprenticeship poses numerous pedagogical and theoretical issues that are relevant to the design of the classroom generally. The research by Collins et al. (1991) developed 'a framework consisting of four dimensions that constitute any learning environment: content, method, sequence, and sociology'. I have summarised these below as a framework that you can use to put cognitive apprenticeship into action in your classroom.

Content

When deciding what content to teach, consider the types of knowledge that are required for expertise in the subject area or topic you are tackling in the lesson. Strategic knowledge is defined as tacit knowledge and is necessary to solve problems and accomplish tasks. This includes:

1. **Domain knowledge:** Concepts, facts and procedures.
2. **Heuristic strategies:** Approaches that are generally considered effective when tackling a certain task.
3. **Control strategies (or metacognitive approaches):** Techniques involved in the process of problem-solving – how to choose between different strategies, when to change strategies, etc.
4. **Learning strategies:** Strategies that help you learn – whether that's how best to acquire knowledge or understanding the most effective process for solving problems.

Method

The methods you are going to use for teaching need to be carefully selected. Collins et al. suggest finding methods that 'give students the opportunity to observe, engage in, and invent or discover expert strategies in context'. They provide six teaching methods which fall into three groups:

1. **Modelling, coaching and scaffolding** enable students to observe, engage and invent.
2. **Articulation and reflection** support students in thinking out loud and comparing their knowledge and understanding with those of their peers.
3. **Exploration** guides students towards autonomy and expert problem-solving.

There's a great teaching and learning methodology right there!

Sequence

Think carefully about how to structure lesson plans and teaching in order to provide meaning to students. Three principles are offered by Collins et al.:

1. **Global before local:** Build a conceptual map that demonstrates the whole task before focusing on each individual component.
2. **Increasing complexity:** Carefully construct a sequence of tasks from basic to more challenging.

3. **Increasing diversity:** Help students distinguish the conditions under which the knowledge, skills and techniques they are learning do and do not apply.

Sociology

The final section of the framework considers the classroom itself. Four recommendations are provided by Collins et al.:

1. **Situated learning:** Complete tasks in an environment that reflects the multiple contexts in which it can be applied. For example, practise a drama performance on a stage.
2. **Community of practice:** Use group activities to develop a sense of ownership and personal investment in specific tasks.
3. **Intrinsic motivation:** Relate the task to an interesting, coherent goal that is relevant and personal to the student (rather than an extrinsic reason).
4. **Exploiting cooperation:** Ask students to work together, both as a powerful motivator and as a mechanism for extending learning resources.

Cognitive apprenticeship

Content Differentiate the types of (tacit) knowledge required for expertise.	Method Give the opportunity to observe, engage in and invent expert strategies.	Sequence To structure lessons to provide meaning within context.	Sociology Immersing students with novice and expert examples.
Domain knowledge Concepts, facts and procedures	**Modelling, coaching & scaffolding** To observe, engage and invent	**Global** Conceptual before the details	**Situated learning** Tasks in the relevant environment
Heuristic strategies A mental shortcut	**Articulation & reflection** To think out loud for comparison	**Complexity** The construction of tasks	**Community of practice** Towards a sense of ownership
Control strategies Metacognitive approaches	**Exploration** Towards autonomy and expertise	**Diversity** Towards a variety of skills	**Intrinsic motivation** Towards a coherent goal
Learning strategies Specific classroom approaches			**Exploiting cooperation** Extending learning resources

The limitations of cognitive apprenticeship

Cognitive apprenticeship is *not* a model of teaching that gives teachers a packaged formula for instruction. Instead, it is an instructional paradigm for teaching. Collins et al. (1991) also emphasise that this is not a relevant model for all aspects of teaching. As ever, my recommendation to any teachers reading this is to consider: what does cognitive apprenticeship look like when teaching a four-year-old child in an Early Years classroom? What does cognitive apprenticeship look like when teaching a 16-year-old at risk of exclusion?

Collins et al. recommend that the teacher does not assume the permanent role of the expert. I have mixed views about this, as teachers do need to understand the nature of expert practice in their field and devise and model methods that are appropriate to teaching and learning that practice. However, I guess we know teaching is nuanced and context will matter depending on what you are teaching, to whom, what they know, when and how.

It's important to note that cognitive apprenticeship is a framework supported by qualitative evidence; there are very few quantitative tests of its efficacy on learning. Central to the success of the model is a clear definition and outcome of what being an 'expert' means. Often expertise shows in different ways and many may argue that learners cannot become experts without rigorous and immersive training.

Nevertheless, the overall message is that if you want to improve a student's memory and performance, developing a cognitive apprenticeship approach is something that you should consider adding to your teaching repertoire.

KEY TERMS

Traditional apprenticeship: Showing students how to do a task and then helping them to achieve it through modelling, scaffolding, fading and coaching.

Cognitive apprenticeship: The teaching and learning of cognitive skills in three steps:

- **Identify**: Make the thought processes visible.
- **Situate**: Make the abstract authentic.
- **Diversify**: Vary the situation and transfer the learning.

PRACTICAL IDEA

Self-explanation

In this chapter I have discussed cognitive apprenticeship for transmitting knowledge, explaining how teachers must make thinking visible to help students move from novice to expert. To support this idea of making thinking visible even further, I want to introduce you to another strategy, known as self-explanation. If we use what we have learned about cognitive apprenticeship, there is a good base of research in the area of self-explanation, which indicates that we can use this specific study skill to help students move from novice to expert. It is a strategy advocated by Dunlosky et al. (2013) as having 'moderate utility', as it has been shown to have effects across a large range of age groups and learning outcomes, although further research is needed to determine its efficacy in the classroom.

Put simply, self-explanation is a strategy for improving comprehension. At its core, self-explanation involves having the students explain – out loud – some aspect of their processing during learning. For example, you could ask them to explain:

- how new information is linked with their prior knowledge
- their thought processes during learning
- the steps they take when solving a problem or completing a task.

In the same way as the teacher is making learning visible in cognitive apprenticeship, self-explanation supports students in making their *own* learning visible. This helps students to integrate new knowledge with prior knowledge and develop the connections they need to move them towards expertise.

One particularly useful method of doing this is encouraging a student to explain new information to someone else. We know that when we learn new information, it has to be based on some prior knowledge. For example, tell me the names of the two volcanoes we have discussed in the book so far. Teachers who ask the right types of questions and offer prompts can help support retrieval for students, which is beneficial to this process. My interpretation would recommend that asking students questions and offering prompts two or three times is a very useful strategy for long-term retention.

As ever, context is key. Students 'with some domain knowledge about a topic may find it easier to use self-explanation' and this is also the case for elaboration (see Chapter 7; Dunlosky et al., 2013). The success of the strategy also lies in the degree to which prompts for self-explanation are content-free versus content-specific, in other words if the prompt is a general one or specific to the content being taught. For example:

Content-free	Content-specific
How does this information relate to what you already know?	Why is using self-explanation as an explicit strategy in your classroom a good idea? How are 'self-explanation moments' identified in your schemes of work and lesson plans?

Repeat it

There is a great strategy that all teachers can use to draw out further details from a student during self-explanation. It's likely to be called a variety of pedagogical names in different parts of the world, but the principle is to ask the student to repeat what they have said for a second time. I am reminded of a conversation I had with cognitive scientist, E. D. Hirsch, where he said, 'Make your classroom a speech community; don't leave knowledge to chance!' If you want to hear more from our conversation, scan the QR code to listen to the podcast episode.

When asking for clarification while a student is self-explaining, whether you're teaching subject terminology or explicit skills, try the simple technique 'Say it again better' by Doug Lemov (2016). Encourage the student to add more detail to their explanation, pinpoint the specifics and use the keywords you have been teaching them.

What I like to add to draw in a little bit of engagement is: 'Repeat what you said again, this time using your [X] voice.' Depending on what I am teaching, the mood of the nation or whatever is in the national press, I ask students to mimic a famous celebrity, a musician or a politician's voice to help them engage and grow more confident. You don't need to do this, but it's another way to support semantic memory because you're linking the concepts, rules and facts being learned with an experience (an episodic memory). Just remember it is a fine line between strengthening content versus the redundancy effect.

1. Encourage students to make their learning visible by using self-explanation.
2. Try asking students to explain out loud how new information is linked to prior knowledge.

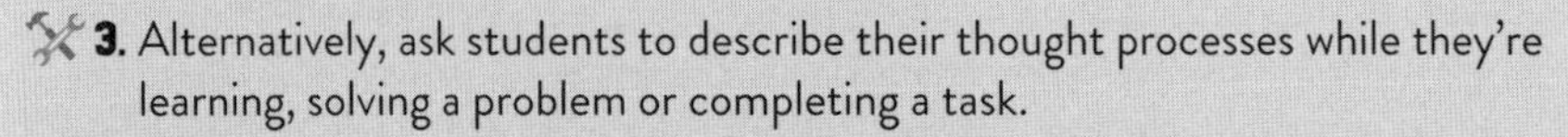

3. Alternatively, ask students to describe their thought processes while they're learning, solving a problem or completing a task.
4. Set up pair, group or whole-class activities where students explain new information to a peer.
5. Use prompts to help students elaborate while they are self-explaining.
6. You could use self-explanation to allow students to become 'experts' in the class. They could 'teach' other students about their expertise. This is motivating, empowering and great retrieval practice.

WORKED EXAMPLE

If we return to my Mount Vesuvius example shared throughout this book, I will show you how you can draw on your own prior knowledge using self-explanation.

First, have a go at retrieving the information we have been learning about Mount Vesuvius by answering this free-recall question:

‘Tell me what you can remember about Mount Vesuvius.’

A student may answer this question with the following (and maybe you did too!):

‘We know that Mount Vesuvius is near Naples, Italy; it destroyed Pompeii.’

A student may say the above sentence when answering a retrieval question at the beginning of a lesson, but I may not be happy with the depth and detail of their sentence. In this case, I may ask them to use the previous technique shared in Chapter 7 to elaborate on specific details – and then self-explain the answer. Some specific cues to support this include:

‘Say your sentence again but this time add:

1. what Mount Vesuvius is

2. when it erupted

3. one more specific fact about what happened.’

What I am hoping to achieve is for the student repeating the original sentence to build the strength of their prior knowledge before introducing any new information. Simple teacher prompts alongside introducing new concepts, rules and facts will help strengthen schemas.

Have a go at this yourself. Say your answer to the free-recall question about Mount Vesuvius again, but this time add the extra three facts above. A model answer might be:

‘We know that Mount Vesuvius is a volcano near Naples, Italy; it destroyed Pompeii in 79 AD, with a cloud of poisonous gas and ash rising 21 miles high into the atmosphere. Today, it is the most densely populated volcanic region in the world.’

Bringing in the theory of cognitive apprenticeship, I might now diversify the examples of volcanoes I'm giving the students (and you!) to help them identify and articulate common aspects, and transfer and reapply what they know to a similar situation. For example, I might introduce Nyiragongo, a volcano that erupted in eastern Democratic Republic of Congo in 2021. My questions to help students compare this with Mount Vesuvius would be:

1. How many people do you think were displaced in the surrounding area?

2. How does this region compare to Naples in terms of infrastructure?

3. What support would you put in place to help the people who were displaced?

If you want, have a go at answering these yourself!

TEMPLATE

Self-explanation

Here's a set of prompts you can use to promote self-explanation in the classroom. Choose the concept you want your students to retrieve and self-explain, for example photosynthesis, and then work through the questions. You could ask the questions verbally or print them out as a prompt sheet for students to work through in pairs or independently.

	Classroom concept, rule or fact to be assessed: _______________
	Methodology
1	Explain the concept out loud.
2	How does this relate to what you already know?
3	What questions does it generate for you?
4	Could you explain this concept in another way?
5	What action should we take next?

Scan the QR code for a downloadable digital copy of this template.

CHAPTER 9
WELLBEING AND MEMORY

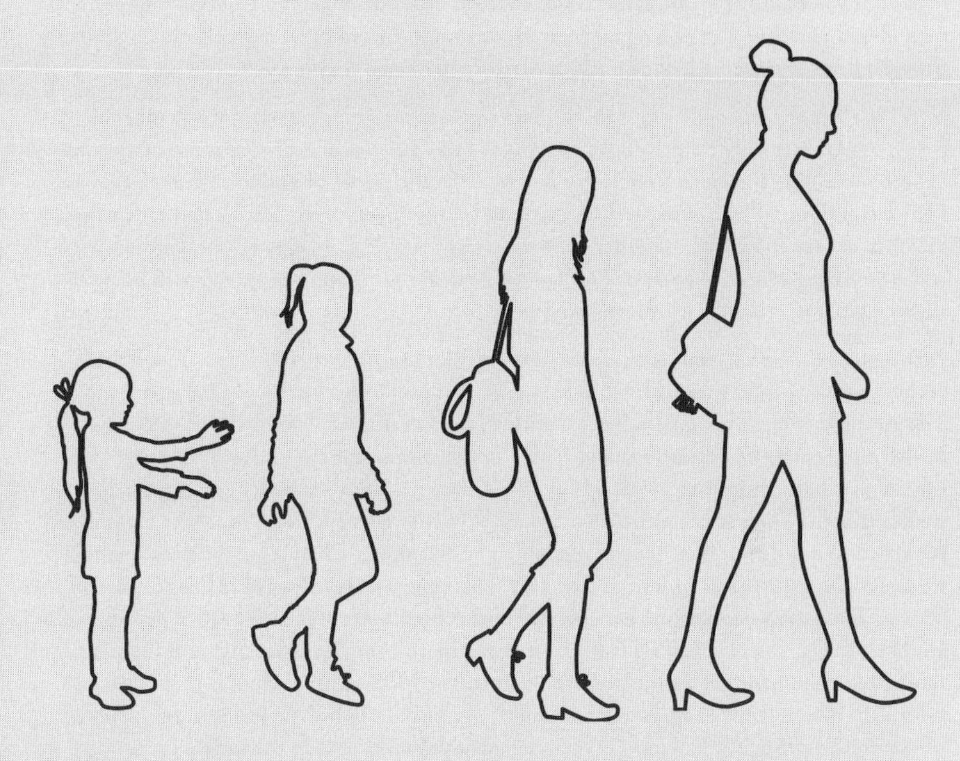

We know that the literature around mental health and physical wellbeing, and its research and evidence base, is growing. We also know that the more we look after our physical and mental health, the better our bodies, particularly the brain, function. If you think back to Chapter 4 (do you remember the topic?), it also becomes clear that putting ourselves in stressful situations affects our performance.

We just have to consider teachers' own experiences to see this in action. When we place our teachers in a stressful environment, with a high contact ratio and little time to eat or drink, a heavy administrative workload and increasing responsibilities to produce good student scores, it's obvious that the role of the teacher is becoming increasingly burdensome and is not yet in keeping with what we now know about mental health and performance. Only a decade ago you would struggle to find much academic research to support improved teacher wellbeing and its links to student outcomes. Today, this is in growing abundance, but it's still not yet advocated for teachers in England. We know that high-performing teams that are trusted and empowered perform better.

Can you imagine a four-day week? Teaching two or three lessons a day? Having ten or 15 students in your class, or being told to provide verbal feedback rather than waste your time recording written statements? How far away are we from our education systems dramatically doing things differently? I am an enormous fan of the teacher as the expert being at the front of the classroom, but I do know that there are many other ways to teach, and there are many other ways that students can learn.

Most of us have been there, working 80-plus hours a week – losing quality time at home, having restless nights and eating a bad diet. It is so easy for us all to jump on 'the hamster wheel' and keep going until our bodies start to send some warning signals. I've been there myself. It will come as no surprise to you to learn that although I was working longer hours, I wondered whether I was being more productive. On the surface, my colleagues probably thought I was producing lots of work, but internally I was burning out.

If this is what the education system is doing to teachers, imagine what the damage is for students. Not only do they have to navigate this system of high-pressure exams and assignments, but they also have to try and learn in the midst of endless other challenges and distractions. With social media all around us, more junk food – with home deliveries easier to access than ever – increased screen time, bullying, images of war, connectivity and everything else in the world, how can we educate our young people to look after themselves and raise the profile of wellbeing?

Today, we are much better at equipping young people with the ability to manage their social, emotional and mental health. However, it is still often a struggle for schools to fit everything into the curriculum, where assemblies, tutor time, PSHE (personal, social, health and economic education) and RSE (relationships and sex education) lessons are the only real opportunities provided for all students to learn explicitly about managing their wellbeing outside of specialist subjects. Whether we agree with teaching facts in our schools or using direct instruction, modelling or chunking, when it comes to wellbeing we need to ask ourselves one small but very important question: what is the purpose of school? Education cannot just be a matter of teaching facts and then testing to assess what students know, can it? How we learn is so much more complex than that and therefore our role as teachers goes beyond this. As educators, the hidden curriculum is just as important: teaching children how to manage their emotions, make the right decisions, take part in a whole-school production or simply learn why they shouldn't skip the lunch queue.

A key question we should all ask is: what is the impact of wellbeing and mental health on learning? Aspects of physically active learning and embodied cognition are embedded in school life in Early Years, primary and special school settings. When pupils reach secondary education, however, this focus across the curriculum decreases. More traditional approaches are perceived as a route to achievement, rather than equipping students with explicit study skills and a good grounding in managing their mental health for a lifetime of success.

In this chapter, we'll explore in further detail the impact of wellbeing on learning by investigating three specific areas: diet, exercise and sleep. We should already know a little about them, but we will consider their impact on our memory. We'll then look at some ideas to help teachers support student wellbeing and holistic development in the everyday classroom environment.

EXPLAINER

Diet

The '5 A Day' campaign was launched by the Department of Health in 2003. The recommendation was that we eat at least five portions of fruit and vegetables each day. Recent studies go further than this recommendation. Researchers at UCL (Oyebode et al., 2014), for example, found that people who ate seven or more portions of fruit and vegetables have a 42 per cent lower risk of early death. The latest child obesity figures released by the NHS (2020) provide data on the height and weight of children with some startling results. At reception age, obesity increased by 0.2 per cent to 9.9 per cent overall in 2019–20, compared with 9.7 per cent in 2018–19. In Year 6, obesity increased by 0.8 per cent to 21 per cent overall in this same period, with boys more likely to be obese than girls and 'children living in the most deprived areas [...] more than twice as likely to be obese than those living in the least deprived areas'.

There is a popular saying, 'You are what you eat', which derives from the French lawyer and politician Jean Anthelme Brillat-Savarin (1755–1826) who published *Physiologie du goût* (translated as *Physiology of Taste*, 1826) and is infamous for coining the phrase, 'Tell me what you eat, and I will tell you what you are.' Given that there is an increased awareness of mental health and research that argues 'obesity is not a disease', we must be very considerate of our assumptions about weight and its connections with health. For example, I'm currently 6'4" tall, weighing 110 kilograms. According to the NHS website body mass index calculator, I am overweight (not obese) and need to lose five per cent of my weight! It is worth mentioning that obesity does have direct links to various illnesses; however there is equally a body of research which suggests that obesity may *not* be associated with death. As with all research, you will find two sides to every argument and multifaceted reasons for associated outcomes.

For the purposes of this book, is it weight or 'what I eat' that influences my memory? If we cast our 'memory' back to those food science lessons we were taught at school, hopefully you may be able to recall some aspects of the food wheel. We know, for example, nuts, seafood and beans, eaten in moderation, are good for our brain and help release **omega-3 acids** and **antioxidants** to improve function. We also know that high-fat diets have been shown to impair episodic memory functions. In an interesting article, Molteni et al. (2004) argued that high-fat diets – think chips and burgers – negatively affect synaptic plasticity and learning efficacy, particularly in relation to neurotrophic factors, which are biomolecules used for the growing and regeneration of axons. Remember those? See page 20. The good news is that exercise reverses the harmful effects of consumption of high-fat foods on synaptic and behavioural activity. The research found that diet and exercise both 'target the hippocampus, a brain region important for learning and memory'. However, diet and exercise derived opposite effects on synaptic plasticity at a molecular level and learning and memory on a behavioural level. It is worth mentioning that this research was conducted on 344 two-month-old rats! It is always more of a challenge to conduct research on children.

A systematic review published by Cohen et al. (2016) reported on whether or not a healthier dietary consumption among children impacted on their executive functioning.

The researchers concluded that eating less healthy snack foods, sugar-sweetened beverages and red or processed meats is associated with poorer executive functioning. In addition, certain vitamins and minerals were found to be 'cofactors for enzymes that synthesise neurotransmitters, thus impacting on cognition throughout childhood'.

Exercise

We can improve our mood, sleep and stress levels, as well as our memory, with exercise. At the time of writing, physical education is a compulsory part of the curriculum for pupils from age five to 16 years old. However, physical education is only statutory in local-authority-maintained schools. The Youth Sport Trust (cited in Foster and Roberts, 2022) reported that: 'Pupils in Key Stage 3 receive an average of 124 minutes of curriculum PE each week. Pupils in Key Stage 4 receive an average of 98 minutes.' Yet the UK Government's (2019) childhood obesity action plan recommends 'moderate to vigorous' physical activity for at least 60 minutes every day! There are countless pieces of evidence to suggest that exercise increases our performance, so why not make this more of a priority in our schools? Or is our curriculum already full to the brim?! Exercise increases the size of our hippocampus and improves memory (Erickson et al., 2011), whilst also reducing the risk of Alzheimer's (Tarumi et al., 2019). We know that in adults, the brain shrinks due to the natural process of ageing, but less is known about the other end of the age spectrum. Nevertheless, the research is clear: 'children who exercise have more brain power' (Cadenas-Sanchez et al., 2020) – the research sources that support this are endless! And this is something teachers, schools and policymakers must seriously consider if we want happier, healthier and better-performing children.

So, if we know exercise is good for mental health, good for our memory and good for a happier life, why do we not insist that our young people do more exercise in school? At a policy level, physical literacy is on the rise. 'At least eight countries' are using the term in policy documents (Martins et al., 2021). If we can teach students how to maintain high levels of movement with confidence, this does affect their 'ability to effectively process knowledge' (Cairney et al., 2019).

As we move forward from the global pandemic (post-2022), all schools are readjusting their curriculum and doing more to support pupils with their mental health. Over the past year, I've been working alongside Teach Active, an online resource designed to deliver English and maths through physically active learning. As a result of this work, I've been immersed in research regarding 'active learning' and have connected with some academics, understanding the importance of a physically active approach to learning, and how this supports our cognition, boosts our moods and supports long-term retention. We all know it to be true, but when we are presented with the hard evidence, uptake in attendance, exam scores and a reduction in mental health issues, the evidence is striking. We simply need more 'active learning' opportunities in all of our schools.

Sleep

We all know that if we don't have a good night's sleep, we suffer the following day. If we are already exhausted, too little sleep will cause cognitive impairment. We will start to find it difficult to balance, to listen carefully and to make clear decisions. This is procedural memory – one's ability to perform actions. If my cognitive abilities are focused elsewhere, for example, trying to sustain my balance because I feel dizzy from lack of sleep, it doesn't take a genius to work out that my learning performance will be hindered. When our executive functions weaken, we struggle with planning, organising ourselves and attempting to problem-solve. Sleep is also when our memories are consolidated and pruned.

You may or may not be familiar with the term **circadian rhythm**. Our internal circadian clock is influenced by night and day, sunshine and the importance of sleep (and darkness). Almost four decades since the first commercial mobile phone was invented, we now understand what impact digital devices have on our circadian rhythm and therefore our wellbeing and our sleep. I have been that person who would take my mobile phone to bed, reading information for hours rather than allowing my body to naturally slow down and fall asleep. Small amounts of light suppress **melatonin**. Melatonin is a hormone produced by the **pineal gland** to help regulate our sleep patterns.

LOCATION OF THE PINEAL GLAND IN THE BRAIN

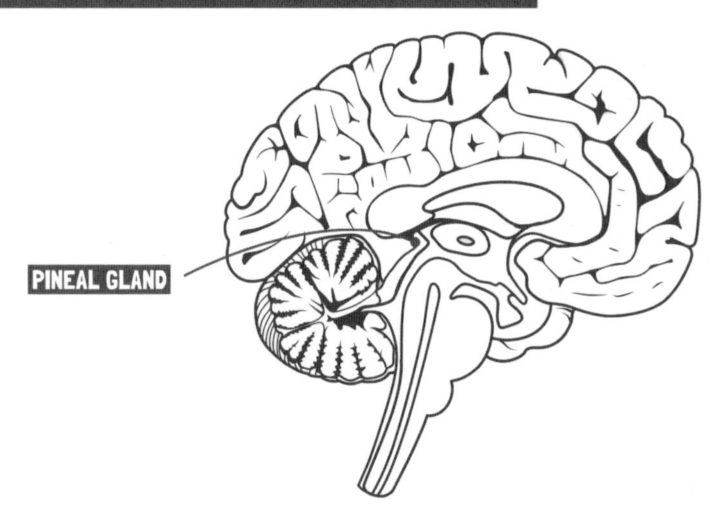

Without enough sleep, our short-term memories simply become overloaded and we can't take on board new information. As a result of lack of sleep, amongst countless other scenarios, the hormone cortisol is produced which is attached to the adrenal glands. As a reminder from Chapter 4, a small dose of adrenaline produces more **glucose** in the blood, which helps us to respond in a 'fight or flight' situation. In a study published in 2015, Hirotsu et al. unpick sleep quality and its relationship with our metabolism. They discuss how our sleep is gradually reducing due to socioeconomic demands and modern society, for example, the need to work longer hours to generate a salary or noisier roads outside our bedroom windows. According to Hirotsu et al., glucose increases during REM (rapid eye movement) sleep, 'leading to negative energy balance in the body'. Disruption to our circadian rhythm is associated with, for example, weight gain, diabetes and an increase in cortisol, glucose and blood pressure. Concerningly, it has also been found that children with a lower socioeconomic status have lower sleep quality (Bruni et al., 2012).

When we have a lack of sleep, we are also more likely to become anxious and stressed because our levels of adrenaline and cortisol are increased, affecting how we respond to other situations. It will come as no surprise that when you are stressed, this decreases your brain functions. If we, for example, use social media and find one or two inappropriate videos or images that increase our terror, stress or trauma, these everyday images send dynamic signals across the brain representing a stress action. Sinha et al. (2016) reported that there is 'acute neuroplasticity during stress, with distinct and separable brain networks that underlie critical control components of the stress response'. However, not everyone has the same levels of neural flexibility during stress and we can begin to understand why it is important that we teach our young people how to be resilient. Another difficulty and abstract challenge schools must address across their curriculum...

What if we have too much sleep? Just like a chocolate bar full of sugar, it impacts on our immune system and therefore our overall physical health. 'The optimal sleep duration appears to be 6 to 8 hours a day' (Linz et al., 2019). An additional detailed study comparing macro and micro sleep architecture and cognitive performance in older adults (Djonlagic et al., 2021) concluded that 'excessive daytime sleeping has also been found to be a marker of cognitive decline and dementia' and sleep disturbances associated with cognitive impairment.

In another fascinating paper, 'Impact of sleep on the risk of cognitive decline and dementia' (Spira et al., 2014), academics sought to evaluate the links between having trouble with falling or staying asleep, and poor-quality sleep, and the risks associated with cognitive decline and dementia, including Alzheimer's disease. It is worth noting that when a person develops Alzheimer's disease, the connections between the billions of nerve cells in the brain start to disconnect. Proteins form abnormal structures that cause the nerve cells to die. According to the Alzheimer's Society in the UK, over half a million people suffer from the disease, and for those that do, this leads to dementia. The research by Spira et al. concluded that poor sleep is a risk factor for cognitive decline compared to healthy sleep, which supports 'maintaining brain health with age'.

The more one digs deeper into the research explaining how we each can lead a healthier lifestyle, the clearer it becomes that there are specific things that we can do to be happier and live longer – and equally, learn better!

KEY TERMS

Antioxidants: Substances that may prevent cell damage in the body and therefore help fight disease.

Circadian rhythm: An internal clock that regulates our sleep patterns.

Glucose: A type of sugar found in the blood; glucose is the body's main energy source.

Melatonin: A hormone produced by the pineal gland that supports our circadian rhythm (sleep patterns).

Omega-3 acids: Nutrients that are essential for the human body and have a multitude of health benefits, including supporting cognitive function.

Pineal gland: A small gland in the brain whose main function is to receive information about light levels in our environment and produce melatonin accordingly.

PRACTICAL IDEA

Prioritising student wellbeing

It is safe to say we need to help our students to sleep better, to exercise more and to eat the right types of food, particularly at a younger age when the body is still growing and when there is an opportunity to embed long-term study skills. I know schools are tackling these issues in the pastoral aspects of their curriculum, assemblies and tutor time, but what can teachers do in their day-to-day teaching to support this?

In the UK, the importance of sleep education has been largely missed off the agenda from a school policy perspective. Why? Well, I suspect delaying the start time to the school day would impact millions of working families and their employment hours. The Teensleep project (supported by the Education Endowment Foundation in 2016) was the biggest study ever to look at teenage circadian delay and the effects of sleep education on academic, health and sleep outcomes. Run by the Nuffield Department of Clinical Neurosciences at the University of Oxford, the Teensleep project found that in adolescence biological rhythms change in such a way that makes it difficult for teenagers to go to sleep and get up early. Therefore, asking an adolescent to get up at 7 a.m to start school at 9 a.m is like asking a 55-year-old to get up at 5 a.m. Whilst there was no evidence that the programme led to improvements in students' sleep quality, they did find some evidence of improvements to students' self-reported behaviours.

Deep sleep is essential for memory formation (Harvard Medical School, 2007). It transfers information from our short-term store (the hippocampus) to long-term memory (the cortex). Scientists and doctors use a term called 'sleep hygiene' (or sleep health) which helps to instil good habits and thoughts for sleep. This table shows the recommended hours of sleep for different age groups (Sleep Foundation, 2021).

Preschool	School-age	Teen	Young adult
3–5 years	8–13 years	14–17 years	18–25 years
10–13 hours	9–11 hours	8–10 hours	7–9 hours

On the next page are some sleep ideas for students. You might like to share these ideas with students and parents and explore them further with your class in tutor time or PSHE sessions.

1. Create a sleep schedule.
2. Exercise for at least 30 minutes on most days, but not before bedtime.
3. Create a good sleeping environment.
4. Have a hot shower or bath before bedtime to help you to relax.
5. Avoid large meals, large beverages and caffeine before bedtime.
6. Have the right sunlight exposure, for example, natural light coming through the curtains in the morning or a lamp which slowly turns on in the morning.

Of course, sleep hygiene is only one part of the wellbeing puzzle, so here are some additional ideas to support nutrition and exercise:

Reward and celebrate

Design systems in school that reward and celebrate healthy eating and active learning, rather than encourage being tied to a screen or eating a burger.

Offer healthy options

Ensure healthy eating options are affordable in your school and available at a much lower price than the usual junk food options.

Promote healthy eating

What do your staff body do to promote healthy eating in the workplace, in their classroom and across the curriculum?

Engage students positively

'Eat Them To Defeat Them' is a colourful and dynamic campaign to encourage young people to engage in a positive way with healthy eating. Check it out at eatthemtodefeatthem.com.

Review your curriculum

Review your school's curriculum provision for physical education. Beyond the government guidelines, what other exposure do your students have with 'active learning', outdoor education and sporting events?

Assess your exercise equipment

In what condition is the exercise equipment available to staff and students? Are they well used? What percentage of students are involved in sport?

TOOLKIT TIPS

1. Help students adopt good habits for sleep, thinking about regular sleep schedules, exercise, the sleep environment and diet.
2. Engage students in healthy eating by promoting this in school and using campaigns such as 'Eat Them to Defeat Them'.
3. Review your school's approach to physical education, the exercise equipment available to students, 'active learning', outdoor education and sporting events.

WORKED EXAMPLE

To encourage students to reflect on their own physical and mental wellbeing, and the healthy habits they could adopt to support their learning, you could encourage them to keep a wellbeing diary. Ask students to respond to certain questions about their exercise, sleep, diet and mood to help them spot any patterns and changes over time. Think about how often you will ask them to complete their diary – set a regular schedule that works in your context. Remember this diary should be personal and confidential to them.

I have devised a template to support you with this. The questions are examples for secondary school students, so please use the blank template on the next page to devise your own questions that are suitable for your students and context.

WELLBEING DIARY

EXERCISE

- How many hours a week do you exercise?
- What's your favourite exercise?
- Can you do 25 squats without losing your breath?
- When did you last take part in a charity sporting event?
- When did you last walk over five miles?

SLEEP

- What's the average number of hours you sleep each night?
- What time do you usually go to bed?
- What time do you usually wake up?
- Do you leave your mobile phone away from your bed?
- How would you rate your sleep quality?

DIET

- Describe a typical:
  - Breakfast
  - Lunch
  - Dinner
  - Snack
- If you ate seven-a-day instead of five-a-day of fruit and vegetables, what would you choose on a regular basis?
- What is your one indulgence that you need to cut back on?

MOOD

- How do you reset your mood when you are feeling anxious or stressed?
- How do you stay balanced?
- When you are feeling moody, are you equipped to recognise the signs or do you rely on others to tell you?
- What are your 'good mood' triggers?

TEMPLATE

Wellbeing

EXERCISE

SLEEP

WELLBEING DIARY

DIET

MOOD

Scan the QR code for a downloadable digital copy of this template.

CHAPTER 10

WHAT NEXT FOR TEACHER CPD?

Ask me 15 years ago or so if I had read any teaching books or research and I would have struggled to give you an answer – and that would have been after ten years of teaching. Of course, I did attend training courses; I completed my master's degree and I was actively reading subject association magazines. But websites were still relatively new (and so was my blog) and the dialogue about teachers becoming research-literate was unheard of.

I listened carefully to presentations and to anyone who was speaking at an event; there were teacher training days and magazines being sent through the post to my classroom desk. The difference today is that there is now an abundance of sources, accessible on our devices and in the palms of our hands. It's easier than ever for teachers to find academic research on cognitive science and psychology. However, with a huge increase in misinformation and disinformation, it's much harder to filter the information and find out what is of use.

Despite the non-stop notifications, it's a good thing to have research at our fingertips. One other aspect of professional development that is worth reflecting on for teachers is how we have all adapted to online CPD throughout the pandemic. Just take a moment to think of how many teacher training sessions you have either presented at or participated in virtually. Which ones made a difference, and why? According to Chen et al. (2017), a lecture duration of 15 minutes is enough to exhaust the working memory.

Teachers want to be given the tools they need to be able to do their jobs more effectively. They already know what they need to do, but accountability, for all its merits in terms of standards and frameworks in all aspects of public life, and bureaucracy often get in the way of innovation. A chapter in *Exploring Teacher Recruitment and Retention* (2020) written by Linda la Velle and Alexandra Kendall discusses the benefits of a high-status, research-informed profession. When it comes to CPD, teacher autonomy is paramount. When all teachers are granted the space to take risks and are provided with training that is grounded in research and cognitive science, our profession will be a better place.

If you're interested in exploring the research about best practice for teacher CPD further, I'd recommend starting with Sims and Fletcher-Wood (2021) and Meesuk et al. (2020). Scan the QR codes to access these papers.

Meesuk et al. (2020)

Sims and Fletcher-Wood (2021)

EXPLAINER

How can you get the most out of CPD?

Training days for teachers can vary from the sublime to the diabolical! A well-planned INSET day can really help bring staff together, motivate them and move their professional learning on, which can have a huge benefit to students. Equally, the opposite is true. Teaching staff are reluctant to take part if they don't feel it will make a difference and is a waste of their time. INSET days are a precious opportunity for training and they must have an impact.

So, for whatever reason you are bringing teachers together, how can you get the most out of the time you have available? Throughout the pandemic, I have been curious to learn how cognitive load theory can be delivered in action for online teacher training sessions. The answer? Regular short sessions. I now work in 20-minute chunks. It's more powerful; teachers benefit more from short, regular content, with time to reflect.

I have been left wondering how this application could be used in our learning opportunities with teachers. I have thought deeply about how I would reshape my teacher training sessions to support the retention of knowledge. Is the traditional INSET day a thing of the past, cramming lots of people into a room to hear one person speak? Instead, we could replace this with short, sharp and punchy CPD sessions throughout the day, the morning or the afternoon with provocations from the floor and all staff contributing to learning which meets their needs and those of the school. It's not an easy feat though! Trying to meet the needs of 100 teachers in a large secondary school is never going to be straightforward.

Considering everything that we have covered in this book so far, in this chapter I would like to present a model for delivering an effective CPD session and show you how the topic of this book can be translated into a teacher training session that you can lead in your own workplace.

The model takes into consideration:

1. The **strategic** elements of CPD, including:
    a. the context of the session in relation to the school improvement plan
    b. the aims and outcomes of the session
    c. the structure of the session
    d. who will present the session
    e. what content will be covered
    f. how the session will be evaluated and reviewed.
2. The **logistical** elements of CPD, including:
    a. resources
    b. location and room arrangements
    c. timings and refreshments.

A model for effective CPD

There are a multitude of different factors you need to consider when you're planning a CPD session. I have devised a model to help you structure your planning, ensure nothing gets forgotten and make your session as impactful as possible.

The different elements of the model are as follows:

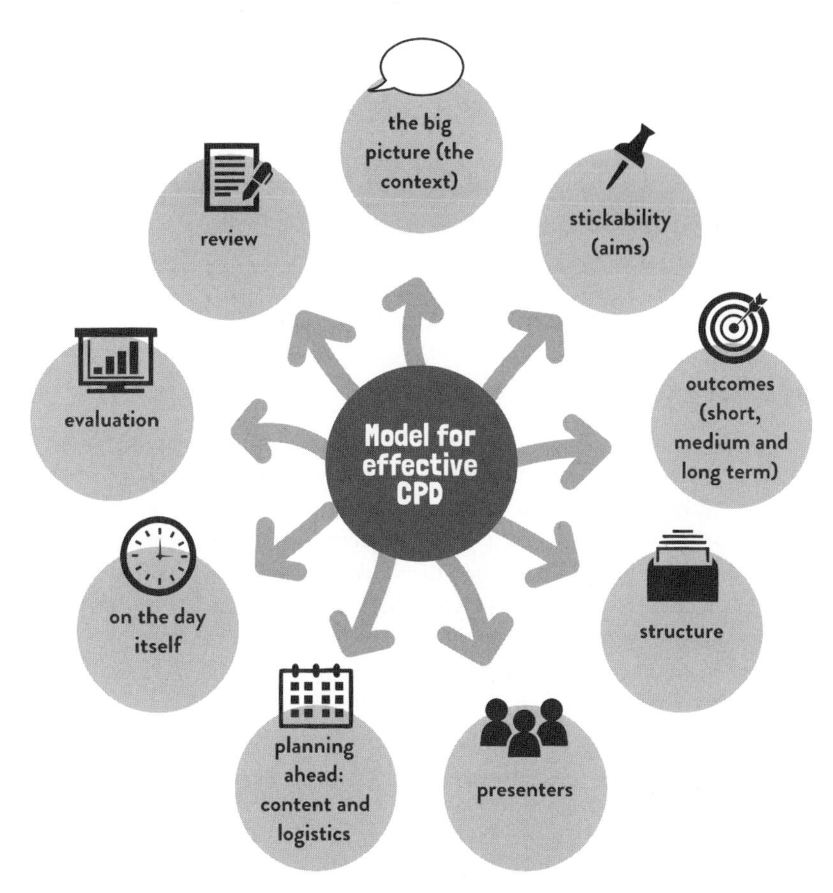

Let's unpick each of these in more detail.

The big picture (the context)

Training days for teachers should not just be a random selection of events, but a series of focused, prioritised and effective opportunities for individuals, teams and the school. When we agree on a context for the day or session, organisers must consider the school's improvement plan; this should be fundamental. It's also essential to take into account participants' existing professional knowledge and expertise.

Some questions you (or your school leader) could ask yourself when organising the next training day are listed on the next page.

1. What professional development will staff require to help them be even more effective in their teaching or role? For example, for a session on memory, what aspects of this book should be shared with staff?
2. What do participants already know about the topic? How can the session be differentiated to take into account the varying levels of knowledge and experience among participants? What was the staff feedback from the last training session?
3. How can part-time staff who may or may not be in attendance be considered?
4. Are there changes at a national or local level that you need or want to incorporate into the day?
5. Will there be an opportunity to consolidate what information is covered on this day, time to implement some of the ideas, and time to revisit key content?
6. Is there any feedback from staff or student voice that may shape what happens?
7. Is there an opportunity for students to attend the day and offer feedback?

Stickability (aims)

It is important to remember, first and foremost, that professional development must be about helping teachers work better. Until you have it absolutely clear in your mind how the training session will enable this, there is little point in pursuing the training. It is also worth seeking teacher feedback to ensure that you have perfectly pitched the objectives for the day to meet their needs. Where I have seen this work very well is when teacher professional development plans are synchronised alongside whole-school priorities which are then aligned with tailored pathways for teachers to pursue. Many training days can become a series of disjointed activities that have no real purpose or gain, and before long, staff will resent the lack of clarity in their learning, and most of all their time being wasted.

Outcomes (short, medium and long term)

Anybody organising a teacher training event must consider the implications of its content versus short-, medium- or long-term outcomes for students based on the time of academic year and school priorities.

You must consider this at an early point; think about what you expect the teachers or staff to produce as an outcome of the day. It could be new curriculum plans; schemes of work; lesson plans or resources; new learning protocols for lessons or for behaviour... the list is endless. What would be the best way for staff to capture their new learning in a way that will help them enhance the outcomes for students (and teachers)? Do your teaching staff keep professional development records, and is this a burden or a professional joy?

It's important to remember that, while the outcomes for the students and the school as a whole may be clearly defined, the outcomes for individual staff members may differ based on their existing professional knowledge and experience. A study at Monash University in Australia (Carpendale et al., 2021) found that highly accomplished teachers ('those who show skilled and sophisticated practice') respond to training in a different way when compared with less skilled or experienced teachers. It's always worth mixing up the audience and the delivery.

Carpendale et al. identified five ways in which teachers may respond to professional development:

Rejection	Replication	Application	Adaption	Amplification
Professional critique of the current status quo and any new ideas being presented.	How do these ideas work in my classroom?	Apply ideas and translate them to suit professional expertise as well as the students in the class.	Think about the pedagogical reasoning of the idea and how it can be modified to suit the application.	How the ideas presented can have a greater impact and be sustained.

When defining the outcomes of your session, think carefully about how individual participants may respond to the session based on these five criteria.

Structure

For a one-off session, think about the overall structure of the day and who is responsible for each section. For a series of shorter sessions, think about the individual structure of each session and who will take responsibility for it. Consider the structure of the content and how staff will learn best, for example, big questions, high-quality input, and opportunities for collaborative or cooperative learning with some time to think and reflect.

Having researched and written this book, I now know that short, sharp sessions are a good option for everyone, providing the people receiving the content with regular opportunities to process what has been said. This enables teachers to build on prior knowledge, making the connections needed to deepen their knowledge and understanding. There is absolutely no point whatsoever in somebody talking endlessly to a room full of people for 30 minutes or an hour without any consideration for how adults learn and retain information.

Presenters

You don't need me to come and visit your school. *You* can now do this for yourself! This model will provide you with the route map that you need to lead the session yourself.

Seeking access to high-quality external speakers is not always easy and can be very expensive. If you want a particular speaker, it is likely you will need to book them months, or possibly even a year, in advance. I know sometimes my teacher training diary has been booked out two years in advance. This is not just because the content is popular, but because days are fixed for schools, and traditionally INSET days tend to happen at the same time of the academic year, meaning there is more demand and less supply.

Take the time to dig deep, discover teachers' passions and nurture individuals to a degree of confidence where they can present in front of a large group of their peers. With practice, your own teaching staff can lead very powerful and inspiring teacher training.

Planning the content and how you will deliver it

In 2021, the EEF published a new guidance report on effective professional development for teaching staff. In the report, the EEF identified 14 mechanisms that should be considered when designing teacher training sessions. These mechanisms will help you to select the content that will be covered in your session and plan for how you're going to deliver it. The mechanisms are split into four sections: building knowledge; motivating teachers; developing teaching techniques; and embedding practice. I have summarised the mechanisms below and offered my thoughts on how to implement them. You can read the report by scanning the QR code.

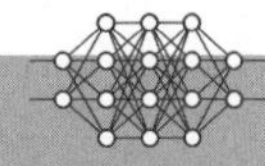

Building knowledge

1

Mechanism 1: Managing cognitive load

- Ensure the content you are presenting and any activities or tasks you set have the right level of intrinsic load for your audience.
- Minimise any extraneous load when you are presenting content.
- Think about what you would be able to take in after a five-period day and work backwards from there.

2

Mechanism 2: Revisiting prior learning

- At the start of the session, recap (or even better, retest) any prior knowledge participants might have about the topic.

Motivating teachers

3

Mechanism 3: Setting and agreeing on goals

- This should be a collective exercise. Key decisions must be communicated and opinions sought publicly.

4

Mechanism 4: Presenting information from a credible source

- Draw on a broad range of credible sources, for example, the Department for Education, a teaching union, research papers or an academic institution.
- Make sure the information is clearly referenced and signpost sources to staff.

5

Mechanism 5: Providing affirmation and reinforcement after progress

- Drip-feed new initiatives, vision and values, and continue to remind staff of the progress being made.
- Remind staff why changes are being made.

Developing teaching techniques

6

Mechanism 6: Instructing teachers 'how to' perform a technique

- Offer clear guided instruction to explain the key concepts and procedures of the approach or technique you are advocating.

7

Mechanism 7: Arranging social support

- Offer opportunities for participants to collaborate with one another.
- Teachers learn more and improve more if they are able to work, plan and make decisions with other teachers (Hargreaves and Fullan, 2012).

8

Mechanism 8: Modelling the technique

- Try 'I do, we do, you do'. Teachers respect the school leader who puts themselves on the front line of a demonstration!

9

Mechanism 9: Monitoring and providing feedback

- Be specific about what you're monitoring and provide clear, supportive and actionable feedback.
- Ensure this is differentiated from high-stakes lesson observations.

10

Mechanism 10: Rehearsing the technique

- Give teachers time to 'plug in and play' with the ideas. What we are hoping for is a change in long-term behaviours.
- Build in time for embedding and retrieval.
- Ask teachers to report back on what's working and what isn't. Lock it in.

Embedding practice

11

Mechanism 11: Providing prompts and cues

- From the original point of exposure, use every opportunity to revisit the material in staff briefings, emails, meetings or 'show and tell' twilights.
- Regular drip-feeding is a good way to help shape culture and habits.

12

Mechanism 12: Prompting action planning

- Offer an opportunity in the session for teachers to plan how and when they will implement an idea in their practice.

13

Mechanism 13: Encouraging monitoring

- Encourage teachers to monitor and record their own performance.
- For example, they could record their goals, the actions they take and how successful they have been. Even better, record short, two-minute videos and circulate them.

14

Mechanism 14: Prompting context-specific repetition

- Offer a range of ideas as to how teachers working with other year groups or subjects can translate the content back into their classrooms.

Planning the logistics: the month/week/day before

I know that there will be many factors that influence the success of a teacher training session, for example, lighting, sound, refreshments, acoustics and of course, the technology. So, it's essential to plan ahead.

When I plan any teacher training day, I always arrange a pre-planning call well in advance to establish objectives and intended outcomes. Depending on the lead-in time, this will determine your priorities and what can realistically be achieved. It can also be really useful to produce a simple countdown list for yourself. This will aid you to organise some things which need to be done much sooner than others. Here's what this might look like.

One month before

At least one month before, I will be sourcing information from the school and the teachers and researching content, strategy and resources to support any desired transformation. I will typically draft the content material, sharing it in advance and seeking feedback before I then refine the resources.

A month before you may want to:

30 DAYS TO GO

1. Make sure parents and students are reminded of the INSET day.
2. Finalise stickability, outcomes and structure for the day.
3. Confirm with guest and/or internal speakers they are still available and what their brief is.
4. Organise catering arrangements – don't be mean here. Tea, coffee, biscuits and a good lunch are crucial. Splash out. The staff deserve it.
5. Consider if the staff on part-time or support contracts should be paid to attend.
6. Plan the location of all events.
7. Think about how you will evaluate the event.

One week before

About one week before, I will do a logistical check on the room, the technology and the infrastructure inside the room to ensure that the content or person presenting is not hindered by external factors which could be considered in advance. For example, this might include the room layout, any password restrictions on the technology, access to video material and the technology being used on the day.

A week before you may want to:

7 DAYS TO GO

1. Publish the programme for the INSET day or CPD sessions.
   You could invite participants to submit sample questions ahead of time.
2. Inform premises staff on locations and seating layouts required.
3. Make sure the AV and heating or air conditioning are working.
4. Arrange access and logins for staff, particularly external guests.
5. Confirm any AV requirements, materials or resources for the sessions. Double check!
6. Prepare your anonymous evaluation. Use feed-forward: 'Have you considered...?'

One day before

The resources for the training day should already be shared, ideally with a one-page summary sheet with links to downloads, further reading and key questions to reflect on. QR codes work wonders too. Prepare printed copies of any resources you need on the day and ensure the physical location is ready – your support team will be able to help with this.

It is important, where possible, to test the technology, and make sure all the facilities are available and refreshments are prepared. Whilst I don't want to splash out in detail what makes a perfect INSET session, all of these factors help teachers become more comfortable after a busy working day, and more importantly, supported cognitively to think deeply about the material being presented in order to make a change in their classroom behaviours.

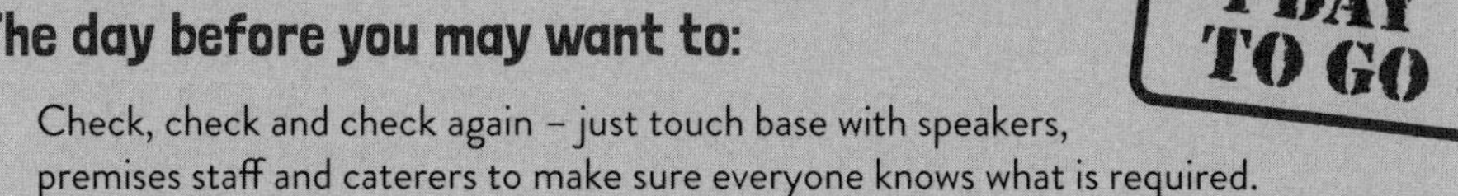

The day before you may want to:

1. Check, check and check again – just touch base with speakers, premises staff and caterers to make sure everyone knows what is required.
2. Ensure the technology requirements and resources are in place and have been tested.
3. Organise registers if required. Don't forget signage and disability access.
4. Upload any resources or links to the school virtual learning environment (VLE) or servers.

On the day itself

Planning for all situations is logistically difficult, especially if there is something already taking place in school that hinders final preparations. For example, you may not be able to set up the teacher training space because there is a lesson or parent consultation taking place beforehand. It doesn't matter how much you prepare, there will likely still be some work to do on the day to ensure your training event can take place without a hitch.

If you have managed to be highly efficient so far, the day should run smoothly and you can focus on the following:

1. Meet and greet speakers and ensure they have car parking available.
2. Ensure all rooms are set and comfortable, and the technology requirements are in place.
3. Touch base with and thank site supervisors, caterers and IT staff.
4. Thank all speakers during the day and explain all hospitality arrangements.
5. Collect staff registers.
6. Send staff evaluations by email link and place a reminder on the staff intranet.

And finally, as soon as the session is over:

1. Draft thank you letters and buy gifts for guest speakers and internal speakers.
2. Update training database or records; offer certificates for professional portfolios.
3. Upload or send any additional or late resources to staff, including those who were absent or who work part-time. Factor in when a follow-up session will be offered.

Evaluation

In setting up the evaluation, look to get different kinds of feedback, both quantitative and qualitative, which can be really useful for thinking and planning future events. The impact of the day on student outcomes should also be seriously considered. You may want to gather information on:

1. the quality of the various sessions – what was most useful and why?
2. the quality of the room arrangements
3. the quality of the catering
4. the impact of the day on staff's future plans
5. the impact of the day on staff wellbeing.

Review

Once the day is over and you have gathered the evaluations, it is important to sit down with some colleagues and consider how to maximise the impact of the day and whether any follow-up work is required. Stick to electronic evaluation rather than paper, which slows down the process. You may also want to consider whether any changes are needed to the content, structure or arrangements of any future training days for the academic year ahead. Most importantly, think about whether any follow-up training is needed for staff who have requested it, for absent or part-time staff, or for those who have stipulated various queries in their feedback.

- Write down when, with whom and how you intend to evaluate the INSET day.
- Why not go really radical and write a blog post for others to read and learn from?

Highly performing schools do this regularly and they show photographs of staff in action too. It's great for recruitment.

The big picture: How does the training session fit into the school improvement plan? What is the context?

Stickability: What are the aims? How will the training session help teachers improve?

Outcomes (short, medium and long term): What impact will the session have for staff and for students and how will this be demonstrated?

Evaluation: Quantitative and qualitative data and feedback on the session and its impact.

Review: Is any follow-up work needed? How could the session be improved in future?

PRACTICAL IDEA

A teacher CPD session on memory

So, how would I lead a training session on the topic of this book: memory? Well, there will be lots of factors to consider. Who is attending, how much time do I have, will it be a one-off, will there be a follow-up session, or will the content be delivered in lots of short and succinct sessions? Here is a simple methodology I would use.

As with all teacher professional development, to change practice there has to be an element of prior knowledge. If you are introducing aspects of this book to a room full of teachers, my first piece of advice would be to establish what your audience already knows. You want to ensure that the session is pragmatic and tailored to meet the needs of staff attending.

Considering there are nine explicit teaching strategies listed throughout this book, I would engineer a series of regular teacher training sessions to align with each of those, with a recap on what has been taught before a new idea is introduced. Analyse what staff know and what they don't, and where there is a need for them to know more. If you can keep the sessions to 20 to 30 minutes maximum, you will be doing yourself and your colleagues a good service. This will be following the methodology I have promoted throughout this book. If you can mix up a range of voices, as well as provide staff with an opportunity to reflect and discuss alongside a cup of coffee and a sandwich, then you will be meeting the minimum expectations. Think carefully about how you can create subgroups for discussion, presentation and feedback alongside whole-school priorities which are published very clearly across your academic calendar. If you want to take it one step further? Invite an external audience.

For each session, take a look through the relevant chapter and determine which key parts of the introduction to memory and the brain are relevant to the school context and need to be shared. If you can dedicate at least a third of your time to sharing this information, with handouts summarising the important points, the rest of the time can be used to model the practical strategy signposted. Below I have provided you with a possible CPD plan using a framework inspired by the 14 mechanisms from the EEF guidance report (2021).

Building knowledge

1. **Time frame:** 20 minutes, covering no more than three pieces of information.
2. **Prior learning:** How does this information connect with school priorities and what has been covered in previous sessions? What do the teachers already know?

Motivating teachers

3. **Goals:** Introduce the content you will be covering and collaboratively set goals for the outcomes of the session based on the starting points of the participants.
4. **Reinforcement:** At the start of the session, do a quick recap on what has already been covered in previous sessions. Retest (do not reteach) in order to help retention, by leading a staff quiz on the topic.

5. **New information:** Pull out three key pieces of information you want to cover this session and give a clear overview of each. Offer dual-coded slides with simple images and keywords, then introduce the practical idea.

Developing teaching techniques

6. **'How to' instructions:** For the practical idea, prepare a beginner, intermediate and advanced level of instructions. Allow individuals to select what would be most useful for them. Provide colleagues with 'what a good one looks like' and a set of scaffolding resources. If you wish to move from this traditional model towards cognitive apprenticeship, make it visible, situate any abstract concepts with concrete examples and help them apply the information in a real-world situation. (For example, discuss a student.)
7. **Social support:** Provide colleagues with time to reflect and discuss one or two key questions. Signpost to where they can find out more information (at varying levels) using QR codes, hyperlinks or a person in the workplace. This social support will be strengthened if the topic is revisited collectively in the future (spaced practice).
8. **Modelling:** Show step by step how the idea can be implemented in the classroom.
9. **Feedback:** Ensure the feedback is context-specific and helps individuals and the group to improve. When will staff be given time to try the ideas and return with reflections?
10. **Rehearsal:** Identify clear time for colleagues to practise trying the ideas in the workplace and report back in the next session. Signal 'what's coming up' in the next session.

Embedding practice

11. **Prompts and cues:** Key personnel can discuss the training in follow-up appraisal conversations, meetings and staff briefings to help retain core messages.
12. **Action plan:** Revisit the goals, set a timeline for action and break down the steps along the way. Ensure everyone sees this information and is part of the planning process.
13. **Monitoring:** Avoid monitoring for the sake of it! Set out clearly from the start how this practice will be quality assured to inform decision-making. If teachers are also involved in this, they are more likely to take ownership. Keep it simple.
14. **Context-specific repetition:** Providing colleagues with time to trial, discuss, refine and reflect on the new ideas is essential.

TOOLKIT TIPS

1. Opt for short, sharp CPD sessions over traditional INSET days. This enables teachers to build on prior knowledge, process their learning and put it into practice.

2. Before planning and delivering a CPD session, always establish what your audience already knows so you can focus on deepening understanding.

3. Always think about how the CPD content relates to student outcomes. Model practical classroom ideas that align with your school's needs and priorities.

WORKED EXAMPLE

A well-planned training session or INSET day in your school can really help bring staff together, move their professional learning to the next level and provide huge benefits for your students. These are precious opportunities to have an impact on outcomes across a school. The **Five Minute Professional Development Plan** on the following page will help you to plan your own training session, guiding you through the logistics and the strategy you need to have in place to make your session a success.

The left-hand side of the plan tackles the logistics, while the right-hand side helps you devise a strategy for an effective training session. Here's how to use each side of the plan.

Logistics

What? When? Where? Who? This is a space to jot down the basics: what is the event? When will it take place? Where's it going to be held? Who's leading the event? Who's attending it? Who's involved in the planning?

Timings: What time will the training start and end? What time will there be a break? The session could be a twilight, a Saturday event, or a full five-hour INSET day.

Number of people: How many people will there be in the whole session? If you're having breakout sessions, how many people will be in each?

Content ratio vs timing: Think about the time you have versus the amount of content you have to present. Remember, it's best to cover one small thing at a time rather than everything all at once.

Logistics: Consider the room, layout of tables and chairs, lighting, sound, connectivity and testing.

Student/staff needs: What impact do you want the training to have in classrooms the very next day, for teachers, teaching assistants and students?

Resources: Prepare some templates and handouts for teachers to play with in their classrooms the next day. Remember to factor in the cost and logistics of printing.

Strategy

School priority: What school priority is the training addressing? How does this training session fit into meeting this priority? How is it communicated? Remember the training should be part of a long-term solution, rather than a bolt-on, sticking-plaster event.

Intended outcomes: What are the intended outcomes for the session? How will this training address student and staff needs that are specific to your context? How can the training be implemented in classrooms the next day? When will there be a follow-up?

Stickability: What are the key takeaways you want people to revisit from your session?

Outcomes and evaluation: How will the impact of the session be evaluated?

Plan B: What if it all goes wrong? Always have a plan B just in case!

TEMPLATE

The Five Minute Professional Development Plan

1. What?

2. When?

3. Where?

4. Who?

Timings

Start

Break

End

Number of people?

More people, less personable

Content ratio vs timing

One message maximum,
one minute minimum

Logistics

Size of room; position, lectern, microphone, sound, ICT, table layout, location...

School priority...

Stickability

Key takeaways

Intended outcomes...

Outcome for the session?

How will this training meet individual/team needs?

Plan for the next day in classrooms?

Follow-up information?

Resources/Structure

Handouts, follow-up online links...

Outcomes/Evaluation

Stickability moment; succinct and memorable

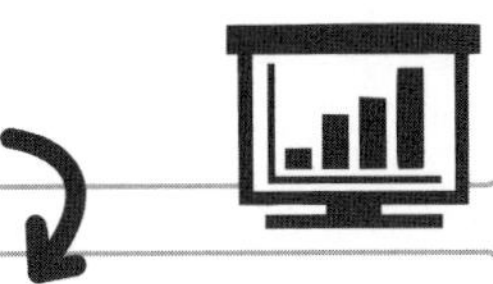

Student/Staff needs?

What would the cynic want that they don't already know?

Plan B

What if the timings change?
The technology lets you down?

Scan the QR code for a downloadable digital copy of this template.

BRINGING IT ALL TOGETHER

What should teachers do now?

Teachers are constantly searching for the elusive strategy that will unlock learning and reduce their workload. Whilst this is desirable, it is probably not helpful. For example, a teacher might select retrieval practice as the number one strategy to use and implement alongside their curriculum design, but continue to use the same retrieval exercises time and time again. We know this is unlikely to work in every classroom context they might come across. The most important thing to stress is that teachers know a wide range of strategies that underpin effective teaching. Understanding the brain and how we learn is top of the list in terms of topics to help all teachers to identify approaches to shape memory and impact learning – and apply them to best effect.

I hope the ideas posed throughout this book provide a starting point. Use these ideas wisely and do not disregard any of the strategies. They will work somewhere according to content, age, stage and time of year. It is important to use all of them as and when required. It's not what you do; it's the way that you do it! And that includes when, where, how and why!

In this concluding section, I want to show you how to 'bring it all together', in other words how the strategies can be deployed throughout an academic year so they complement and build on one another.

Let's take a moment to recap the ten practical ideas presented in this book:

Technique	What is it?
1. Direct instruction	Presenting new material using modelling, chunking and dual coding
2. Retrieval practice	Desirably difficult, low-stakes quizzing
3. Spaced practice and interleaving	Scheduled and mixed content and retrieval practice over time
4. Spaced and active rereading	Restudying text material at intervals and highlighting key content
5. Summarising	Creating a bitesize overview of content
6. Mnemonics	Mental models to learn key concepts, processes or terminology
7. Elaboration	Explaining *why*
8. Self-explanation	Students explaining new information
9. Prioritising student wellbeing	Ensuring students take care of themselves physically and mentally
10. Teacher CPD on memory	Teacher training on how learning happens

Considering each of these ideas to support the acquisition of knowledge, how can your team, department or school map these out coherently across an academic year, considering all the pressures of curriculum coverage, exams and associated challenges of working in a school?

To begin this process, there are a number of questions I would like you to ask yourself:

1. How confident do you feel about using each technique?
2. Do you recognise when in your teaching you offer the study strategies to your students?
3. If so, which ones do you use the most?
4. Do you have any proof to suggest a particular technique works better than another in your context and at a particular time of the year?
5. How do we evaluate our perception of each of these techniques in terms of learning versus performance?
6. Are these techniques explicitly referenced in your scheme of work?
7. If so, are they connected to other areas of the school at a macro level?
8. Does your school leadership team have these strategies highlighted by year group and by subject throughout the academic year?
9. If so, how is this overview adopted to suit teaching and learning needs?
10. When does teacher training take place to enable the deployment of these strategies?

In some of the experiences I have had with other teachers, I can see clearly where each of these techniques is referenced within individual schemes of work. I suspect there will be one or two schools that not only have these strategies identified in schemes of work, but have also mapped them across the school. Wouldn't this be a **great thing to have** in every school? Not only would this build a whole-school curriculum plan based on how we learn, but it would also give teachers the opportunity to explicitly teach students these techniques as valuable skills for self-study and revision. It's not just about teaching students 'what' but 'how'. This overview could be a strategy which is then communicated with parents and which would, ultimately, develop study skills with our young people at a much earlier age.

The result?

Students will be less anxious when high-stakes exams arrive. They will develop a degree of metacognition as they learn which technique to use for a task and when. Our young people leave full-time education with a love for learning and the ability to self-regulate their learning for the future. This can only be a good thing for our society. The challenge is, as you and I both know, how to reliably reward all students regardless of their ability, and consider societal subject bias and how we can change the narrative on this, for example, maths and art being considered equally as a worthy qualification.

You will see from the diagram on the next page that I have provided you with an example of what an academic calendar may look like in one subject month by month and how these techniques can be explicitly referenced in curriculum maps and schemes of work.

September	October	November	December	January	February	March	April	May	June
Direct instruction	Direct instruction	Direct instruction	Direct instruction	Direct instruction	Direct instruction	Direct instruction	Direct instruction	Direct instruction	Direct instruction
	Spaced & active rereading	Spaced & active rereading	Spaced & active rereading	Spaced & active rereading	Spaced & active rereading	Spaced & active rereading	Spaced & active rereading	Spaced & active rereading	Spaced & active rereading
		Summarisation	Summarisation	Summarisation	Summarisation	Summarisation	Summarisation	Summarisation	Summarisation
			Self-explanation	Self-explanation	Self-explanation	Self-explanation	Self-explanation	Self-explanation	Self-explanation
				Elaboration	Elaboration	Elaboration	Elaboration	Elaboration	Elaboration
					Mnemonics	Mnemonics	Mnemonics	Mnemonics	Mnemonics
Retrieval practice	Retrieval practice	Retrieval practice	Retrieval practice	Retrieval practice	Retrieval practice	Retrieval practice	Retrieval practice	Retrieval practice	Retrieval practice
Spaced practice/ interleaving	Spaced practice/ interleaving	Spaced practice/ interleaving	Spaced practice/ interleaving	Spaced practice/ interleaving	Spaced practice/ interleaving	Spaced practice/ interleaving	Spaced practice/ interleaving	Spaced practice/ interleaving	Spaced practice/ interleaving
Student wellbeing focus				Student wellbeing focus				Student wellbeing focus	
Teacher CPD session		Teacher CPD session		Teacher CPD session		Teacher CPD session			

If schools can have this mapped out, with supporting resources and teachers confident enough to know what the techniques are and how to deploy them in practice, our classrooms will be a much more effective space for teaching and learning.

It's important to note that this route map is offered as an example and should not debilitate your autonomy to select specific teaching techniques for your students and the context in which you work. It's important to think about how the strategies on offer align with your curriculum sequence and the rhythm of your academic year. Once you have these things thought through, you can then consider what the techniques look like, what training needs to be considered for the teachers around you, and then allow time to

implement these carefully so that they become embedded as part of the school culture. You will also need to consider how the technique needs to be adapted between subjects, age groups and time of year. Scan the QR code on the left for a blank calendar for you to scribble ideas down for your own context, keeping all this in mind.

To support the implementation of the ideas in every classroom, I have created a unique **Five Minute Memory Plan**. This tool brings together all the ideas in the book and will help every teacher to plan how they will use the ideas in their classroom. On page 142 is an outline of the plan. Scan the QR code at the bottom of this page for a full version of the plan that you can download, print off and scribble notes on.

Identifying and using these techniques will ripple through the school building. They will be evident in lesson plans, curriculum overviews, teacher training sessions and pedagogical strategies in the classroom. More importantly, students will be able to articulate to the teacher which technique they are using, why and at what points. It will be even better if families are supported by schools to learn this knowledge, taking into consideration how long it may or may not have been since they were last in a school themselves. We know that the family unit at home plays a big part in the long-term success and outcomes of a child, but this is rarely evident or reported in league tables. I think it's a duty of all schools to provide their local community with this information so that they can support their children in school. Whilst most schools will do this, equipping families with these explicit skills to use during homeschooling, homework or revision periods should lead to a more productive environment, improve mental health, build better connections between school and home, and make for happier students.

I also recognise that there are multiple factors that schools are managing to support all students to succeed, and these strategies being implemented alone aren't a one-size-fits-all for improving student achievement. This is certainly not a panacea, but at least by providing you with this beginner's guide to memory, I hope the information and strategies presented will benefit your students if you are motivated and capable of using them. The challenge is, as always, to establish these effective techniques without much effort, so they are used more consistently with disadvantaged students who probably would benefit more from the strategies.

Scan the QR code for a downloadable digital copy of the Five Minute Memory Plan.

TEMPLATE

The Five Minute Memory Plan

1. Objectives...

2. Assess prior knowledge

Last lesson we... ?

Last week we... ?

Last month we... ?

3. Mnemonics

The surprise?

The structure?

The simplicity?

The specificity?

The subtext?

4. Direct instruction

What abstract ideas must be concrete?

How will you chunk information?

What modelling will you provide?

What dual coding is required?

5. Interleaving

What context?

When?

Why?

6. Spaced retrieval practice

What short-answer questions will you ask?

What free-recall tasks will you plan?

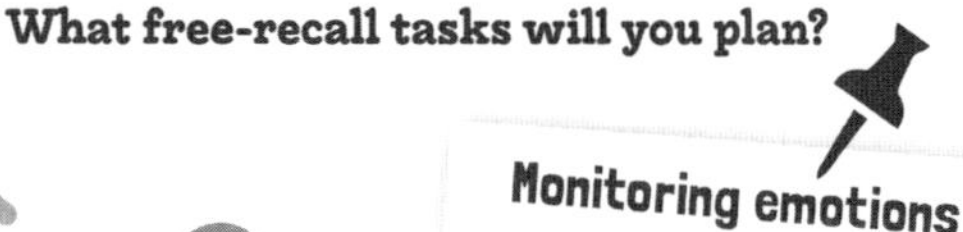

Monitoring emotions

Intense focus

Clear objective

Immediate feedback

7. Questioning for...

What elaboration will you seek?

What self-explanation will you require?

8. Cognitive load theory

How will you balance intrinsic load?

How will you reduce extraneous load?

9. Assessment

How is your assessment manageable?

How will you make it motivational?

How will the information be meaningful to take action?

Are you providing feedback, feed-up or feed-forward?

Verbal or non-verbal cues?

CONCLUSION

CONTINUING YOUR JOURNEY WITH MEMORY

Despite receiving a detailed and comprehensive introduction to teaching during my training, one aspect of pedagogy that was missing was understanding how we learn and how to translate this information in the classroom. With the abundance of research, access to professional development and many new teachers being exposed to cognitive science at an earlier stage of their career, I am optimistic about the future quality of our teachers entering the classroom.

However, as with all things teaching, educators do not necessarily need to know more information to help change their behaviours. Teachers need time to practise and find out what works well in their classroom. For example, when posing a question, how long should they wait before providing the answer? What type of feedback should a teacher provide to a demotivated student? There are a million and one different scenarios and approaches.

When a teacher qualifies, they are on a continued trajectory to master the classroom. This is a career-long process. As a teacher develops secure subject knowledge and a wide repertoire of behaviour management strategies, what needs to follow soon after is a deep understanding of how to learn. As I've highlighted in this book, how we can shape our brain is the crux of everything we must share with teachers. It rests with their understanding of theory and being given the time to translate the necessary concepts into pedagogical techniques for the classroom.

We are all on a journey in our understanding of memory, whether we do this consciously or unconsciously, and as I have highlighted, this book showcases my own journey. You reading this book now becomes part of your journey too! If I could add more information to this book or write a follow-up, it wouldn't necessarily be anything more on memory, rather on why we forget. To explore this further, I'd recommend watching Robert Bjork explain his concept of retrieval-induced forgetting. Scan the QR code to access the video.

As we reach the end of this book, I want to provide a series of reflection questions for you to consider to help you reflect more deeply about where you and your students are in your journey and to think about where you might need to go next.

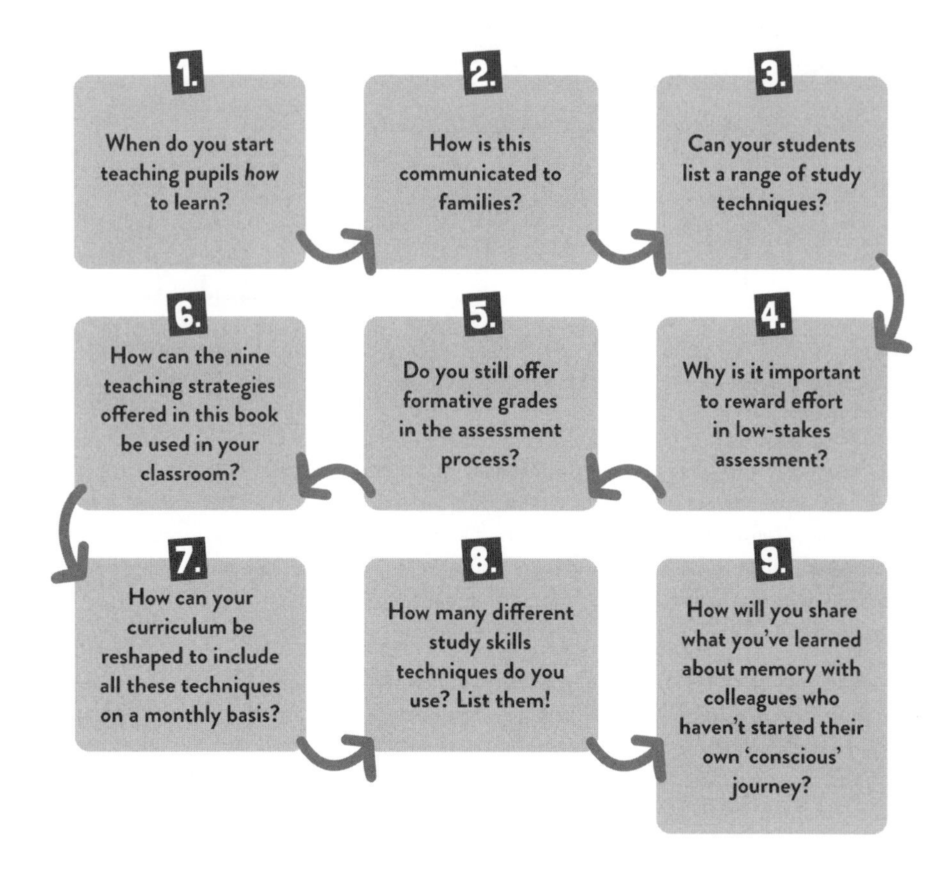

Taking it further

Here is a list of sources that have inspired my journey with cognitive science and understanding the brain. If you want to take your learning further, I heartily recommend you take the time to delve into these publications yourself.

If I were to write an 'intermediate guide to memory for teachers', some of the things I would like to include in a follow-up resource would be:

1. understanding the teenage brain
2. implications for teachers working with vulnerable students
3. additional learning needs
4. how the brain repairs itself (or not) during illness or injury
5. how we impair memory
6. why we forget and more about retrieval-induced forgetting.

You might like to choose one of these topics to explore further in your own research.

Understanding the Brain, an audiobook by Jeanette Norden

'Improving students' learning with effective learning techniques: Promising directions from cognitive and educational psychology', by Dunlosky et al. (2013)

The work of the Learning Scientists: **www.learningscientists.org**

Stop Talking, Start Influencing, by Jared Cooney Horvath

Connect the Dots, by Tricia Taylor

Why the Brain Matters, by Jon Tibke

Powerful Teaching, by Pooja Agarwal and Patrice Bain

An Introduction to Cognitive Psychology, by David Groome

The Future of Teaching, by Guy Claxton

How Learning Happens, by Paul Kirschner and Carl Hendrick

Some ethical questions

To conclude, I'd like to share one final piece of research which throws up some ethical questions as well as highlights what little we all know about the organ in our skull that enables *you* to read this text and *me* to write it.

We know the brain is the central organ in our nervous system. We know that it is full of billions of neurons, sending electrochemical signals to form up to one hundred trillion connections. Yet we know very little about what happens to our brain when we die.

If you can forgive me for ending on a somewhat morbid story, I would like to tell you about a world first, when neuroscientists (inadvertently) recorded an 87-year-old man's dying brain while he was suffering from a cardiac arrest. Over a period of 15 minutes, using electroencephalography (EEG), they found that 'the brain may pass through a series of stereotyped activity patterns during death' (Vicente et al., 2022), meaning our lives literally flash before us as we pass away! Measuring 30 seconds of activity either side of when the heart stopped beating, researchers found that changes in neural activity (brainwaves) continued after death. From an ethical perspective, we are not in a position to gather such data from humans who are on their death bed, yet these findings suggest that we still have much to learn about how this organ – and our memory – functions from the moment we begin to grow as an embryo in the womb, right up to the moment we leave Earth as we know it.

As I stated in the opening chapter of this book, I'm a teacher, not a cognitive psychologist or neuroscientist. However, as an educator, I believe we can use what we know about the brain to help us live a healthier and more fulfilled life, as well as reflect on what techniques and strategies help us to strengthen the brain and its functions. We all have much to learn, but as teachers we can work together to collate what we know and devise strategies to help students remember concepts, rules and facts. Not only will this make us more effective at teaching, but it will also provide all students with the opportunity to learn better, have a more fulfilled experience at school, and develop a deep love for learning that can become lifelong.

One area of concern I have with emerging government policy on knowledge acquisition and memory is that it could fail to factor in all the aspects of learning related to social, emotional and mental health. We have to work hard to ensure that our vulnerable students are not left behind. Amidst the league tables and exam pressures that all our young people face, by using what we know to equip our young people with the study strategies outlined in this book, we can at least put them in a stronger position to be successful throughout life, not just at the moment our education system tests their ability to recall in a high-stakes exam.

There are nine children in every classroom living in poverty across the UK. That's 4.3 million students (CPAG, 2021). Using what you and I both now know about memory, sharing this widely, and in particular sharing strategies to help our young people learn more effectively, is a social justice issue. For these children, supporting them to learn how to study effectively in school – and showing them how they might use these strategies at home, whatever that may look like for the most vulnerable – is more than just teaching kids stuff. Teaching children *how* to learn, not just *what* to learn, is something we should all take seriously.

REFERENCES

Adams, C. D. (1868), *The Genuine Works of Hippocrates*. New York, NY: Dover.

Agarwal, P. K., D'Antonio, L., Roediger III, H. L., McDermott, K. B. and McDaniel, M. A. (2014), 'Classroom-based programs of retrieval practice reduce middle school and high school students' test anxiety', *Journal of Applied Research in Memory and Cognition*, 3, (3), 131–139.

Alzheimer's Society, 'Facts for the media', www.alzheimers.org.uk/about-us/news-and-media/facts-media

APA, 'transfer-appropriate processing', https://dictionary.apa.org/transfer-appropriate-processing

Atkinson, R. C. and Shiffrin, R. M. (1968), 'Human memory: A proposed system and its control processes', *Psychology of Learning and Motivation*, 2, 89–195.

Bahrick, H. P. (1979), 'Maintenance of knowledge: Questions about memory we forgot to ask', *Journal of Experimental Psychology: General*, 108, (3), 296–308.

Bjork, E. L. and Bjork, R. A. (2011), 'Making things hard on yourself, but in a good way: Creating desirable difficulties to enhance learning', in: M. A. Gernsbacher, R. W. Pew, L. M. Hough and J. R. Pomerantz (eds.) and FABBS Foundation, *Psychology and the Real World: Essays illustrating fundamental contributions to society*. Broadway: Worth Publishers, pp. 56–64.

Blakemore, S.-J. (2019), *Inventing Ourselves: The secret life of the teenage brain*. London: Transworld.

Blanchette Sarrasin, J., Brault Foisy, L.-M., Allaire-Duquette, G. and Masson, S. (2020), 'Understanding your brain to help you learn better', Frontiers for Young Minds, https://kids.frontiersin.org/articles/10.3389/frym.2020.00054

Bruni, O., Kohler, M., Novelli, L., Kennedy, D., Lushington, K., Martin, J. and Ferri, R. (2012), 'The role of NREM sleep instability in child cognitive performance', *Sleep*, 35, (5), 649–656.

Cadenas-Sanchez, C., Migueles, J. H., Erickson, K. I., Esteban-Cornejo, I., Catena, A. and Ortega, F. B. (2020), 'Do fitter kids have bigger brains?', *Scandinavian Journal of Medicine and Science in Sports*, 30, (12), 2498–2502.

Cairney, J., Dudley, D., Kwan, M., Bulten, R. and Kriellaars, D. (2019), 'Physical literacy, physical activity and health: Toward an evidence-informed conceptual model, *Sports Medicine*, 49, (3), 371–383.

Carpendale, J., Cooper, R., Berry, A. and Mitchell, I. (2021), 'Balancing fidelity with agency: Understanding the professional development of highly accomplished teachers', *Professional Development in Education*.

Centre for Education Statistics and Evaluation (2017), 'Cognitive load theory: Research that teachers really need to understand', https://education.nsw.gov.au/about-us/educational-data/cese/publications/literature-reviews/cognitive-load-theory

Chen, O., Woolcott, G. and Sweller, J. (2017), 'Using cognitive load theory to structure computer-based learning including MOOCs', *Journal of Computer Assisted Learning*, 33, 293–305.

Claxton, G. (2021), *The Future of Teaching*. Abingdon: Routledge.

Coe, R. (1998), 'Can feedback improve teaching? A review of the social science literature with a view to identifying the conditions under which giving feedback to teachers will result in improved performance', *Research Papers in Education*, 13, (1), 43–66.

Cohen, J., Gorski, M., Gruber, S., Kurdziel, L. and Rimm, E. (2016), 'The effect of healthy dietary consumption on executive cognitive functioning in children and adolescents: A systematic review', *British Journal of Nutrition*, 116, (6), 989–1000.

REFERENCES

Collins, A., Brown, J. S. and Holum, A. (1991), 'Cognitive apprenticeship: Making thinking visible', *American Educator*, 15, (3), 6–11.

CPAG (2021), 'Child poverty facts and figures', https://cpag.org.uk/child-poverty/child-poverty-facts-and-figures

de Groot, A. (1966), 'Perception and memory versus thought: Some old ideas and recent findings', in B. Rleinmuntz (Ed.), *Problem Solving*. New York, NY: Wiley.

Department for Education (2016), 'Standard for teachers' professional development', www.gov.uk/government/publications/standard-for-teachers-professional-development

Department for Education (2021a), 'Small-scale research projects: summaries', www.gov.uk/government/publications/analytical-associate-pool-summary-of-projects

Department for Education (2021b), 'Early career framework', www.gov.uk/government/publications/early-career-framework

D'Esposito, M. (2008), 'Working memory', in: M. J. Aminoff, F. Boller, D. F. Swaab, G. Goldenberg and B. L. Miller (eds.), *Handbook of Clinical Neurology*, vol. 88. Amsterdam: Elsevier, pp. 237–247.

Djonlagic, I., Mariani, S., Fitzpatrick, A. L., Van Der Klei, V. M. G. T. H., Johnson, D. A., Wood, A. C., Seeman, T., Nguyen, H. T., Prerau, M. J., Luchsinger, J. A., Dzierzewski, J. M., Rapp, S. R., Tranah, G. J., Yaffe, K., Burdick, K. E., Stone, K. L., Redline, S. and Purcell, S. M. (2021), 'Macro and micro sleep architecture and cognitive performance in older adults', *Nature Human Behaviour*, 5, 123–145.

Duckworth, S. (2018), *How to Sketchnote*. Elevate Books Edu.

Dudley, D., Dean, H., Cairney, J. and Van Bergen, P. (2020), 'Pedagogical constraints of physical literacy based on cognitive load theory', *Prospects*, 50, (1–2), 151–164.

Dunlosky, J., Rawson, K. A., Marsh, E. J., Nathan, M. J. and Willingham, D. T. (2013), 'Improving students' learning with effective learning techniques: Promising directions from cognitive and educational psychology', *Psychological Science in the Public Interest*, 14, (1), 4–58.

Dweck, C. S. (2007), 'The perils and promises of praise', in: M. Scherer (ed.), *EL Essentials on Formative Assessment*. Alexandria, VA: ASCD, pp. 66–75.

Ebbinghaus, H. (1885), *Memory: A contribution to experimental psychology*. New York, NY: Teachers College, Columbia University.

Education Endowment Foundation (2018), 'Teaching and learning toolkit', https://educationendowmentfoundation.org.uk/education-evidence/teaching-learning-toolkit

Education Endowment Foundation (2021), 'Effective professional development', https://educationendowmentfoundation.org.uk/education-evidence/guidance-reports/effective-professional-development

Endres, T., Kranzdorf, L., Schneider, V. and Renkl, A. (2020), 'It matters how to recall – task differences in retrieval practice', *Instructional Science*, 48, 699–728.

Erickson, K. I., Voss, M. W., Prakash, R. S., Basak, C., Szabo, A., Chaddock, L., Kim, J. S., Heo, S., Alves, H., White, S. M., Wojcicki, T. R., Mailey, E., Vieira, V. J., Martin, S. A., Pence, B. D., Woods, J. A., McAuley, E. and Kramer, A. F. (2011), 'Exercise training increases size of hippocampus and improves memory', *Proceedings of the National Academy of Sciences of the United States of America*, 108, (7), 3017–3022.

Evidence Based Education (2020), 'The great teaching toolkit', www.greatteaching.com

Ezzati, A., Katz, M. J., Zammit, A. R., Lipton, M. L., Zimmerman, M. E., Sliwinski, M. J. and Lipton, R. B. (2016), 'Differential association of left and right hippocampal volumes with verbal episodic and spatial memory in older adults', *Neuropsychologia*, 93, 380–385.

Farley, P. (2020), 'Long-term learning requires new nerve insulation', University of California San Francisco, www.ucsf.edu/news/2020/02/416621/long-term-learning-requires-new-nerve-insulation

Foot, P. (1967), 'The problem of abortion and the doctrine of the double effect', *Oxford Review*, 5, 5–15.

Foster, D. and Roberts, N. (2022), 'Physical education, physical activity and sport in schools', House of Commons Library, https://researchbriefings.files.parliament.uk/documents/SN06836/SN06836.pdf

Francis, C. D. (1868), *The Genuine Works of Hippocrates*. New York, NY: Dover.

Gansemer-Topf, A. M., Paepcke-Hjeltness, V., Russell, A. E. and Schiltz, J. (2021), '"Drawing" your own conclusions: Sketchnoting as a pedagogical tool for teaching ecology', *Innovative Higher Education*, 46, 303–319.

Ginott, H. (1972), *Between Teacher and Child*. Scribner.

GL Assessment (2018), 'Children's wellbeing: Pupil attitudes to self and school report 2018', www.gl-assessment.co.uk/media/294651/childrenswellbeingreport2018.pdf

Grant, H. M., Bredahl, L. C., Clay, J., Ferrie, J., Groves, J. E., McDorman, T. A. and Dark, V. J. (1998), 'Context-dependent memory for meaningful material: Information for students', *Applied Cognitive Psychology*, 12, (6), 617–623.

Greene, J. D., Sommerville, R. B., Nystrom, L. E., Darley, J. M. and Cohen, J. D. (2001), 'An fMRI investigation of emotional engagement in moral judgment', *Science*, 293, 5537, 2105–2108.

Hargreaves, A. and Fullan, M. (2012), *Professional Capital*. New York, NY: Teachers College Press.

Harvard Medical School (2007), 'Sleep, learning and memory', http://healthysleep.med.harvard.edu/healthy/matters/benefits-of-sleep/learning-memory

Hattie, J. and Timperley, H. (2007), 'The power of feedback', *Review of Educational Research*, 77, (1), 81–112.

Hesse, H. (1922), *Siddhartha: An Indian Poem*.

Hirotsu, C., Tufik, S. and Andersen, M. L. (2015), 'Interactions between sleep, stress, and metabolism: From physiological to pathological conditions', *Sleep Science*, 8, (3), 143–152.

Hobert, L. and Binello, E. (2017), 'Trepanation in Ancient China', *World Neurosurgery*, 101, 451–456.

James, W. (1890), *The Principles of Psychology*. New York, NY: Henry Holt.

Kak, S. C. (1997), 'On the science of consciousness in Ancient India', *Indian Journal of History of Science*, 32, 105–120.

Karpicke, J. D. and Bauernschmidt, A. (2011), 'Spaced retrieval: Absolute spacing enhances learning regardless of relative spacing', *Journal of Experimental Psychology*, 37, (5), 1250–1257.

Kim, S. K. and Webb, S. (2022), 'The effects of spaced practice on second language learning: A meta-analysis', *Language Learning*, 72, (1), 269–319.

Kirschner, P. and Hendrick, C. (2020), *How Learning Happens*. Abingdon: Routledge.

Kirschner, P. A., Sweller, J., Kirschner, F. and Zambrano, R. J. (2018), 'From cognitive load theory to collaborative cognitive load theory', *International Journal of Computer-Supported Collaborative Learning*, 13, 213–233.

Ku, Y. (2018), 'Selective attention on representations in working memory: Cognitive and neural mechanisms', *PeerJ*, 6, e4585.

Lave, J. (1988), *Cognition in practice: Mind, mathematics and culture in everyday life*. Cambridge: Cambridge University Press.

la Velle, L. and Kendall, A. (2020), 'A high-status, research-informed profession', in T. Ovenden-Hope and R. Passy, *Exploring Teacher Recruitment and Retention*. Abingdon: Routledge, pp. 46–58.

Lemov, D. (2016), *Teach Like a Champion 3.0*. Hoboken, NJ: Jossey-Bass.

Linz, D., Kadhim, K., Kalman, J. M., McEvoy, R. D. and Sanders, P. (2019), 'Sleep and cardiovascular risk: How much is too much of a good thing?', *European Heart Journal*, 40, (20), 1630–1632.

Lokhorst, G.-J. (2013), 'Descartes and the pineal gland', Stanford Encyclopedia of Philosophy, https://plato.stanford.edu/entries/pineal-gland/

Major, L. E. and Higgins, S. (2019), *What Works?* London: Bloomsbury Education.

Martins, J. E., Onofre, M., Mota, J., Murphy, C., Repond, R.-M., Vost, H., Cremosini, B. Svrdlim, A., Markovic, M. and Dudley, D. (2021), 'International approaches to the definition, philosophical tenets, and core elements of physical literacy: A scoping review', *Prospects*, 50, 13–30.

Meesuk, P., Sramoon, B. and Wongrugsa, A. (2020), 'Classroom action research-based instruction: The sustainable teacher professional development strategy', *Journal of Teacher Education for Sustainability*, 22, (1), 98–110.

Mehmood, R. and Khan, S. (2018), 'Siddhartha: A modern man of Ancient India', *South Asian Studies*, 33, (1), 305–314.

Molteni, R., Wu, A., Vaynman, S., Ying, Z., Barnard, R. J. and Gómez-Pinilla, F. (2004), 'Exercise reverses the harmful effects of consumption of a high-fat diet on synaptic and behavioral plasticity associated to the action of brain-derived neurotrophic factor', *Neuroscience*, 123, (2), 429–440.

Neisser, U. (1976), *Cognition and Reality*. San Francisco, CA: Freeman.

Nielsen, J. A., Zielinski, B. A., Ferguson, M. A., Lainhart, J. E. and Anderson, J. S. (2013), 'An evaluation of the left-brain vs. right-brain hypothesis with resting state functional connectivity magnetic resonance imaging', *PLOS ONE*, 8, (8): e71275.

NHS (2020), 'National child measurement programme England 2019/20 school year', https://digital.nhs.uk/data-and-information/publications/statistical/national-child-measurement-programme/2019-20-school-year

Norden, J. (2019), *Understanding the Brain* (audiobook). Wolverhampton: The Great Courses.

Nuthall, G. (2007), *The Hidden Lives of Learners*. Wellington: NZCER Press.

Oyebode, O., Gordon-Dseagu, V., Walker, A. and Mindell, J. S. (2014), 'Fruit and vegetable consumption and all-cause, cancer and CVD mortality: Analysis of Health Survey for England data', *Journal of Epidemiology and Community Health*, 68, (9), 856–862.

Oxford Learner's Dictionaries, 'plasticity', www.oxfordlearnersdictionaries.com/definition/english/plasticity

Oxford University Hospitals, 'Teensleep: Improving educational attainment in adolescence through sleep education', www.ouh.nhs.uk/research/patients/trials/teensleep.aspx

Paivio, A. (1990), *Mental Representations: A dual coding approach*. New York, NY: Oxford University Press.

Pan, S., Mayoral, S. R., Choi, H. S., Chan, J. R. and Kheirbek, M. A. (2020), 'Preservation of a remote fear memory requires new myelin formation', *Nature Neuroscience*, 23, 487–499.

Roediger, H. L. (1980), 'Memory metaphors in cognitive psychology', *Memory and Cognition*, 8, (3), 231–246.

Rosenshine, B. (2012), 'Principles of instruction: Research-based strategies that all teachers should know', *American Educator*, www.aft.org/sites/default/files/periodicals/Rosenshine.pdf

Shao, S., Guo, H., Mou, F., Guo, C., Zhang, L. (2020), 'The records of Anatomy in Ancient China', *Chinese Medicine and Culture*, 3, (4), 210–215.

Silaj, K. M., Schwartz, S. T., Siegel, A. L. M. and Castel, A. D. (2021), 'Test Anxiety and Metacognitive Performance in the Classroom', *Educational Psychology Review*, https://link.springer.com/article/10.1007/s10648-021-09598-6

Sims, S. and Fletcher-Wood, H. (2021), 'Identifying the characteristics of effective teacher professional development: a critical review', *School Effectiveness and School Improvement*, 32, (1), 47–63.

Singh, C. (2009), 'Problem solving and learning', *AIP Conference Proceedings*, 1140, 183.

Sinha, R., Lacadie, C. M., Constable, R. T. and Seo, D. (2016), 'Dynamic neural activity during stress signals resilient coping', *PNAS*, 113, (31), 8837–8842.

Skene, K., O'Farrelly, C. M., Byrne, E. M., Kirby, N., Stevens, E. C. and Ramchandani, P. G. (2022), 'Can guidance during play enhance children's learning and development in educational contexts? A systematic review and meta-analysis', *Child Development*.

Sleep Foundation (2021), 'How much sleep do we really need?', www.sleepfoundation.org/how-sleep-works/how-much-sleep-do-we-really-need

Spira, A. P., Chen-Edinboro, L. P., Wu, M. N. and Yaffe, K. (2014), 'Impact of sleep on the risk of cognitive decline and dementia', *Current Opinion in Psychiatry*, 27, (6), 478–483.

Sweller, J. (1988), 'Cognitive load during problem solving: Effects on learning', *Cognitive Science*, 12, (2), 257–285.

Sweller, J. (2012), 'An interview with John Sweller', www.youtube.com/watch?v=3bZOdZ8qBOk&t=960s

Sweller, J., Ayres, P. and Kalyuga, S. (2011), *Cognitive Load Theory*. New York, NY: Springer.

Tarumi, T., Rossetti, H., Thomas, B. P., Harris, T., Tseng, B. Y., Turner, M., Wang, C., German, Z., Martin-Cook, K., Stowe, A. M., Womack, K. B., Mathews, D., Kerwin, D. R., Hynan, L., Diaz-Arrastia, R., Lu, H., Cullum, C. M. and Zhang, R. (2019), 'Exercise training in amnestic mild cognitive impairment: A one-year randomized controlled trial', *Journal of Alzheimer's Disease*, 71, (2), 421–433.

Tarver, S. G. (1998), 'Myths and truths about direct instruction', *Effective School Practices*, 17, (1), 18–22.

Taylor, T. (2019), *Connect the Dots*. Woodbridge: John Catt.

Teacher Toolkit (2020), 'Podcast 94: Teaching knowledge, skills and cultural literacy' (podcast with E. D. Hirsch), www.teachertoolkit.co.uk/2020/10/18/podcast-94

Tibke, J. (2019), *Why the Brain Matters*. London: Sage.

UK Government (2019), 'UK chief medical officers' physical activity guidelines', www.gov.uk/government/publications/physical-activity-guidelines-uk-chief-medical-officers-report

US Foreign Office, 'Foreign language training', www.state.gov/foreign-language-training

Verkoeijen, P. P. J. L., Rikers, R. M. J. P. and Özsoy, B. (2008), 'Distributed rereading can hurt the spacing effect in text memory', *Applied Cognitive Psychology*, 22, (5), 685–695.

Vicente, R., Rizzuto, M., Sarica, C., Kazuaki, Y., Sadr, M., Tarun, K., Mostafa, F., Moien-Afshari, F., Haw, C. S., Llinas, R. R., Lozano, A. M., Neimat, J. S. and Zemmar, A. (2022), 'Enhanced interplay of neuronal coherence and coupling in the dying human brain', *Frontiers in Aging Neuroscience*, 14, 813531.

Willingham, D. T. (2017), 'A mental model of the learner: Teaching the basic science of educational psychology to future teachers', *Mind, Brain, and Education*, 11, (4), 166–175.

Willingham, D. T. (2010), *Why Don't Students Like School?* San Francisco, CA: Jossey-Bass.

Yilmaz, R. M. (2020), 'Effects of using cueing in instructional animations on learning and cognitive load level of elementary students in science', *Interactive Learning Environments*.

Zaromb, F. M. and Roediger, H. L. (2010), 'The testing effect in free recall is associated with enhanced organizational processes', *Memory and Cognition*, 38, 995–1008.

INDEX

A

abstract concepts 12–14, 36, 96
action potentials 52–3
active learning 116
active rereading 63
adolescence 57–8
adrenal glands 58, 117
adrenaline 58–9, 117
Alzheimer's disease 116, 118
amygdala 9, 36, 40, 55–6
antioxidants 115
anxiety 48, 57–8, 61–2, 117
  see also stress
apprenticeship 103–5
  see also cognitive apprenticeship
Aristotle 5
assessment 46–7, 61–2, 82
Atkinson, R. 33
audience effect 51
axon hillocks 20–1
axons 20–2, 52, 115
axon terminals 20–1

B

Bananarama Principle xii, 25, 62
Blakemore, S. J. 51
boxology 33
brain
  limbic system 9, 32, 55–6
  neurons 19–23, 52–3, 92
  parts of 6–9, 32, 117
  plasticity 21, 23, 60, 90–4, 115, 118
  see also cognitive psychology; neuroscience
brain stem 7–8, 91
breaktime 57
Brillat-Savarin, J. A. 115
Buddha 4

C

caudal 7
cell body 21
central nervous system 91
cerebellum 7–8
cerebral cortex 8–9
Chinese medicine 5
chunking 12–13, 42–3
Cicero ix
circadian rhythms 117, 119
Claxton, G. 33, 73, 102
coaching 103
Coe, R. 27
cognitive apprenticeship 45, 102–11
cognitive architecture 33
cognitive load theory 16, 39, 68–73
cognitive neuroscience *see* neuroscience
cognitive psychology 3, 8, 33
communication 60
compulsion 55
conditioned responses 36
context-dependent memory 40
continuous professional development (CPD)
 1–2, 123–35
cooperation 107
cortisol 58–9, 117
cramming 24, 44, 62
curriculum planning xvi, 44, 94, 139–41

D

declarative knowledge 37
  see also explicit memory
dementia 118
dendrites 20–1
depression 57
  see also mental health
Descartes, R. 5
D'Esposito, M. 73
diencephalon 7, 9
diet 115–16, 120
direct instruction 10
  chunking 12–13
  dual coding theory 14–17
  myths and facts 11
  see also instruction
discovery learning 69
disengagement 57
distributed practice 44
domain knowledge 106, 109
dopamine 55
dorsal 7
dual coding theory 14–17, 76
dual store model 33
Duckworth, S. 76
Dunlosky, J. xvii, 62, 63, 64, 109
Dweck, C. 55

E

Ebbinghaus, H. 41, 73
eidetic memory 40
elaboration methods 82, 94–100
emotional memory 40
emotions
  fight or flight response 36, 55–6, 58–9
  and hormones 57–9
  and learning 50–2, 54–7, 61
  and memory 52–9
  negative 57
  role of teachers 54, 56–7
  see also mental health; wellbeing
episodic memory 35–6, 52, 59, 92, 115
ethics 146
exams 61–2
exclusions 57
exercise 116, 120
  and memory 116
explicit memory 34–6
extracurricular experiences 57
extraneous load 70–1, 72, 74

F

fading support 103
feedback 27–8, 55, 81
feedback loops 81
feed-forward 27, 81
feed-up 27, 81
fight or flight response 36, 55–6, 58–9
5 A Day campaign 115
Foot, P. 53
forgetting curve 40–1, 73
formative assessment 47
fornix 9, 56
frontal lobe 8
Frontiers for Young Minds 22–3

G

Galen 4, 5
Gall, F. J. 4, 6
Gansemer-Topf, A. 76
germane load 71–2, 74
Ginott, H. 54
glucose 60, 117
Great Teaching Toolkit xiii–xiv

H

health 57, 59, 115, 118
  see also wellbeing
Health Survey for England (2021) 57
Hesse, H. 4
heuristic strategies 106
hidden curriculum needs 57
highlighting 63–4
hippocampus 9, 32–3, 56, 115, 116, 119
Hippocrates xi, 5
Hirotsu, C. 117
hormones 57–9, 117
hypothalamus 9, 56, 58

I

immune system 118
implicit memory 34, 36–7
INSET days 124
  see also continuous professional development (CPD)
instruction 46–7
  see also direct instruction
interleaving practice 44–9
intrinsic load 70, 72, 74
intrinsic motivation 107
isolation effect 63

J

James, W. 91

K

Kendall, A. 123
key information, identifying 64

L

language 60
la Velle, L. 123
learning
  definitions of 69
  and emotions 50–2, 54–7, 61
  and plasticity 92–4
  and problem-solving 69–70
  situated 107
left-brain dominance 9
Lemov, D. 110
lesson planning 72
  see also curriculum planning
limbic system 9, 32, 55–6
long-term memory 32, 33–6, 92, 119
lunchtime 57

M

massed practice 44
massed rereading 63
means-end analysis 69–70
medulla oblongata 8
melatonin 117
mental health 57–8, 61–2, 113
  see also emotions; stress
mental models 81–4
mesencephalon 7
metacognitive approaches 106
metencephalon 7
midbrain 8
milestones 35
mnemonics 82, 83–8
Mnemosyne 83
modelling 14, 64, 98, 103
moral dilemmas 53–4
motivation 26, 55, 57, 107, 133–4
music, and concentration 40
myelencephalon 7–8
myelin 20, 22
myelination 22
myelin sheaths 20–2

N

National Institute for Direct Instruction 10
neuromyths ix
neurons 19–23, 52–3, 92
neuroplasticity *see* plasticity
neuroscience 3
  history of xi, 3–6
  how memory is shaped 19–24
  limbic system 9, 32, 55–6
  parts of the brain 6–9, 32, 117
  plasticity 21, 23, 60, 90–4, 115, 118
  right/left-brain dominance 9
neurotransmitters 21, 23, 55, 92, 116
nonsense syllables 41, 73
Norden, J. 3, 6, 60, 94
nucleus 21
Nuthall, G. 50, 56

O

obesity 57, 115, 116
observation 103
occipital lobe 8
off-rolling 57
omega-3 acids 115

P

Paivio, A. 14, 76
Pareto Principle 82–3
parietal lobe 8
peripheral nervous system 91
phrenology 4, 6
physical health *see* health
pineal gland 5, 117
pivot points 82
plasticity 21, 23, 60, 90–4, 115, 118
Plato 5
poverty 146
praise 55
prefrontal cortex 32–3
presynaptic terminal 92
priming 37
priorities, for teachers xiii–xiv
prior knowledge 16, 45, 96, 109
problem-solving 3, 32, 45, 53, 69–70, 106
procedural knowledge 37
  see also implicit memory
propositional theory 84
PSHE (personal, social, health and economic education) 114
Pylyshyn, Z. 84

R

recall xvi, 25, 41–2
redundancy effect 16, 39, 110
rehearsal xvii
 repetition 24, 110–11
  see also retrieval practice; rote learning
rereading 62–6
retention 44
  see also forgetting curve
retesting 25
retrieval practice xvi–xvii, 22, 25–9, 41, 46–7, 64
right-brain dominance 9
Roediger, H. L. xv
rostral 7
rote learning 22, 24
RSE (relationships and sex education) 114

S

sadness 57
scaffolding 72, 74, 103
schemas xvi, 12, 45, 69–70
  see also mental models
scripts 82
self-explanation 82, 109–11
semantic memory 35–6, 59, 110
sensory memory 40, 52
Shiffrin, R. 33
short-term memory 32–3, 41, 117, 119
situated learning 107
sketchnoting 76
sleep 116–20
  recommended hours 119
spaced practice 44, 47–9, 64
spaced rereading 63
spatial memory 32
special educational needs 57
spinal cord 91
Spira, A. P. 118
stress 27, 40, 52, 58, 113, 116, 117–18
subconscious, and memory 36
summarising 64, 74–7
summative assessment 61
Sweller, J. 45, 68–70, 73
symbols 84
synapse pruning 21, 92, 115
synapses 21–3, 115
  and plasticity 92–4
synaptic cleft 23

T

tacit knowledge 106
Tarner, S. 10
Taylor, T. xv
Teach Active 116
teachers
  coaching 103
  continuous professional development (CPD) 1–2, 123–35
  modelling 14, 64, 98, 103
  role in managing emotions 54, 56–7
  scaffolding 72, 74, 103
teaching priorities xiii–xiv
Teensleep project 119
telencephalon 7–8
temporal lobe 8, 55
testing 61–2
  see also assessment
thinking
  made visible 104
  mental models 81–4
  see also abstract concepts; cognitive apprenticeship
timings, of lessons 57
trolley problem 53–4

V

ventral 7
verbal memory 32

W

wardrobe metaphor xv, 31
wellbeing
  diary 121
  diet 115–16, 120
  exercise 116, 120
  and memory 113–20
  prioritising 119–21
  sleep 116–20
  see also health; hormones; mental health
Willingham, D. ix, 2
Willis, T. 4, 5
working memory 38–9, 53–4, 57, 68, 70–3
Wren, C. 5

ABOUT THE AUTHOR

Ross is a qualified teacher who, across three decades, has worked in some of the most challenging secondary schools in London as a design technology teacher and as a deputy headteacher. Throughout his school leadership, Ross has been responsible for improving the quality of teaching and learning and has an international profile as a leading contributor and organiser of professional development, research and teacher wellbeing within a growing community of education professionals.

As the most followed educator on social media in the UK, Ross offers unique social media insights and support for schools and organisations. He is frequently asked to speak at national conferences and has worked with teachers all over the UK and in many parts of the world. He is regularly asked to reflect on educational developments in multiple publications about education policy. Through his website, he advocates teaching and supports thousands worldwide. He is a PGCE tutor and visiting tutor at the University of Buckingham and when not completing action doctoral research, he is either teaching teachers, reading, writing or tweeting @TeacherToolkit! Ross is the bestselling author of *Mark. Plan. Teach. 2.0*, *Teacher Toolkit* and *Just Great Teaching*.